Cambridge Studies in Social Anthropology

General Editors

M. FORTES, J. R. GOODY, E. R. LEACH, S. J. TAMBIAH

NO. 6

BUDDHIST MONK, BUDDHIST LAYMAN

OTHER TITLES IN THE SERIES

Buddhist monk, Buddhist layman

A STUDY OF URBAN MONASTIC ORGANIZATION
IN CENTRAL THAILAND

JANE BUNNAG

CAMBRIDGE
AT THE UNIVERSITY PRESS
1973

Published by the Syndics of the Cambridge University Press
Bentley House, 200 Euston Road, London NW1 2DB
American Branch: 32 East 57th Street, New York, N.Y.10022

Library of Congress Catalogue Card Number: 72–86420

ISBN: 0 521 08591 8

Printed in Great Britain by
Western Printing Services Ltd
Bristol

Contents

List of tables

List of illustrations

MAPS

FIGURES

Preface

This book is based upon material collected in Ayutthaya between September 1966 and August 1967 for use in my doctoral dissertation which was presented to London University in May 1969. This fieldwork was carried out under the auspices of the London–Cornell Project for East and South-East Asian Studies which is financed jointly by the Carnegie Corporation of New York and the Nuffield Foundation. I would like therefore to thank the authorities concerned most warmly for their generous sponsorship of my research programme.

I would also like to express my gratitude to Dr S. J. Tambiah of the Faculty of Archaeology and Anthropology, University of Cambridge, as it was he who first inspired my interest in Theravada Buddhism, and provided constant stimulus and support throughout my studies. I am also heavily indebted to Dr E. M. Mendelson and Miss Barbara Ward who supervised and encouraged my postgraduate work at the School of Oriental and African Studies, University of London, and to Professor E. H. S. Simmonds, Head of the Department of South-East Asia and the Islands, for his warm support throughout.

My thanks are also due to the officials of the National Research Council, Bangkok, who gave me permission to carry out my research programme in Ayutthaya, and to Dr Puey Ungaphakorn, Governor of the Bank of Thailand, who kindly sponsored my application.

I would like, furthermore, to express my gratitude to Dr Jacques Amyot of the Department of Social Sciences, Chulalongkorn University, Bangkok, for his valuable advice on certain aspects of fieldwork, and to Khun Sulak Siwarak for introducing me to the town and people of Ayutthaya. Of these latter I am particularly indebted to Khun Thep Sukkharattani and his family who welcomed me into their home, and to Khun Siri Imchai whose continuing and expert guidance was invaluable. Indeed, I must acknowledge my gratitude to all residents of Ayutthaya, both monk and lay, whose co-operation made my fieldwork an experience both fruitful and memorable.

The Thai terms used in the following chapters are transliterated according to the 'general' system laid down by the Royal Institute of Thailand, and presented in an article entitled 'Notification of the Royal Institute concerning the Transcription of Thai Characters into Roman', *Journal of the Siam Society*, vol. 33, pt. 1 (1941), pp. 49–65.

ix

Preface

The transcription of Pali terms follows the system used in the *Concise Pali–English Dictionary* compiled by A. P. Buddhadatta Mahathera (Colombo, 1957), although the diacritical marks have been omitted here.

Throughout the text the terms monk and *bhikkhu* (Pali) are used interchangeably; the Pali word *bhikkhu* being used in preference to the Thai term *phra*, also meaning monk, as the former is more generally known. I have used the Pali term *Sangha* (monkhood) in preference to the Thai derivatives for the same reason. The Thai term *wat* meaning monastery is however both brief and fairly familiar, and has therefore been used as an occasional substitute for the English equivalent.

Members of the laity are in some places referred to by the alternative term 'householders' (Pali: *gahapati*; Thai: *kharawat*), a term which expresses the fact that their religious role is complementary to that of the homeless *bhikku* (lit. mendicant).

Monks and laymen mentioned in the text have been given fictitious names, except where the individuals involved requested that their real names should be used.

Jane Bunnag

Bangkok
September 1972

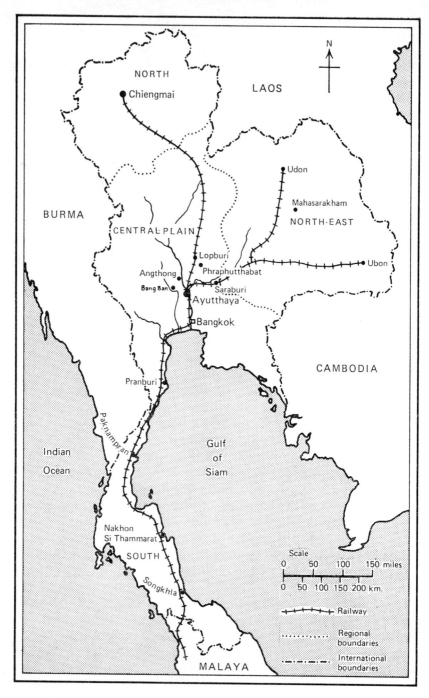

Map A   Thailand

xii

Introduction:
The Thai social system

The Siamese are a people incapable of retaining one spark of animosity, and during my stay in Bangkok I do not remember a single instance of seeing two Siamese come to blows and seldom even quarrel. They have been taught from their infancy to obey and respect every grade, from the King to those just one degree above them; and from their inferiors they in their turn receive that homage they pay to others; hence even were they so disposed opportunities seldom offer which would admit of a dispute.

From *Residence in Siam* by Frederick Arthur Neale (London, 1852, p. 148)

For the majority of the Thai population it is axiomatic that to be Thai is to be Buddhist. Nevertheless, and not unnaturally, different individuals exhibit different degrees of religious commitment and interest and respond in a variety of ways to the religious opportunities available. The differences in temperament and personal inclination which to some extent condition this variety lie beyond the scope of the present study. Instead I have tried to analyze religious role performance in terms of its correlation with the social and economic status of individual actors. As will presently become clear a person's income, educational qualifications, and present life-style provide fairly reliable indicators as to how he will conceive of his role as a Buddhist: men from a rural background are for instance more likely than their urban fellows to make a career for themselves in the Buddhist *Sangha*. Similarly the enactment of the role of Buddhist layman or householder varies according to the income and orientations of individual actors.

Initially it will be necessary to establish the broad boundaries within which individual role performances may vary, without being regarded as deviant. Which is to say that I shall in the first instance be concerned with the ways in which the roles as defined in the Pali scriptures are interpreted on a practical level, and with the assessment of the degree of leeway permitted to the performers. Then and only then can one look beyond individual interpretations to the socio-economic correlates which to a large extent condition them.

Pursuant to these specific aims it will be necessary to present material susceptible of analysis in terms of the more general effects of Buddhism on Thai society. It has been a fairly common practice amongst social scientists working in Thailand to assume, either from ignorance or conviction, that the emphasis in Theravada Buddhism on individual salvation leads to the breakdown and dissolution of personal relationships, and the loosening of social ties. On the other hand I shall argue that to analyze the elements of social interaction which involve the transfer of merit, a primary concept in Theravada Buddhism, is to trace the veins and arteries of Thai society. Which, expressed as anthropology rather than metaphor, is to say that the actions regarded by the actors as meritorious are those which the anthropologist sees as tending to maintain social solidarity. The fact that so many of my colleagues maintain a contrary position is due in part to their assumption that the tenets of Theravada Buddhism are interpreted in an unaltered form on the practical level, in part to their relying on the religious ethos to explain all, whilst neglecting historical and politico-economic features which could prove more illuminating.

The framework for analysis in this study and its central theme will be the relationship between Buddhist monk and Buddhist layman as I observed it during my stay in Ayutthaya, Central Thailand, between September 1966 and August 1967. My aim will not be to analyze religious ceremonies and rituals, but to look at the people involved, both within and without a specifically ceremonial context; to ascertain the nature of their relationship, the motivations for their involvement, to describe the economic transfers taking place.

In presenting data illustrative of these points I hope, without being tediously anecdotal, to transmit some of the flavour of provincial Thai town life – an essence which, unlike that of Thai village society, is little known. Accordingly, I have used the case-history method of presenting a good deal of the material; in certain chapters I give calendars of activities, budgetary details, and guest lists for attendance at ceremonials as an integral part of the text, rather than relegating such data to obscurity in appendices. My presentation of a good many primary data not available elsewhere will of course be of primary interest to the serious student of Thai anthropology, but I hope that it will also be of value to the more general reader. Today Everyman is an amateur anthropologist, and because of its present political prominence Southeast Asian society is particularly vulnerable to the sort of journalistic half-exposure which disseminates misinformation most efficiently. The *bhikkhu* in his saffron robe is an obvious target for this treatment; consequently Thai monks are variously expected to be better, worse, more numerous, more inflammatory, more inflammable, than is in fact the case. I found in beginning my study that I was approaching a landscape whose features were half-known and much misunderstood. This book is of necessity a work of social topography.

The material presented in subsequent chapters is based on fieldwork carried out in Ayutthaya, Central Thailand, though the conclusions reached are I believe susceptible of generalization to a much wider social arena. The town of Ayutthaya is situated some fifty-five miles north of Bangkok and was itself the capital of the kingdom of Siam from 1350 until 1767 when it was sacked by invading Burmese forces. It is interesting to see that this disastrous event is regarded by the present inhabitants of the city as being a relatively recent occurrence. It was repeatedly emphasized by informants that there existed in Ayutthaya something which was hostile to the modern world, an inveterate hatred of change. Tales were related concerning fabulous hoards of gold, and priceless Buddha images which had been buried in the ground, or cast into a pond or canal when news of the Burmese advance reached the terrified town. These treasures remain undisturbed however, it being the belief that certain death awaits the bounty hunter who dares to tamper with Ayutthaya's jealously guarded past.

This insistence that Ayutthaya turns her back on the present day can be regarded as a justification for the stagnation of the modern town. Although very different both in style and in spirit from sophisticated Bangkok, Ayutthaya is yet too near to the new capital to sustain any real independence. This is particularly noticeable in the economic sphere where Ayutthaya was once pre-eminent in the production of knives, swords and iron-work of all kinds. Nowadays cutlery is brought from Bangkok for sale in Hua Ro, the market place of the old town. The freshwater fish for which Ayutthaya is famous is however transported in the reverse direction, and is scarcely to be found outside Bangkok. Furthermore, though she is situated in the centre of one of the richest rice-growing areas in Southeast Asia, Ayutthaya is largely by-passed by the resultant trade as most of the grain is shipped, in caravans of slow-moving barges, down the river Chao Phraya to the mills and markets of the present capital.

Ayutthaya's own industrial sector at the time of my stay comprised little more than a tobacco factory, a paper mill, and two small family businesses, specializing in the production of cheap cotton cloth. The local distillery had lately gone out of operation.

In recent years the town has become increasingly oriented towards the tourist trade, but the effects of this upon the ordinary inhabitants are still quite marginal. Most of the tourists are day-trippers, people spending one

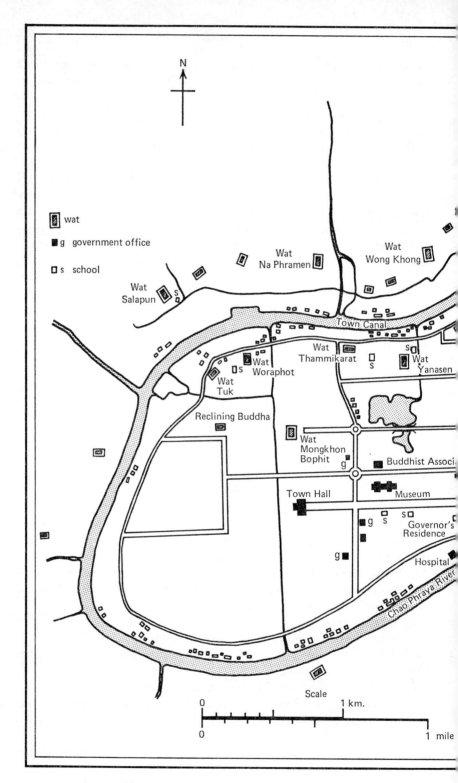

Map B   Ayutthaya, Central Thailand

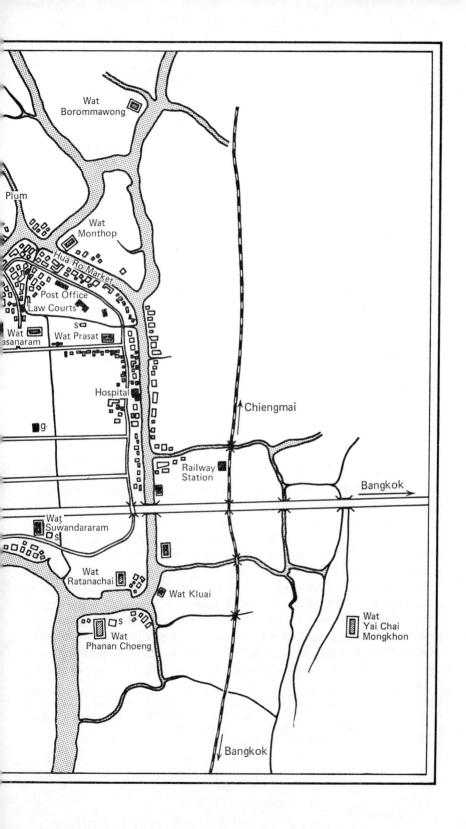

of their days allotted to Thailand scrambling around the ruined monasteries of the old capital. *Farang* (Western)[1] residents of Bangkok, in search of antiques at bargain prices, compose another category of more regular visitors.

Ayutthaya's accessibility to Bangkok – it is less than two hours' journey by road – makes it ideally situated for commuters in both directions. A good number of Ayutthaya's residents travel daily to work in business firms or in government offices in the capital, whilst many of the provincial town's most eminent officials – the judge, the bank manager, and several doctors for example – make the same journey in the reverse direction from the Bangkok suburbs. Indeed, Ayutthaya's few private cars belong to these commuters from the capital; the majority of permanent residents traverse the comparatively short distances between home and work place by bicycle, moped, or on foot, or commit themselves into the hands of the drivers of the buses and motor-*samlors* which throng the narrow roads.

The town's rather minimal commercial activity centres on Hua Ro market place which is represented on the map (see Map B) as the densest area of settlement in the north-eastern corner of the main island. It is here, in Hua Ro, that the influences of Bangkok on the one side and of the rural hinterland on the other, can be seen most clearly to meet and mingle. The shops, which as is common in Thailand are largely Chinese-owned, stock medicines, groceries and manufactured goods brought from the capital. On the other hand, most of the vendors of vegetables, fruit and sweetmeats who set up their stalls in the narrow lanes and alleys between these shops are Thai villagers who have come to town for the day to sell their produce.

The distinction of present-day Ayutthaya derives mainly from her position as the capital of the Province of the same name, which makes her a centre of bureaucratic and educational activity. There are today more than sixty schools and other teaching establishments in the town, and a substantial proportion of the 30,000 people resident in the municipal area are employed in the state-run hospitals and banks, or in any one of the numerous government offices.[2]

From the point of view of research into religious behaviour moreover, Ayutthaya is of particular interest. Within the *Amphoe* or District of Ayutthaya, which comprises both the municipality and some of the neighbouring rural settlements, there are some seventy-two Buddhist monasteries or *wats*. The most important ecclesiastical offices are attached to the larger urban foundations and the ecclesiastical heads of both the Province and the

---

[1] *Farang:* Thai equivalent of *Feringhi*, which according to Webster's New Collegiate Dictionary, is derived from the Persian *Firinghi*, from the Arabic, *Faranji*, a corruption of the Old French, *Franc* – a Frank. In Thailand, as throughout most of the East, the word means a European, or more broadly a Westerner.
[2] Statistics from the Town Hall, Ayutthaya.

District of Ayutthaya are resident in the town. There are also in this provincial capital special schools for the instruction of the ordained which attract monks from the outlying rural villages, as well as from further afield, outside the Region. In addition to the numerous inhabited monasteries there are in Ayutthaya many deserted monuments and *stupas*[3] which, as was mentioned, now provide a major attraction for both Thais and foreign tourists visiting the town.

It is necessary however, to place the Ayutthaya data to be analyzed in subsequent chapters in their broader context. To this end the former paragraphs of the introduction are given over to describing in outline the main features of the Thai social system, and to indicating the sources of more detailed information for those who require it.

POLITICS AND ADMINISTRATION

After the Revolution of 1932 a constitutional monarchy was established in Thailand, and the initiative in political affairs passed into the hands of the small group of military leaders who had successfully opposed the old regime. But, despite the fact that it has been shorn of any real political power the monarchy retains its function as an important symbol of identity for the Thai people, who, it should be remembered, have never been subjected to colonial domination.

The Thai kingship has many facets; its incumbent is at one and the same time a semi-divine being, to be addressed and referred to by the elaborate terms reserved for royalty, and also a father to his people. A portrait of the present King is to be found in the most ramshackle farmhouse of the remotest rural settlement in the country. Often it is placed on or near to the Buddhist altar, or by the side of a picture showing a famous Buddha image, or an eminent monk renowned for his spiritual powers. On the other hand, the villager is not too surprised if the King comes in person to inspect an irrigation project being undertaken in the area, and it is considered only natural that a pop-song penned by the royal hand should reach the top of the charts. Although, therefore, in status terms the Thai Monarch is very remote from the ordinary people, he is yet able to exercise a great deal of personal influence.[4]

For the purposes of administration Thailand is divided into 71 Provinces (*Changwat*) which are further subdivided in 509 Districts or *Amphoe*; each

---

[3] *Stupa*: a reliquary, a monument built to contain relics or ashes of a deceased person.
[4] The Thai King and Queen are models for their subjects in every way and set the standards of excellence. The Queen coaches the Thai entrants for the Miss Universe contest, advises them on make-up, deportment and so on.

Amphoe consists of a number of *Tambon* or Sub-Districts, which are in country areas split into constituent villages (*Mu Ban*).[5] The District Office with the *Nai Amphoe* at its head is the lowest level in the central government hierarchy which is staffed with civil servants. The headman of the Sub-District (the *kamnan*) and the village headman or *phu yai ban* are local government officials, the latter being elected by popular vote within the village, whilst the *kamnan* is chosen by the *Nai Amphoe* (District Head) from amongst the headmen of the villages in that Sub-District or *Tambon*.

Within the civil service itself positions are awarded according to a variety of criteria, success in examinations and personal recommendation being the most important conditions for eligibility, although seniority of service may also be taken into account. With respect to the first of these qualifications it should be noted that Thai society is still highly stratified in terms of opportunities for education. The State provides for four, or in some areas for seven, years of free education only. Consequently only those individuals in the upper levels of the socio-economic hierarchy can afford to give their children the secondary education which is a necessary prerequisite for the most senior civil service posts. These people are also the most likely to have influential contacts who will lend their support to any application.[6]

It is perhaps at the District level where the central government reaches out into the Provinces that the gulf between the elite of the civil service and the junior grades becomes most noticeable. Most of the senior officials in the District (*Amphoe*) Office have graduated from a university, or from some other institution of higher education. They are highly mobile, being transferred from place to place at intervals of two or three years. The eventual aim of most high-ranking civil servants is of course to be posted to Bangkok.

It is usual however for the more junior officials in government offices to be drawn from the local population. Many of these individuals have had little if any secondary education, but they have, by a combination of ability and practical experience, managed to become fairly efficient clerical workers. Such people provide a vital link between the higher government officials and the local community; their superiors rely upon them to provide them with a working knowledge of conditions in the area, whilst they also facilitate communication in the other direction by guiding their fellow citizens who are unfamiliar with bureaucratic procedures. The following quotation from an article by Jeremy Boissevain in 'Patronage in Sicily' (*Man*, March 1966) is also applicable to the Thai situation.

[5] Ayutthaya Province is divided into fourteen Districts or *Amphoe*. *Amphoe* Ayutthaya, which is composed of the municipal area and some outlying rural settlements, is divided into eleven *Tambon* or Sub-Districts.

[6] There are however a few government scholarships for children whose parents cannot afford to pay for secondary education.

'In such a society the lines of communication through the formal system are tenuous and difficult to follow because of the social distance between those who wish to make their voices heard on high, and those who control the channels through which such messages necessarily must pass.'

In Thailand, people do not apply for civil service posts nor for visas or permits of any kind without mobilizing links they may have with a sponsor or patron of superior status. Similarly, most bureaucrats, for their part, neglect applications which come without personal recommendations, preferably in oral form. A vicious circle can be seen to be operative here. The bureaucrat is inefficient because positions are allotted and business conducted on a personal basis, and because of this inefficiency people must continue to by-pass the official channels and use other means to gain their ends. As a result of this the patron/client system retains its importance despite the existence of the ideally impersonal bureaucratic structure.

Although in the foregoing paragraphs I have been concerned only with the patron/client system as it operates in the administrative sphere, I should make it clear that personal sponsorship is necessary, and sometimes sufficient, for effective action in most areas of Thai social life. This point receives ample illustration in subsequent paragraphs.

ECONOMICS

By far the largest proportion of the Thai population (an estimated 84%) is engaged in the agricultural sector of the economy, rice being the staple crop. Indeed over the last fifty years the country has become one of the world's largest rice exporters, yet the changes in the economy which have made this possible are generally said to have been 'in volume rather than in kind' (Ingram 1955, p. 209).[7] This is to say that in response to the world-market demand for rice the Thais have improved very little on their traditional techniques of production, and have not increased the proportion of capital to labour used. It is true, however, that much more land has been taken into cultivation, though even today it is probable that only between 10% and 11% of the total area is cultivated (Ingram 1955, p. 55). Furthermore the typical peasant cultivator aims primarily to produce sufficient rice to support his family and only when their needs are satisfied does he sell the surplus.

In his book *Politics in Thailand*, D. A. Wilson states that in rural areas

[7] The statistics used in this section are taken largely from the book *Economic Change in Thailand since 1850* by J. C. Ingram (Stanford 1955); and an article by J. C. Caldwell entitled 'The Demographic Structure', in *Thailand: Social and Economic Studies in Development*, ed. T. H. Silcock (A.N.U. 1967).

'the relative importance of cash in the household economy varies with the amount of rice available for sale. The tendency in areas of substantial rice surplus, particularly in the Central Region, is for the household to live on its own rice supplemented by fish and vegetables gathered from the lush countryside. Any other goods such as cloth, meat, tools, animals and luxuries are bought with cash from the proceeds of the sale of surplus rice' (Wilson 1962, p. 40).

The typical Thai family is thus basically self-sufficient in terms of the labour-force used, and the food produced. Furthermore, land is by and large individually owned throughout Thailand, and though the size of holdings varies from region to region (Wijeyewardene 1967, p. 76) nowhere in the country as a whole is the pressure on land comparable with that experienced in some other Asian countries. The frequently repeated phrase 'There's fish in the water, there's rice in the fields' (*Nai nam mi pla, nai na mi khao*) expresses quite succinctly the Thai's awareness of the natural abundance of the surrounding countryside, as well as his justifiable confidence that he can survive there quite comfortably without having to work too hard.[8]

The most prestigious form of employment for the towndwelling Thai is to be engaged in government service, and it is estimated that there are over half a million government employees in Thailand (Caldwell 1967, p. 51). It must be remembered that most banks, schools and hospitals are state-owned, with the result that the distinctive khakhi uniform of the civil servant is by no means confined to officials in the administration.

Most of the urban Thais who are not *kharachakan* (lit. servant of royal works) are employed in the service industries, which is to say they make a living as servants, labourers or hawkers, as ferrymen, taxi-drivers and so on. Between these people and those who occupy senior positions in the civil service there is a marked distinction not only in income but also in life-style, though in these terms the ranks of the more lowly government officials merge imperceptibly with those of the service workers.[9] The gulf which exists between people at opposite ends of the socio-economic scale forms the basis for discussion in chapter 5, where details of the religious expenditures made by individual Buddhist laymen are presented for analysis.

It is generally true to say that 'the Thai have not shown much enthusiasm for business enterprise' (Ingram 1955, p. 217), and as was mentioned earlier with specific reference to Ayutthaya, the commercial and business sector is

---

[8] This expression is derived from an inscription authorized by the Thai monarch Ram Kham Haeng *c.* A.D. 1292 (see G. Coedès, 1966). It has since been incorporated in a popular song, and is often heard in common speech.

[9] Many of these individuals in the lower ranks of urban society are partially self-sufficient in that they grow their own fruit and vegetables, and may keep a few chickens.

almost completely dominated by the diligent Chinese population, which comprises more than 3 million individuals in Thailand today (Caldwell 1967, p. 33). Thus although the Thais grow the rice the marketing and milling of grain is largely in Chinese hands.

The Indians, Pakistanis and Ceylonese in Thailand, who comprise the other most sizeable alien ethnic minority, also occupy a special niche in the urban economy.[10] It is usual to find individuals from this group making a living by selling carpets or cloth, as owners of butchers' shops, or as money-lenders, though the Sikhs, in Thailand as elsewhere in Southeast Asia, are traditionally employed by businesses or by private individuals as night-watchmen, perhaps because of their height and fine physique.

It was earlier remarked that there have been very few qualitative changes in the Thai economy, although the country has in recent decades become increasingly involved in international trade. One aspect of this conservatism is that the spending patterns of the average Thai have also changed very little. Ingram reports that 'People prefer to keep their savings in the form of gold or cash and they have not made much use of banks, postal savings or co-operatives for this purpose. Nor are they willing to invest in the stock of a corporation which they do not understand or trust' (Ingram 1955, p. 218). My own observations from Ayutthaya would indeed support this contention. Furthermore it can be added that surplus cash which is not used to buy jewellery, clothes or, increasingly, western luxury goods, is often spent in the fulfilment of a variety of social obligations. It is for example incumbent upon a wealthy individual to support numerous clients, and other dependents, some of whom may be poor relations. Such expenditure not only serves to validate his social status but also brings spiritual benefits in that charitable actions of any kind are felt to be highly meritorious in religious terms. It is believed however, that people at all levels of society derive the maximum spiritual and social benefits by investing their savings in support of the Buddhist *Sangha*, in any one of the variety of ways which are discussed below.

KINSHIP

'The chief features of the kinship system beyond its bilaterality, short depth and collateral relation are the emphasis on relative age within generation, distinction between generations and the regard for the sex of persons linked' (Nash 1965, p. 62).

This statement made by Nash with reference to Burmese society, is equally applicable to the Thai situation. Thai kinship terminology is presented in

[10] This minority-group numbers about 7,000 individuals (Caldwell 1967, p. 29).

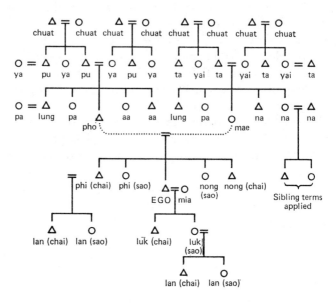

Fig. 1.1.   Thai kinship terminology

Notes:
Translation of kin terms

chuat:	great-grandparent	phi chai:	older male sibling or cousin
pu:	paternal grandfather	phi sao:	older female sibling or
ya:	paternal grandmother		cousin
ta:	maternal grandfather	nong chai:	younger male sibling or
yai:	maternal grandmother		cousin
pho:	father	nong sao:	younger female sibling or
mae:	mother		cousin
lung:	elder brother of either parent	luk:	child
pa:	elder sister of either parent	lan:	nephew/niece, grandchild
aa:	father's younger sibling (both sexes)	mia:	wife (*phanraya*, elegant form)
na:	mother's younger sibling (both sexes)		

N.B.
i. The four terms used for kinsmen in the grandparental generation are used in combination to refer to ancestors in general, i.e. *pu-ya-ta-yai*: ancestors, forbears.
ii. Similarly, the expression *luk-lan* refers to descendants and junior relatives in general.

Fig. 1.1. The terms set out in this figure are also applied to affinal relations, although when used in reference the suffix *khoei* (m) or *saphai* (f) meaning 'affine' may be added if it is necessary to be more specific. Unrelated persons with whom one is on intimate terms are also designated by an appropriate kinship term. The lack of interest in establishing the precise kinship relationship which exists between different individuals in Thai society can to some extent be explained with reference to political and economic factors. Because Thailand has a state-system of government, kinship status is not important for establishing individual rights to citizenship, as it is in many societies studied by anthropologists. Nor is it necessary to allocate rights to scarce economic resources by the operation of the hereditary principle; as was illustrated in the previous section there is in the country as a whole little or no material deprivation of any kind. This lack of emphasis on kinship and genealogy is strikingly illustrated by the fact that family names were only introduced into Thailand by government decree some fifty years ago, and even today their use is largely restricted to bureaucratic affairs.

Amongst a few high-ranking Thai families however, there is, as might be expected, a greater emphasis on pedigree. Although political power has, since the Revolution, passed out of the hands of both royalty and aristocracy, individuals from these groups still form a privileged elite with a background and style of life in common. Within this elite many marriages are arranged with a view to consolidating the property interests of the families concerned. The high incidence of intermarriage can be seen both to reflect and to reinforce the internal cohesiveness of this privileged minority.

Considerations of seniority both within and between generations are more important for the conduct of social relations than is the question of the degree of kinship existing between the parties. The premise that one should respect one's elders indeed provides a primary basis for action, and one which applies even to relations between siblings where the age difference may be very small. Like most dyadic relationships in Thai society, that which exists between elder and younger kinsmen of the same or of different generations, takes a very generalized patron–client form; the senior member is expected to provide counsel and moral guidance, as well as material assistance when the need arises; whilst the junior partner should in turn pay heed to this advice, and give more tangible evidence of his deference by acting as general factotum for his superior.

In Thailand, as in other Theravada Buddhist countries, women are believed to be the inferior sex, because they epitomize those sensual pleasures which form the chief obstacle to any man's spiritual advancement. It is interesting to see that this ideal disparity in status is to some extent reflected in the use of kinship terms in other spheres of activity. The word *mae* (mother) for example forms part of the common nouns *mae khrua* (cook), *mae kha* (vendor) and *mae chi* (nun), all of whom are individuals of relatively lowly social status. The terms *mae* (mother) and *yai* (maternal grandmother) are similarly used in addressing any woman who is senior in age, but of lower social status than the speaker; a passenger on a ferry-boat might for instance address the elderly oarswoman as *mae* or *yai*. The word *pa* meaning the elder sister of either parent is more rarely used in this context, but the term *ya* (father's mother) is never employed in this way, a circumstance which may reflect the ideal superiority of the male, and the associated belief that senior kinsmen on one's father's side of the family are expected to be more sternly authoritarian than the corresponding maternal relatives.

In addressing an elderly man of lower social status the words *lung* (elder brother of either parent) or *ta* (maternal grandfather) may be used to express a similar mixture of familiarity and respect, although the terms for father (*pho*) and paternal grandfather (*pu*) are not extended in this way. The word *pho* is however incorporated in the expression *luang pho* (Revered Father), a respectful term of address and of reference applied to eminent monks, and one which may also be used when talking about famous Buddha images, or the Buddha himself where the reference is clear from the context.

The term *mae* on the other hand figures in the names of various non-Buddhist supernatural phenomena, the Goddess of the Rice Fields is for example known as *Mae Phosop*, and the word *mae* is also attached to the proper names of *phi*, the unhappy and malevolent spirits of people who met an inauspicious end.

Nevertheless, despite these and other similar linguistic usages, Thai women appear to enjoy a considerable measure of equality both in law and in behavioural terms. With respect to rural society for example, it has often been remarked that there is extraordinarily little division of labour along sexual lines; it is equally possible for men to act as midwives and for women to turn their hands to the plough (Hanks 1963, p. 436). This substitutability of roles (Nash 1965, p. 57) is however less apparent in an urban context where male and female spheres of influence are usually more disparate. The middle-class Bangkok housewife knows no more about her husband's office job than does her English or American counterpart, and may similarly spend her time in making visits to the hairdresser, or attending classes on cookery or painting. But in Thailand, as in western society, the most educated and enterprising women can also achieve positions of real power and influence, both in business affairs, and in the national bureaucracy.

Marriage. The marriage customs described in this section are essentially those of the Central Plain, which may differ in some respects from those of other regions.

Unless there are political or property interests at stake marriage is usually a matter of individual choice.[11] In some instances however the marriage is arranged by the two sets of parents simply by reason of the friendship which exists between them. Indeed, several of the young people I knew expressed a preference for this procedure, believing that their elders could more accurately assess the worth of a prospective spouse than they could themselves. Moreover, should the relationship prove to be unsatisfactory, neither partner need bear any responsibility for its rupture.

When the initiative is taken by the young people themselves, parental consent is necessary if either party to the marriage has not reached the age of majority; and indeed the approval of one's seniors is desirable whatever the circumstances. Nevertheless, where the choice of the couple does not accord with the wishes of one or both sets of parents, elopement provides the most common expedient (Kaufman 1960, p. 151).

Ideally the union should be solemnized by a civil ritual, preceded by a ceremony of blessing performed by a chapter of Buddhist monks. Furthermore, according to a law which was passed in 1935, all marriages should be registered at the District (*Amphoe*) Office, but this has not yet become common practice, particularly in country areas. Indeed the material available on Thai village life suggests that in many cases the assumption of the marital relationship is marked neither by any kind of public ceremony, nor by official registration, 'the fact of the young couple's living together being the seal of marriage in the eyes of the community' (de Young 1955, p. 63). My own observations suggest however that towndwellers may be somewhat more punctilious in these matters, in that the marriages I attended in Ayutthaya were marked by both religious and civil ritual, and were subsequently registered at the *Amphoe* Office.

In many cases a common fund is established for the new couple by both sets of parents. In legal terms the husband is regarded as being both the head of the conjugal union and the manager of the joint conjugal estate, although he must in the second capacity obtain his wife's consent before disposing of any part of their joint property which she has brought to the marriage. Either partner may in addition possess personal property which is his or her sole concern. Furthermore the law provides that 'where a wife has been carrying on a profession before marriage she may continue to carry on such a profession without the consent of her husband'.[12] Thus, as

---

[11] Between members of high-ranking Thai families marriages are arranged with a view to consolidating property interests.

[12] Civil and Commercial Code of Thailand, Bk v, Chap. III, Sect. 1456.

was stated earlier, the Thai woman may enjoy a position of considerable freedom, and of equality with her husband – although in deference to the inherent superiority of the male, many Thai wives address their husbands as *phi*, or elder sibling!

With respect to the children the husband also has parental power, although neither in law nor in fact is the marriage of the mother crucial for the child's legitimacy; there is in effect no such thing as bastardy. Thai law clearly states that 'a child born of an unmarried woman is deemed to be the legitimate child of such a woman',[13] and indeed fatherless children seem to be easily absorbed into the mother's kin group, such ill-feeling as exists being directed not against the child but against the father for not having married the girl.

Inheritance. It appears that land and property belonging to both parents are equally divided between their male and female offspring according to the principles of bilateral inheritance, although there is some evidence of preferential ultimogeniture, according to which principle the youngest child inherits the family home as well as his share of the land or other possessions (Yano 1968, p. 860). Should an individual die intestate the children and the surviving spouse have equal rights of inheritance.[14]

Divorce. Most anthropologists report that divorce in Thailand is relatively easy and frequent, and that, like marriage itself, it often entails no civil procedure (Wijeyewardene 1967, p. 68). As in the majority of cases marriage is not used to create an on-going alliance between two families but to establish a single conjugal bond, it is perhaps not surprising that marital breakdown should be fairly common. If the couple prove to be incompatible it is usual for them to return to their respective families. The children of a broken marriage usually but not invariably remain with their mother.

Residence. A newly married couple may take up residence with the parents of either partner, although there appears to be some preference for uxorilo-cality at least in the early years of the marriage (Wijeyewardene 1967, p. 69). A similar trend observable in Burmese family relations has been explained by Nash in the following terms:

> 'the mother–daughter bond may be considered the keystone relationship. Marriage does little to attenuate it, and it serves as the chief linkage between households ... the role of mother is a stable, house-oriented role. Mothers and daughters spend much time in close proximity and

---

[13] Civil and Commercial Code of Thailand, Bk. v, Chap. i, Sect. 1525.
[14] The special arrangements made for the disposal of the property of a deceased monk are discussed below in chapter 4: see p. 119.

the daughter is under constant guidance and surveillance ... Unlike the father–son relationship in which there is the element of replacement along the age axis or the element of separation when the young man comes into full maturity, and the older man passes out of the control and command phase of his life, the mother–daughter role is without the threat of replacement or separation' (Nash 1965, pp. 51–2).

This explanation may well hold good for Thai society, although there are other factors to be taken into consideration. It seems from the material available that it is unusual for two or more married siblings to remain in the parental home (Caldwell 1967, p. 49) and thus the choice of residence for newly-weds might well depend to some extent on the age status of either partner in his or her sibling group. Bearing in mind that ultimogeniture is a common principle of inheritance, it is probable that if either spouse is the youngest child of the family, then the young couple will go to live with that set of parents from whom they will ultimately inherit the house and its effects.

The typical household group also includes individuals of the grand-parental generation who have retired from active life, as well as siblings and cousins of the household head who are unmarried or divorced, and other assorted relatives; orphaned or illegitimate children are also easily accommodated in a kinship group of this kind.

In country areas this assorted grouping of relatives (*phi nong*) who share the same compound[15] usually forms the basic labour unit. Because of the abundance of land, and the present state of technological simplicity the actual size of this labour unit is fairly flexible. Although the demand for labour is not infinitely elastic, an increase in the number of people employed usually results in a sufficient increase in output.

In an urban setting on the other hand, the traditional pattern of residence may be modified for a variety of reasons, the most important of these being the fact that a towndweller's wage or salary is naturally graded according to the position he holds, and without any regard for his family commitments. He cannot therefore afford to support indefinitely a large number of dependents, and it is more usual for individuals who are committed to the modern monetary economy to live in a simple elementary family. The greater pressure on land in the town, as well as the considerable geographical and social mobility of individuals in the middle and upper levels of urban society, must be regarded as contributing to the changes visible in the traditional patterns of residence described above. It is notable in this con-nection that the people occupying an inferior position in the urban social

[15] Within the compound there may be one large house or several smaller houses occupied by members of the extended family group.

hierarchy, who are only partially committed to the cash economy and remain to some extent self-supporting, live in extended family groups exactly similar to those described above for rural areas. Furthermore, amongst families at the uppermost end of the social scale the ethic of 'noblesse oblige' may work to produce residential groups of the same traditional type; which is to say that a member of the old aristocracy who lives in town on the income of his income may feel compelled to validate his privileged position by supporting numerous clients and poor relations. It is usual for such individuals to possess both the space and the financial resources to make this possible.

In conclusion, it can be said that kinship relations are of smaller significance in Thailand than they are in other less mobile societies where birth status determines social position. Nevertheless there are a number of very general premises relating to kinship behaviour which are regarded as being of primary importance for the maintenance of smooth social relations. Thais believe that not only should one respect one's senior kinsmen who, having lived longer, are assumed to know better, but also that relatives should assist each other in all matters. But in Thailand as in other societies where kinship is reckoned bilaterally, kinship relations are only significant when they are activated, and a great deal of freedom is given to the individual in selecting the people whom he will regard and treat as kin.

RELIGION

Philosophical aspects of Theravada Buddhism. There seems to be no doubt that Theravada Buddhism was made the state religion when the first Thai kingdom was founded at Sukhothai (*c.* A.D. 1238), which suggests that it must already have been well-established before this date. Some authorities consider that this form of Buddhism may have been introduced from Ceylon at some time during the third century B.C., though this opinion is difficult to substantiate (Wells 1960, p. iv).

The scriptures of the Theravadins, which are written in the Pali[16] language, are arranged in three parts or *pitakas* (lit. Baskets) known collectively as the *Tripitaka*, the Three Baskets of the law. The *Vinaya-pitaka*, generally considered to be the eldest of the three, contains rules and regulations pertaining to the conduct of Members of the *Sangha* or Order of Buddhist Monks; the *Sutta-pitaka* is concerned with the *Dhamma* (Word of the Buddha) and consists of discourses and sermons said to have been delivered by the Buddha himself, and by his earliest disciples; the third *pitaka*, known as the *Abhidhamma-pitaka*, was compiled at a considerably

16 Cf. *An Introduction to Pali Literature* by S. C. Banerji (Calcutta 1964), p. 14 and passim.

later date than the other parts of the canon, and contains books of exegesis and explication of the doctrine (Dutt 1957, p. xviii).

The teachings of Theravada Buddhism aim primarily to show the adherent the way in which he can escape from this suffering world by achieving Enlightenment or *Nirvana* (lit. Freedom from Desire). The Buddha (lit. the Enlightened One) taught that this state of Salvation can only be attained by an individual who renounces attachments to all worldly things, material or immaterial. It is felt that man's involvement in the sensory world can bring him only suffering by reason of the *Dukkha* (impermanent, transitory) nature of all things; emotional attachments bring suffering when the loved one dies, or changes or moves away; devotion to material possessions also causes unhappiness, as such objects may be stolen or simply perish and decay in the course of time; and furthermore even the ideals to which a man is committed can soon become tarnished and lose all value. Even the entity which we call the 'Self' or 'I' is believed to have no permanent existence, being merely a combination of ever-changing physical and mental forces. Indeed, the craving for the World, for its ideas, opinions and beliefs, and for its sensual delights, is based on the mistaken idea of the Self which arises out of man's ignorance of the transient (*Dukkha*) quality of worldly things.

The selfish desires (*Tanha*) of the individual cause him to take volitional actions or *Khamma* which inevitably entail some kind of reaction and thus constitute a force for continuity. As long as he performs *khammic* acts the actor cannot achieve *Nirvana* and will continue to be reborn into this suffering world, where he must reap the harvest of his previous deeds and misdeeds.

Khamma may be relatively good or relatively bad; good *Khamma* brings merit (Pali: *punna*, Thai: *bun*) for the actor whilst evil actions result in demerit (Pali: *papa*, Thai: *bap*). The reaction to either type of activity may take place almost immediately or after a longer interval of time, and indeed, as was implied above, this *khammic* force persists even after death when the balance of merit and demerit on the actor's spiritual account determines his subsequent status; he may return to the World in any animal or human form. On the other hand, his return will be delayed if he is forced to spend an intervening period in Hell in expiation for previous wrongs done, or if alternatively, he is rewarded for meritorious action by being allowed to stay for a while in one of the many Heavens of sensuous pleasure.

According to orthodox Theravada doctrine, only a monk (*bhikkhu*), that is to say a man who has renounced secular society, can have any hope of achieving *Nirvana*; the layman or householder who remains firmly rooted in the material world can entertain no such aspirations. In practice however, none of the Thai monks to whom I spoke appeared to consider *Nirvana* a relevant goal for which to strive; those who considered that Salvation was attainable in modern times, believed that only after billions of years of tireless effort could they or their contemporaries achieve this state. The majority of monks however, chose to rationalize their limited spiritual horizons by saying that only the Buddha and few of his disciples had become Enlightened, and that this facility was no longer available.

Thus both the Buddhist *bhikkhu* and the Buddhist householder pursue the same end, though by different means; each 'seeks the secondary compensation of a prosperous rebirth' (Tambiah 1968, p. 41) by doing good and avoiding evil. The acquisition of merit is also felt to bring immediate benefits in the form of happiness and peace of mind. Those feelings of euphoria can be seen by the outside observer to be the direct result of performing some socially approved meritorious action.

For the monk the primary merit-making activity is the study of the *Dhamma*, though the pastoral services he performs for the lay community also result in an increment to his spiritual store. The avoidance of demerit on the other hand, entails adhering as closely as possible to the rules of conduct defining his role which are contained in the *Vinaya-pitaka*.

For the layman, Buddhism provides a special and less exacting ethical code (contained in essence in the Five Precepts), according to which he should shape his actions if he is to avoid acquiring demerit. Whereas, a positive increment of merit results from his performing various charitable works, the most significant of these being the provision of material support for members of the Buddhist *Sangha*, who may not participate in secular activity and thus depend for their existence upon donations made by the laity. According to Buddhist belief however, any act of giving is meritorious, and thus a patron can further improve his spiritual status by acknowledging, in some tangible form, that society requires him to assist his friends and relatives.

It is possible moreover for one individual to make merit on another's behalf. When, for instance, a boy is ordained as a monk some of the merit thus made is automatically transferred to his parents. In other cases the living transfer merit to the dead, and 'thus enhance the salvation prospects of the latter' (Obeyesekere 1968, p. 26). This transfer is accompanied by the action of *yat nam* (pouring water out onto the ground) and is an integral part of many merit-making ceremonies performed by the monks (Tambiah 1968, p. 99).

It can be seen from the foregoing discussion that the theory that an individual accumulates merit or demerit by his *khammic* actions provides in very general terms an explanation for his present social status and for the vicissitudes of life which may befall him, in that 'the past determines the present which (combined with the past) determines the future' (Obeyesekere 1968, p. 21). But it must be stressed that as a theory of causation *Khamma* is very indeterminate; merit is not comparable, the actor is unaware of the precise value of his past and present actions, and nor does he know when their effects will be made manifest. The fruits of *Khamma* may ripen instantaneously, or on the other hand it may take several billions of years before they come to maturity.[17]

Whether or not the *khammic* ideology is used to explain and to justify individual circumstances depends a great deal upon the viewpoint of the speaker; a wealthy man can regard his own success as clear evidence of the meritorious actions he has performed in the past, whereas an envious neighbour who suspects him of chicanery and sharp dealing can console himself with the thought that the effects of evil action are not to be avoided. The individual who feels that he has failed in life might similarly explain this misfortune with reference to events which took place in a previous existence which he cannot remember. However such a person is perhaps more likely to rid himself of every shadow of responsibility by citing ill-luck or some other non-Buddhist phenomenon as the causative factor.

It is interesting to see that Buddhist beliefs and those which are commonly labelled 'Hindu' or 'Animistic' to some extent fulfil complementary functions. The *khammic* theory does for example provide only a very generalized explanation of the individual's social condition, an explanation which is psychologically inadequate in a situation of crisis. In such circumstances Hindu techniques of astrology can be used to isolate the immediate source of the trouble, and in the case of illness, a cure, also regarded as being *khong sasana phram* (part of the religion of the Brahmins), can be applied.[18] Belief in the intervention of ghosts or *phi* as well as folk-scientific theories derived from scanty medical knowledge also furnish the individual Buddhist with alternatives to the *khammic* explanation of events. Whatever agency

---

[17] See *The Dhammapada*, verses 119–22, for graphic illustration of this point:

> v. 119 'Even an evil-doer sees good so long as evil ripens not; but when it bears fruit, then he sees the evil results.
>
> v. 120 Even a good person sees evil so long as good ripens not; but when it bears fruit, then the good one sees the good results.
>
> v. 121 Despise not evil, saying "It will not come nigh unto me"; by the falling of drops even a water-jar is filled; likewise the fool, gathering little by little, fills himself with evil.
>
> v. 122 Despise not merit, saying "It will not come nigh unto me"; even by the falling of drops a water-jar is filled; likewise the wise man gathering little by little fills himself with good.'

(Narada Thera 1959, p. 40)

[18] Buddhism is not concerned with alleviating immediate physical suffering. Suffering of all kinds is considered to be a necessary condition of existence. Nevertheless there is a Buddhist ceremony sometimes performed in time of illness with a view to improving the merit balance of the sufferer (Wells 1960, p. 209).

is instrumental in causing illness, the fact that one becomes ill, is of course, in theory, ultimately explicable with reference to the state of one's merit balance, although this link is rarely traced by the sufferer.

The Thais consider that any person can acquire the ability to heal or to tell horoscopes by diligent study of the text-books where these Hinduistic practices are revealed. Nevertheless, my observations in Ayutthaya showed that more credence was given to the specialist who was also a Buddhist monk. But although such talents are traditionally associated with the monkly role they are in fact exercised by a very small proportion of the *bhikkhus*; which is to say that although most *saiyasat* (magical practitioners) are monks, relatively few monks are *saiyasat*. Furthermore the members of the monastic community in Ayutthaya did not participate at all in other Hindu rituals, such as 'calling the *khwan* (soul essence)' (Wells 1960, p. 137), which were performed by lay specialists, as were the seances and rituals of exorcism associated with animistic beliefs. Nor did the *bhikkhus* of Ayutthaya have any dealings with the house-spirits (*phra phum*) to which most laymen make offerings from time to time.[19]

With regard to the theological position it is interesting that the Buddha did not deny the existence of the angels and deities of the Hindu pantheon, nor of ghosts, spirits and other supernatural phenomena, but simply that he regarded the associated beliefs and practices as irrelevant and as a hindrance to salvation. Thus the monks, who are in theory devoted to the attainment of *Nirvana*, should have no truck with these unorthodox (i.e. non-Buddhist) religious elements, whilst 'the lay masses by virtue of their involvement in the social system are incapable of salvation anyway; therefore the practice or non-practice of magic and deity propitiation make little difference to their ultimate future prospects' (Obeyesekere 1968, p. 23).

Although the *bhikkhus* of Ayutthaya did not hope to achieve Enlightenment, they tended on the whole, with the exception of a few magical practitioners, to be more dismissive of 'Magical Animism'[20] than their lay fellows and their counterparts in rural areas, who are familiar from a number of anthropological studies.[21] For this reason, in discussing monk/layman relations I shall confine myself to examining interaction which is generally recognized to relate to the practices of Buddhism.

This task is not as simple as it may seem at first sight.[22] Notwithstanding the general interest in merit-making, opinions differ as to which activities are of relevance in this connection, according to the depth of awareness and

[19] This is not true of all Thai monks (cf. Ingersoll 1966, p. 60, and Kaufman 1960, p. 107).
[20] See Ames (1964, pp. 21–52).   [21] E.g. Kaufman (1960); Tambiah (1968).
[22] See Mendelson (1965, p. 217) on the difficulties of distinguishing between the different elements.

philosophical understanding of the individual actor. Although the distinction between the sophisticated and the naive to some extent cross-cuts the division between the monkhood and the laity, it is true to say that most of the people with any degree of doctrinal expertise are monks of long-standing.[23] In some instances monks must appear to maintain a dual standard in that they give their tacit approval to certain items of religious behaviour which they consider to be inefficacious. It was believed in Ayutthaya for example that if one visited a neighbouring shrine which housed a replica of the Buddha's foot-print, on seven separate occasions, then one would have acquired sufficient merit to avoid having to go to Hell whatever evil actions one committed in the future. Several *bhikkhus* expressed to me their scepticism with regard to this theory but said that they could not speak out for fear of losing lay support. Furthermore they recognized that the laymen still needed to perform these activities, which they as monks had been able to renounce.

Neither monks nor laymen questioned the validity or necessity of the merit-making rituals, performed for laymen at critical turning-points in the individual life-cycle,[24] although a few people, most of them monks, recognized that certain basic ritual elements, such as the sprinkling of lustral water, the use of the sacred thread and so on were clearly derived from the Hindu tradition.[25] Nevertheless these and other disparities in intellectual awareness were not reflected with any accuracy on the behavioural level. Even the *bhikkhu* who realized that merit-making was irrelevant to the central religious goal could scarcely refuse requests to perform ceremonies for members of the lay community upon whom he depended for material support. Furthermore a layman who took an existentialist position with regard to Buddhist philosophy might hesitate before contracting out of all social obligations, which involve amongst other things, attendance at merit-making rituals held by friends and relations.

[23] Though not all monks had expert knowledge of the doctrine.

[24] And in any case 'the performance of all Buddhist rituals can be justified with reference to the sacred texts' (Obeyesekere 1968, p. 31).

[25] 'On the occasion of the national ceremonies in commemoration of the twenty-fifth Buddhist Century there was an argument about whether to allow the holy water to have its usual role in this special occasion or not... those who opposed its being used considered that... "Its inclusion may have a place in private observances but not in this historical one. For it would be a source of undesirable remarks if seen by thoughtful Buddhists from all over the world."

'The dispute was then submitted to the Ecclesiastical Chief Minister Somdet Phra Vanarat who pronounced that the holy water together with the rites connected therewith be suspended from the ceremony (the rites connected with the holy water here were the encirclement of a thread of spun but untwisted cotton around the scene of the ceremony. This was thought to be a protection against the incursion of evil spirits into that area.)' (Punyanubhab 1965, p. 173).

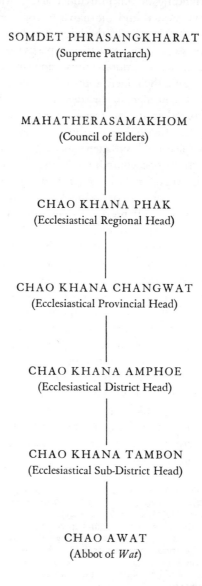

SOMDET PHRASANGKHARAT
(Supreme Patriarch)

MAHATHERASAMAKHOM
(Council of Elders)

CHAO KHANA PHAK
(Ecclesiastical Regional Head)

CHAO KHANA CHANGWAT
(Ecclesiastical Provincial Head)

CHAO KHANA AMPHOE
(Ecclesiastical District Head)

CHAO KHANA TAMBON
(Ecclesiastical Sub-District Head)

CHAO AWAT
(Abbot of *Wat*)

Fig. 1.2.   Outline chart of the Thai *Sangha*
(According to the Act on the Administration of the Buddhist Order of Sangha, 1962)

The Thai Buddhist Monkhood (Sangha). I should like to conclude this chapter by describing fairly briefly the formal organization of the *Sangha* in Thailand in modern times. Between 1902 and 1903 a series of bills were enacted pertaining to the administration of the *Sangha* as the Church of Thailand.[26] The regulations thus established however, in no way interfere with the operation of the rules of discipline contained in the *Vinaya-pitaka* which are binding upon Theravada Buddhist monks in all countries. The purpose of these Acts on the Administration of the Buddhist Order of Sangha (1902, 1941, 1964) was to organize the monkhood as a national institution and indeed to bring the Order under State Control. This aim is clearly stated in the preamble to the first Act which came into force in 1902 during the reign of Rama V, where it is written that

'Whereas the amendment of the law and the reformation of the administrative system of the State have brought about manifold developments and outstanding progress to the country it is obvious that the religious affairs of the Buddhist Church are of no less importance to the development and prosperity both of Buddhism and of the country, in that systematically administered they will serve to attract more people to the study and practice of Buddhism under the guidance of *Bhikkhus* (phikkhu), thereby leading them to the right mode of living in accordance with the Buddha's instructions.'[27]

Following this legislation a hierarchy of ecclesiastical offices was created, along the lines of the Thai civil administration. The King who has the final authority in all Church affairs appoints the Supreme Patriarch (*Somdet Phrasangkharat*) who stands at the apex of the ecclesiastical pyramid. In his turn the Supreme Patriarch appoints, with the King's approval, a number of senior *bhikkhus* to serve on the Council of Elders (*Mahatherasamakhom*), a body which combines legislative, administrative and judicial functions (Sobhana 1967, p. 14).

Local ecclesiastical administration is in the hands of the church officials in charge of the various administrative areas into which Thailand is divided, the largest and most inclusive of these being the nine Regions (*Phak*) each of which has at its head a *Chao Khana Phak* or Ecclesiastical Regional Head. The next official in declining order of rank is the Ecclesiastical Provincial Head (*Chao Khana Changwat*) followed by his subordinates at the District (the *Chao Khana Amphoe*) and Sub-District levels (the *Chao Khana*

---

[26] For details of pre-modern legislation pertaining to the *Sangha*, see article entitled 'The Government of the Thai Sangha' by Phra Sasana Sobhana in *Visakha Puja* (1967), publication by Buddhist Association of Thailand, Bangkok. For historical development of the *Sangha*, see Dutt 1957 and 1960.

[27] See Acts on the Administration of the Buddhist Order of Sangha (The Mahamakuta Educational Council, The Buddhist University, Bangkok 1963).

Tambon). The most junior ecclesiastical official is the abbot of the individual monastery or *wat* (*Chao Awat*), which forms the smallest unit of administration.[28]

The civil servants employed in the Department of Religious Affairs in the Ministry of Education are occupied almost exclusively with matters pertaining to the *Sangha* as Church of Thailand. The Director-General of this Department is ex-officio Secretary-General to the Council of Elders and all senior ecclesiastical appointments must be ratified by his immediate superior, the Minister of Education.

A most important function of the officials in the Department of Religious Affairs is to organize, in conjunction with senior *bhikkhus*, the courses of ecclesiastical education; the three grades of the primary course known as *Nak Tham* (Student of the *Dhamma*) were introduced in 1910 whilst the more advanced *Barian* or Pali Course (Grades 3–9) was established somewhat earlier, in 1893 (Wells 1960, pp. 14–15). In his article 'Church and State in Thailand', Yoneo Ishi writes that

'The adoption of a system to give the monks an official status by state examinations helped to strengthen the state control of the monks. This system which aimed at deepening the monks' knowledge of Buddhism, enforced a sort of orthodoxy by banning free interpretations of the Buddhist doctrines which are liable to bring about schism within the Buddhist Order. Thus, the Thai monks' understanding of Buddhism became stereotyped, and the monks' subjugation to the state was strengthened' (Ishi 1968, p. 866).

My own observations support these statements in that the *bhikkhus* of Ayutthaya did not appear to indulge in anything approaching philosophical speculation or debate, and for them *Dhamma* study meant working for the annual ecclesiastical examinations.

The Department of Religious Affairs is also concerned with the administration of Central Church Property, which consists largely of disused monasteries and the associated estates. It is through these channels moreover that the government budget for the support of religious affairs is administered, the major items of expenditure being the restoration of both deserted and inhabited *wats*, and the costs of ecclesiastical education over the whole country (Wells 1960, p. 31).

A yearly record of the number and status of the residents in all the monasteries in Thailand is preserved in the Department of Religious Affairs in Bangkok. Each abbot is required to submit an annual report to the

---

[28] There are approximately 24,105 monasteries in Thailand, which housed during the Lenten season 1966 a total of 175,232 monks (statistics from the Department of Religious Affairs, Bangkok).

Department giving detailed information about the members of his *wat* community, their age, academic qualifications and so on. He must also report on the activities organized by the monastery for the laymen in the vicinity, and comment on the extent of lay participation in these services.

The *Chao Khana Amphoe* (Ecclesiastical District Head) is a pivotal figure with regard to communication taking place between the civil administration and the *Sangha*. He collects the reports of individual abbots in his District and tabulates the information contained before forwarding it, through the Education Section in the *Amphoe* office, to the Department of Religious Affairs in Bangkok.

Furthermore the *Chao Khana Amphoe* plays an important part in the allocation of ecclesiastical offices which fall vacant within his area of juris-diction. Final appointments for positions below the level of Ecclesiastical District Head are granted by the Ecclesiastical Head of the Province (*Chao Khana Changwat*), but it is impossible for an officer of this standing to have personal knowledge of all the *bhikkhus* in the province and he must rely upon the opinion of his subordinates at the District level in making these appointments. Messages are also relayed in the other direction through the medium of the *Chao Khana Amphoe* in that he is responsible for the local organization of the annual ecclesiastical examinations when he receives his directive from Bangkok, and it is his duty to see that Buddhist ceremonies held to mark national holidays are performed at the proper time and place.

It must be mentioned in conclusion that though there exists in Thailand a single system of ecclesiastical administration the Thai *Sangha* is divided into two sects. A movement of reform begun under King Mongkut (1851–68) resulted in 1894 in the Buddhist Monkhood's splitting into two *nikai* (sects); the smaller reform group was known as the *Thammayutika-Nikai* (The Sect of these who uphold the *Dhamma*, or Reform Sect), whilst the main body called themselves the *Mahanikai* (The Greater Sect). The chief points of difference between the two lie in the fact that the *bhikkhus* of the *Thammayutika* sect adhere more strictly to the rules of conduct laid down in the *Vinaya-pitaka* and in general place a greater emphasis on study rather than on pastoral services performed for the laity. Although there is necessarily a considerable degree of overlap in behavioural terms between the strictest *Mahanikai* monk and the most liberal members of the *Thammayutika* sect, the latter can on the whole be seen to adhere to the more rigorous standards which they profess.[29]

[29] See article in Thai in the journal *Sangkhomsatporithat* (The Social Science Review) by S. Siwaraksa on the causes and implications of the differences existing between the two sects (Special Edition no. 4, August 1966 (Social Sciences Press, Bangkok), p. 89).

Monks of the two sects cannot perform rituals pertaining to disciplinary affairs together because of the stricter interpretation of the Word of the Buddha which is followed by the *Thammayutika* sect. Nevertheless, *Mahanikai* and *Thammayutika* monks can jointly officiate at merit-making rituals performed at some layman's invitation. Where both sects are represented on such occasions the chants are recited in the *Sanyoga* mode following *Mahanikai* practice, although for ceremonies performed exclusively by *Thammayutika* monks a recitative form (*Magadha* or *Mogodh*) assumed to be closer to the original Pali intonation is often adopted (Wells 1960, p. 129). In terms of outward appearance monks of the two sects are usually indistinguishable. Originally monks of the Reform Sect adopted a different way of carrying the begging-bowl, and wore their robes in a different style, but these diacritical emblems have largely been abandoned as the original practices of the *Mahanikai* are generally considered to be more convenient and comfortable.

A few of my informants insisted that the *Thammayutika* monks came only from the upper levels of Thai society. As the reform movement was begun and completed under royal leadership it is true that the sons of aristocratic families were the first to be ordained into the new sect. But at no time have humbler individuals been excluded, and my work in Ayutthaya indicates that at the present time there exists no difference between *bhikkhus* of the two sects in terms of social background. For the average layman sectarian differences are of no significance whatsoever, and several of my informants were unaware that the Buddhist *Sangha* was so divided. Furthermore, for many of the ordinary *bhikkhus* the basis of this division and its implications are far from clear. It is not unknown for a man to be ordained as a *Mahanikai* and as a *Thammayutika* monk at different times in his life.

1

'The way of the monk'

Shed thou householders' finery
As coral tree its leaves in fall:
And going forth in yellow clad,
Fare lonely as a rhinoceros.

Verses from the *Patimokkha* translated by
Edward Conze (Conze 1959, p. 80)

The role of the Buddhist monk or *bhikkhu*, both as it is defined in the
scriptures, and as it is enacted on the ground, forms the critical focus of the
present chapter. It is not surprising to find that there are certain discrepancies
between the ideal and its practical realization; it is perhaps surprising that
there are not more of them. A second and closely related issue concerns the
integration of this role into the total social system. I shall examine the
antecedent qualifications which go to permit, promote or prohibit a man's
assumption of this role, occupancy of which may vary from a few days to a
lifetime. And indeed, this close analysis of the recruitment process will in
itself help us to pinpoint the factors which go to influence an individual's
length of tenure as a monk. A further point for discussion turns on the
significance of his period of service in the *wat*, for the man who later chooses
to disrobe. As will become clear, qualifications earned, talents developed,
and contacts made as a monk can be employed to advantage in other social
roles.

Early Buddhist doctrine was the property of a religious elite of mendicant
monks whose aim was to reach *Nirvana* by perfecting their understanding
of the *Dhamma*, or Word of the Buddha, the Enlightened One. According
to Pali scholars one of the oldest parts of the canon is the *Patimokkha* section
of the *Vinaya-pitaka* which comprises 227 highly specific rules of conduct
for the *bhikkhu*. Adherence to these remarkably comprehensive ascetic
proscriptions is necessary but not sufficient for the attainment of the highest
spiritual goals, as it is intended only to aid the monk in his pursuit of
Salvation by removing him as far as possible from the ordinary world.

The question as to how far it is considered possible or desirable in the
Thai context for any individual to renounce society will receive due consideration in the next chapter; our immediate concern is with the social
interpretation of the role of the monk as it is defined by the *Patimokkha*

29

code. A point which will be emphasized repeatedly is that the ascetic regime of the monk, though intended to remove him from lay society in fact renders him dependent on that very society for material support and is believed furthermore to enable him to confer merit (*bun*) upon any house-holder who offers alms. This functional interdependence of the monastic and lay sectors of society has important implications for role performance; with respect to the monkly role, operating as it does with a more specific brief, a certain range of leeway is allowed, even institutionalized, but monks who stray too far from what is generally regarded to be the norm may be checked by the withdrawal of lay support. Conversely, those *bhikkhus* with powerful personal charisma, from whatever source, usually receive more than adequate material reward.

Although the material used in this chapter is based on my Ayutthaya experience, many of the generalizations I shall make have application beyond the limits of this specific area of study, as will be clear to those readers acquainted with other literature on related topics.

It is both impossible and unnecessary to discuss in turn each of the 227 rules in the *Patimokkha*, a good number of which are in any case only relevant to the conditions prevailing in India during the early days of the development of the Buddhist *Sangha*. Consequently the scope of the discussion can be limited to those proscriptions, proffered by informants both monk and lay, as being the most important criteria for distinguishing the 'way of the monk' (*thang phra*) from the 'way of the world' (*thang lok*).

THE MONKLY ROLE

One of the most significant differences between a monk and his lay counter-part is that sexual activity of any kind is forbidden him on pain of immediate expulsion from the Order. This injunction does not prohibit men who have been married from becoming ordained, even whilst their wives are still living, although it does mean that they must remain celibate whilst wearing the yellow robe.[1] It was my impression that the members of the Thai *Sangha* adhered very closely to this rule of celibacy and few cases of its alleged infraction came to my hearing.

Aside from their intrinsic human interest, these stories were of value in that they illustrated the reluctance both of members of the lay community and of the ecclesiastical authorities to take the responsibility of bringing disgrace upon any *bhikkhu* – and by extension to the *Sangha* as a whole –

[1] Over 27% of my informants in Ayutthaya monasteries had been married. See Appendix 2 for details.

where it is at all possible to avoid doing so.[2] The attitude maintained by most laymen is that if the saffron robe becomes 'too hot' (*pha ron*) for its wearer for whatever reason then he should rejoin the lay world which he yearns for. Nor is there any barrier to his doing so, as the ordinand takes no binding vows of any kind; the man who earns the disapproval of the laity may well forfeit their continuing material support.

There were in Ayutthaya two or three *bhikkhus* described by some lay informants as showing 'too much interest in the way of the world' but they appeared to restrict its expression to casting a few bold glances in the direction of the young female members of the congregation gathered to witness any ceremony; families desirous of borrowing ritual equipment (altars, images and so on) necessary to hold a merit-making ceremony centred in the home, sent their prettiest representatives as suppliants to those abbots, who were liable to respond more generously under such circumstances.

Despite these contrary examples however, the proscription against sexual activity appears to be quite strictly observed; according to many Thai monks it is their scrupulous adherence to this rule which distinguishes them from their Burmese counterparts who are reputed to be guilty of a double misdemeanour, in that they escort girls to places of public entertainment. Although this allegation is just one manifestation of a more widespread national prejudice it does appear to have some slight basis in fact. In his book on village life in contemporary Burma, Manning Nash speaks of the 'arrogant wearers of the yellow robe who are seen at football matches . . . or with women' (Nash 1965, p. 143). These *bhikkhus* who are known as *khit pongyi*, meaning literally 'modern monk, not worthy of respect', are however few in number and sternly disapproved by the majority of their fellows. As far as I know there is no Thai equivalent for the term *khit pongyi* which suggests that, though there are monks who contravene rules restricting contacts with women, they are very few in number, and manifest their interest in 'worldly ways' less publicly.

A second austerity which is regarded as being particularly hard to endure is the *bhikkhu*'s practice of taking no nourishment after midday; members of the Buddhist *Sangha* take only two meals each day, eating for the first time at approximately seven o'clock in the morning, and timing their last meal to finish just before noon. After this time they are allowed to smoke or chew betel, or to drink any liquid which is unsweetened, and which does not contain milk; this means in practice that the *bhikkhu* can take any beverage to which he has added neither sugar nor milk himself, consequently soft drinks such as Coca Cola or Orangeade are regarded as quite acceptable,

[2] See Appendix 1a for a case of alleged infraction of the rule against celibacy which involved legal action.

since the *Sangha* does not enquire into the conditions of their manufacture. But with regard to the rule against taking an evening meal, as with respect to the ban on taking alcoholic drinks, the monks of Ayutthaya appeared to be quite scrupulous – unlike Michael Moerman's informants in Ban Ping (Moerman 1966, p. 154). Nor did they appear to suffer any disability in the form of listlessness or exhaustion; indeed several *bhikkhus* whom I knew practised the additional austerity of eating only once each day. This is in fact one of the thirteen *Dhutanga,* or Austere Practices, which will be discussed at length below.[3]

A third criterion which serves to distinguish the way of the monk most markedly from that of the average layman, lies in the fact that the former does not earn his living in any ordinary way, but by and large subsists on presentations of food made by the householders, who live along the route taken by him on his daily alms-round. The prohibition against taking life, though it applies to all Buddhists, is given a stricter interpretation in the case of the *bhikkhu*; and one implication of this is that members of the *Sangha* cannot subsist by cultivating such land as belongs to the monastery because such activity would inevitably entail the destruction of innumerable small organisms in the soil. Consequently monastic land-holdings are usually loaned or rented out to the laity for cultivation.[4]

In addition, Theravada Buddhist monks may not indulge in commercial activity of any kind, though this does not mean that in Thailand the *bhikkhus* do not possess small sums of money for their personal use. The ideal is that on ordination the monk renounces all worldly possessions beyond the Eight Requisites allowed to him. But in practice the articles considered necessary are considerably more numerous than the stipulated items – namely, one set of robes (three garments: 1–3), one alms-bowl (4), a razor (5), a needle and thread for patching his robes (6), a filter for straining living organisms from water used for drinking or bathing (7), and a girdle or belt to secure the lower garment of his robe (8). The articles numbered 6, 7 and 8 in the preceding list are in fact owned by comparatively few monks, but most *bhikkhus* possess additional items such as a quilt, a pillow and a mosquito-net to suspend above his sleeping mat; an umbrella, a kettle, a cup and saucer and some cutlery – to name just a few of the most common items.[5]

Over and above these initial personal effects *bhikkhus* also receive small

---

[3] See chapter 2 (p. 54) for further treatment.

[4] *Bhikkhus* should also filter drinking water, or water used for bathing, in order to remove 'living things' from it. My observations showed that very few monks observe this practice, though in this, as in other respects, members of the *Thammayutika* sect tend to be more strict.

[5] The monk whose ordination I helped to finance needed 25 Requisites. See below, chapter 5.

amounts of money and other material goods (items of grocery or objects used in ritual, e.g. candles, incense-sticks, lotus buds, etc.) in return for their performance of merit-making ceremonies on behalf of members of the lay community. As far as the money is concerned the amounts given are quite small, the traditional sum being somewhat between ten and thirty *baht* for each monk taking part in a particular ritual performance.[6] Furthermore the fiction that Buddhist monks do not handle money may to some extent be maintained by the use of an intermediary, both in the act of donating and of spending the money concerned. That is to say that the layman initially presents the money to a lay-bursar (*waiyawachakon*) attached to the monastery where the intended recipient resides; the *waiyawachakon* in turn conveys the money to the monk or alternatively buys on his behalf any articles he should need up to that amount. On the other hand the *bhikkhu* who wishes to spend some of his money – newspapers, cigarettes, or supplementary food being the most usual items of expenditure – usually takes with him one of the small boys who help with chores around the *wat* (*dek wat*),[7] to carry out the transaction for him.

We have already remarked that there is a basic conflict in the position of the monk, springing from the fact that the *bhikkhu*'s abstinence from worldly activity renders him capable of conferring spiritual benefits in the form of merit upon those still enmeshed in secular affairs, who in turn express their reverence and gratitude by making presentations of the material objects ideally renounced by all members of the *Sangha*. The further implications of this paradoxical state of affairs will be explored more fully in the following chapter. At this point it is sufficient to note that the Buddhist monk must behave with great circumspection as regards his worldly possessions; it is common practice for *bhikkhus* to share such money and goods as they are given with their fellows whenever possible, and where such distribution is not possible to strive to maintain an attitude of indifference towards the objects in question.

In drawing attention to some of the discrepancies between the rules of the *Patimokkha* code and their practical implementation my intention is not to discredit the Thai monk, but rather to draw attention to the difficulty of realizing the original ascetic ideal. On the contrary I was impressed by the generally high standards of conduct maintained by the monks of Ayutthaya, and it would seem that the rewards – both material and immaterial – which are entailed in entering the Order, are for the most part fairly earned, in

---

[6] At the time of fieldwork (1966–7) £1 sterling=57 *baht*; at the time of writing there are 50 *baht* to the pound.

[7] *Dek wat* are usually boys from poor families who receive board and lodging at the *wat* in return for performing domestic chores for the monks (see below, p. 87).

the sense that most *bhikkhus* observe a genuinely more ascetic way of life than do their lay fellows. There are comparatively few monks who can be regarded as malingerers.

These men who have entered upon 'the way of the monk' are separated from the rest of society not only by their residence in the *wat* but by diacritical features of dress and personal appearance. The Buddhist *bhikkhu* wears saffron-coloured robes and his head and eyebrows are shaved immediately prior to the Ordination Ceremony and thereafter once each month for as long as he remains in the Order.[8]

Furthermore, the monk is differentiated from the laity in matters of etiquette and deportment, which are also regulated by the *Patimokkha* rules; he should be careful of his table manners, and 'not eat stuffing out (the cheeks like a monkey)'; he should wear his robes in a decorous and modest manner and not 'sit laughing loudly in inhabited areas' (Ven. Nanamoli Thera 1966, p. 14). These minor regulations are observed quite strictly and Thai monks do tend to be of quieter and more dignified mien than their lay fellows. It is quite remarkable that boisterous young men assume at least the outward trappings of their new role immediately and without self-consciousness on being ordained. The significance of the monkish façade for monk–laity relations cannot be overemphasized, as the reputation of many an eminent monk in Ayutthaya was based more on his conformity to the formal stereotype of the calm and passive *bhikkhu* than on his knowledge of the scriptures, his aptitude for teaching and preaching, or any other clerical skill.[9]

In the context of interaction between a member of the *Sangha* and a person belonging to the lay community the status superiority of the former over the latter is acknowledged by numerous linguistic usages; in such a situation both monks and laymen use special terms of address and self-reference to express their awareness of the spiritual disparity which exists between them. There is in addition a special vocabulary of terms to describe ordinary actions as performed by monks (see Table 1.1).

Furthermore the layman's respect for the monk is expressed in greeting-patterns and in seating arrangements at mixed gatherings where priority is always given to members of the *Sangha*; when a layman encounters a *bhikkhu* he knows, in the street, he raises his hands in the *wai* gesture of respect which the monk may acknowledge with a few words of blessing but will never return. And, should a householder visit a monk in his *kuti* or living quarters in the *wat* he shows his respect by prostrating himself on

---

[8] The fourteenth day of the waxing moon in each lunar month, *Wan Kon* (Shaving Day), marks the occasion when all monks shave their heads and eyebrows.

[9] See below, pp. 69–70 and passim.

the floor. The head of a layman should never be higher than that of the monk, his superior.[10] Nor may a member of the lay community eat at the same time as the ordained but must wait until the latter finish their meal, the men standing by to present (*phrakhen*) each dish, as *bhikkhus* may not partake of any food which is not formally offered.

TABLE 1.1. *Linguistic usages operating between monks and laymen*

The Monk	The layman

i. Term of self-reference when speaking to a layman:
    atama
	i. Term of self-reference when speaking to a monk:
	    phom (m)
	    dichan (f)
	    (also polite usage between laymen)

ii. Term of address when speaking to a layman:
    yom, or *khun* (also used between laymen)
	ii. Term of address when speaking to a monk:
	    than
	    or *Luang Pho* (Reverend Father)
	    or specific title

iii. The verb to eat: *chan*
    to sleep: *cham wat*
    to bathe: *song nam*
	iii. *kin*, or *than* (polite)
	    non lap
	    ap nam

NOTE:
In the Thai language each noun has an associated classifier which may be used in association with the noun, or on its own where the reference is clear. The word *khon* is the classifier used when speaking about ordinary people, e.g.

    Three farmers: *Chao na   sam   khon*
               Farmer   three   person

But in speaking about monks the classifier *ong* is used, e.g.

    Three monks: *Phra   sam   ong*
              Monk   three   person (or religious person)

The classifier *ong* is also used when speaking about the Buddha or a Buddha image, angels and deities of the Hindu pantheon (though not of malevolent spirits or *phi*) and when referring to royalty. Novices (*nen*), or junior members of the *Sangha*, who are less than 20 years of age, and observe only 10 of the 227 rules of the *Patimokkha*, are also *ong* rather than *khon*, e.g.

    Three novices: *nen   sam   ong*
               novice   three   person

Nuns or *mae chi* are however regarded as ordinary people, e.g.

    Three nuns: *mae chi   sam   khon*
              nun   three   person

Laymen and women accord these respectful forms of behaviour and address to all members of the Buddhist monkhood although it would be surprising if they did not revere some *bhikhus* more than others, on the basis of their length of service in the *wat*, of their scholarship and learning, or because of personal charisma springing from some other source. Nevertheless, as all members of the lay community – even the Monarch – are of

[10] Similar patterns of behaviour also obtain between laymen, and between monks within the monastic community. The head is regarded as sacred, being the seat of the individual's *khwan* or soul-essence (Rajadhon 1961, p. 171; Tambiah 1968, pp. 52-3).

35

inferior spiritual status to any member of the *Sangha*, they adjust their behaviour accordingly.

Since women are regarded as the major obstacles to any man's renunciation of the sensory world female members of the laity must be particularly circumspect in their dealings with *bhikkhus*, taking care to avoid all physical contact even of an indirect nature. One of the implications of this avoidance is that a woman who has occasion to pass any object – such as a book, or a glass of water – to a monk, must place it, not in his hand but upon a cloth (*pha phrakhen*) which he carries for the purpose. Furthermore, on all the trains and buses special seats are reserved for members of the *Sangha*, to minimize the risk of their coming into contact with female passengers. However, as will later become clear, this ban on physical contact with monks does not prevent women from making daily offerings of cooked food to the mendicant *bhikkhu*, nor from attending ceremonies and services in the *wat*. Indeed, at least with respect to these two kinds of activity the female members of the lay community are generally more diligent than the males, for a variety of reasons to be explored at length below.

ENTRY INTO THE ORDER OF MONKS

It is obvious from the foregoing paragraphs that the man who becomes a *bhikkhu* enjoys a position of great prestige in society, at the same time as deriving other benefits of a transcendental kind from this most meritorious act of renunciation. In Thailand, according to popular belief, all young men who have reached the age of twenty should enter the *wat* for at least a brief period of time; unlike monks of the Christian tradition the Buddhist *bhikkhu* is not asked to dedicate his life to the Order and indeed may return to lay life at any time. The Thai practice whereby young men enter the *wat* for a short period of time (*chua khrao*) has rightly been regarded as a kind of *rite de passage* by many anthropologists (Rajadhon 1961, pp. 68–9; Tambiah 1968, p. 58), as to become a monk for even a brief period is thought to transform young men who are immature or 'unripe' (*dip*) into fully adult members of society. In former days – and in some country areas to this day – it is said that a young man's prospects for marriage might depend upon whether or not he had spent a season in the *wat*.

Thai men who are ordained on a temporary basis 'according to custom or tradition' (*ben prapheni*) usually spend a part or the whole of one Lenten season (*phansa*) in the monastery, which is to say from mid-July until mid-October, a period coinciding with the heaviest monsoon rains. During this time the Buddha is believed to have ordered his disciples to go into retreat lest they damage the growing rice.

In contemporary Thailand monastic communities often double in size during *phansa* with the influx of newly ordained monks and unless a man has been in the *wat* during this Lenten season he cannot properly be said to have been a *bhikkhu* and, indeed, his name will not appear in the official records of the Religious Department in Bangkok.[11]

For another group of Thai men, ordination, far from preceding the assumption of social maturity, marks the end of their active participation in the world, as it is a fairly common practice to retire into the monastery in old age. But, over and above the men who become ordained on a temporary basis and those who spend only their final years as members of the *Sangha*, there are some individuals who can be regarded as 'permanent' or 'career' monks, in that they remain in the Order for many years, and in some cases for most of their lives. It is these monks and their relationship with the lay community who form the focus of this study.

Because these so-called permanent monks may also re-enter lay society at any time, and indeed rarely know or state for how long they intend to remain in the *wat*, they can in a formal sense only be distinguished by the fact that they do not refer to themselves as having *buat chua khrao* or 'been ordained for a short time'; nor are they known to the lay community as 'temporary' monks.[12] In practice most of the *bhikkhus* who remain in the monastery after the end of *phansa* are permanent in the sense defined above.

The situation which thus exists in Thailand today is one whereby about one-half of the adult male population has spent some time in the monastery,[13] and where a much smaller proportion remains in the *Sangha* on a more long-term basis. Some idea of the ratio of 'permanent' monks to laymen can be gained from the fact that in the District of Ayutthaya there were approximately 30,000 men who were over twenty years of age and thus eligible to become *bhikkhus*, and within the same administrative area at the time of my fieldwork there lived some 434 monks whom one could describe as permanent.[14]

[11] Boys under twenty years of age may be ordained as novices (junior members of the *Sangha* who observe Ten Precepts) on a temporary basis during this period, whilst others remain in the Order for many years so that they might pursue their studies at monastery schools. (See below, chapter 3.) During Lent (*phansa*) 1967 the number of monks in the *wats* of Ayutthaya District (*Amphoe*) increased from 434 to 817, and the number of novices from 97 to 161.

[12] The term *chua khrao* may be used rather disparagingly by 'permanent' monks and by some laymen to refer to those temporary members of the *Sangha*, although in theory to be ordained for any period is meritorious.

[13] See Tambiah (1968, p. 58) and Fitzsimmons (ed.) (1957, p. 113) for comparative figures.

[14] We should beware of attaching too much importance to these figures in that a number of monks in Ayutthaya came from outside the *Amphoe* area (see Appendix 2), whilst on the other hand Ayutthaya men were living in monasteries elsewhere,

Bearing these figures in mind it is reasonable to enquire whether or not there are any factors – beyond personal disinclination to abandon 'the way of the world' – which prevent some men from becoming ordained, and conversely whether the permanent monks have anything in common other than the length of their service in the *wat*.

The Ordination Ceremony (*ngan upasombot*) whereby a man is admitted into the Buddhist *Sangha* is described in greater detail in the chapters concerned with the religious behaviour of the Thai householder, but certain aspects of this procedure must be examined at this point in order to assess to what extent, if at all, it can be regarded as a mechanism of selection.

An important point to remember is that in order to leave the lay society the ordinand (*nak*) requires the active co-operation of a number of people from the lay community and of at least five members of the *Sangha*, who form the quorum necessary for a valid act of ordination.

Of householders who participate in the ceremony of *upasombot* one or more acts as the sponsor or *chao phap* by financing the affair, which may cost between three hundred and three thousand *baht*, or more (Kaufman 1960, p. 129), depending upon the pocket and preferences of the people concerned. In the majority (55%) of cases I witnessed the father of the ordinand acted as *chao phap*, although in some instances this title was given more in recognition of the fact that the preparations for the ritual and the post-ceremonial festivities took place in his house (which was near to the *wat*) than because he shouldered all the expenses himself. In any case it is believed that the parents of the ordinand, and in particular his mother who bore him, automatically make the most merit.[15] In fact, in Ayutthaya the expenses of ordination were rarely if ever defrayed by a single person although it was usual for two or three people to make significantly larger contributions than the other guests.[16] It may be remembered that according to Buddhist ideology, gifts in any form bring merit to the donor; it is regarded as particularly meritorious to contribute to the costs of an ordination ceremony.

particularly in Bangkok. The only figures which would have any real meaning would be those for the 'permanent' monks in the country as a whole at any one time, compared with the total male population eligible to become monks (i.e. of twenty years or older). As a census of the monastic population is taken only during Lent when large numbers of men become ordained temporarily it is impossible to get even a rough estimate of the total number of permanent monks in Thailand at any one time. The national figures for the *Lenten* season 1967 were as follows: 175,232 monks, 87,661 novices (statistics from the Department of Religious Affairs, Bangkok).

[15] 5.3% of the total number of monks interviewed gave filial obligation as their reason for becoming ordained.

[16] See Moerman (1966, pp. 150–1) for a different practice.

'The way of the monk'

As will be made clear in subsequent chapters, the necessity of holding periodic life-crisis rituals, of which ordination is one of the most important, gives rise to a system of reciprocal exchanges between laymen, sanctioned by the ideology of merit-making; which is to say that if individual X contributes 100 *baht* to the cost of a cremation ceremony sponsored by individual Y, who may be a kinsman or merely a friend or business associate, then Y should reciprocate by bringing an equivalent amount when X's son enters the *Sangha* the following year. A breakdown in reciprocity expresses or may well create a rupture of the relationship between the two parties concerned. On the other hand, if social obligations are fulfilled on both sides by the exchange of contributions then both parties make merit, and also gain the good opinion of society for having observed the correct social forms. Because of this system it seems unlikely that, except in the case of the desperately poor, the lack of necessary funds acts as a limiting factor in excluding some men from the Order of Monks. Indeed even when the relations and friends of the aspiring ordinand are themselves poverty-stricken, hope is not at an end as the *bhikkhus* in the *wat*, or some wealthy philanthropist, usually take it upon themselves to assume the honour and the financial responsibilities of acting as sponsor. During my period of fieldwork I attended two ordination ceremonies which were financed by the abbot of the *wat* of ordination, and a third, the expenses of which were shared between the *bhikkhus* and a wealthy spinster, who said that having no sons of her own, she was pleased to make merit by sponsoring the ordinand.

The candidate for ordination however requires the backing of a number of householders, in another than financial form. According to a series of Acts on the Administration of the Buddhist Order of Sangha which were passed in the first half of the present century (betwen 1902 and 1941) the ordinand must present to the *bhikkhu* who is to confer ordination upon him, a completed certificate of application. This form vouchsafes that the candidate is aged twenty years or over, and in good health; that he is not in debt nor guilty of any other crime; and that both his parents, and his wife, if he is already married, have consented to his entering the monkhood. The signature of the ordinand must be underwritten by those of three other laymen. Furthermore if the ordinand is a government employee he must submit another document which grants him leave of absence from the civil service for a certain period.[17]

The application forms are issued by the Department of Religion in Bangkok to *bhikkhus* holding the office of *upacha* and are in turn given by the latter to the ordinand when he comes with his sponsor to request

[17] After four years' employment in any branch of the service a Thai civil servant is entitled to spend one Lenten season in the *Sangha* without forfeiture of pay.

ordination. The completed forms are usually returned to the *upacha* on the day of the ordination ceremony.[18]

It is clear that this formal application procedure, which is just one aspect of the institutionalization of the Thai *Sangha*, goes a long way towards ensuring that the monkhood does not provide a sanctuary for men who are fleeing social responsibilities or the consequences of previous misdeeds. Nor indeed are *bhikkhus*, once ordained, beyond the reach of the ordinary law of the land, as we shall see.

The ceremony of ordination by which a man is admitted into the *Sangha* must be performed in the *bot*[19] of the *wat* by a quorum of at least five monks one of whom, the *upacha*, has been authorized by the Department of Religious Affairs to confer ordination.[20] In theory the *upacha* should attempt to ascertain the suitability of the candidate prior to the actual ceremony, by making sure that he is able to read and write, so that he can pursue the ecclesiastical study courses available. The seriousness of the ordinand's intentions is generally measured by his ability to memorize the Pali responses which he must make during the ceremony. It is probable that the majority of younger men who apply for admission into the Order can meet the minimal requirement of literacy, though this may not be true of older individuals, particularly those from rural areas, who enter the *wat* on retiring from active social life.[21] Certainly, several of my older informants seemed scarcely to be able to write, though they were at pains to disguise this disability. It is obvious, then, that this ruling is not very stringently applied, and in none of the cases I observed did the *upacha* actually test the capacity of the ordinand to read and write.

Nor does the inability to repeat the Pali formulae, used in the ordination procedure, ever appear to form a serious obstacle to admission to the *Sangha*; for one ceremony I attended there had clearly been very inadequate rehearsal, and the ordinand was prompted throughout by an older relative who had previously spent several years in the *wat*.[22] It used to be the practice for young men to spend several weeks of preparation in the monastery prior to ordination, but this is clearly not possible at the present time, particularly in the urban situation where the ordinand is often employed in his office or workship until the eve of the ordination. Only one instance came to my notice of an *upacha*'s refusing to ordain a young man on the

[18] See Vajirananavarorasa (1963, pp. 112–13) for lay-out of application forms.
[19] The building in the *wat* which stands within the consecrated area marked by the *sima* or boundary stones.
[20] See also the Laws of the Council of Elders (*Kot Mahatherasamakhom*), Vol. 3, Bk 7, Sect. 1.1 – 1.162, for procedure for the appointment of the *upacha*.
[21] In Thailand an estimated 71% of the population over ten years of age is literate (Caldwell 1967, p. 53).
[22] For full details of the Ordination Ceremony see Vajirananavarorasa (1963).

grounds that he was insufficiently prepared. The *bhikkhu* in question lived in a sparsely populated area in the Southern Region of Thailand. He was the only monk for many miles who was empowered to confer ordination, and consequently had virtual control of entries into the Order. He appeared to enjoy this power and prided himself on his strictness in applying the rules for admission. But such a situation appears to be rather rare, and in Ayutthaya at least I heard of no comparable incidents. Within the municipal area there were eleven monks who had received the appointment of *upacha* and none of them made it their practice or their principle to turn away aspiring monks, though one or two expressed reservations with regard to the value of being ordained for a short time (*chua khrao*) both for the ordinand himself and for the community he joined on this temporary basis.[23]

After the ceremony, during which the ordinand is formally cross-examined by the *khu suat*[24] as to his eligibility to enter the *Sangha*, the *upacha* presents the new *bhikkhu* with an identity card. This is a kind of monk's passport which gives all the details of his past and present statuses.[25] The date and location of the ordination ceremony, and the names of the monks who officiated are entered on this document; the Pali name bestowed on the new monk by the *upacha* is also set down, though such names are rarely used except in official contexts[26] or when they are incorporated as part of an honorific title. If the monk should subsequently move to live in another monastery the abbots of the *wats* concerned should give their written consent to his transfer by signing his passport; furthermore the *bhikkhu*'s academic grades and any other titles received are recorded in this document.

In summary, then, the ordination ceremony can be said to act as a selective mechanism in so far as it requires the consent of a number of laymen and of members of the *Sangha*; interestingly enough during the procedure of ordination the people present in the *bot* are asked to voice any objections they may have to the ordinand's entry into the *Sangha* or to be

---

[23] At one ordination ceremony I attended a monk gave a sermon in which he spoke of the inestimable value of ordination. He told the *nak* who was to remain in the Order for fifteen days that the spiritual and mental benefits derived from having been a monk remained with the man throughout his life whether or not he chose to spend it in the *wat*. Several days later the same *bhikkhu* remarked in conversation that individuals who *buat chua khrao* have no time for worthwhile study and cause needless readjustment within the community as the other monks must at least attempt to teach them how to behave as monks (how to wear the robes, etc.) and instruct them in the rudiments of the *Dhamma*.

[24] *Khu suat*: generally translated as 'tutors' or 'witnesses'; during the ordination ceremony the two *khu suat* enquire into the ordinand's fitness to become a monk.

[25] For the form of the identity card see the *Kot Mahatherasamakhom*, Vol. 3, Sect. 2.34.

[26] For example, in any dealings the monk may have with the bureaucracy or with higher ecclesiastical officers.

silent thenceforth (Vajirananavarorasa 1963, p. 35). Thus although men who are obviously suffering from gross physical, mental or social disabilities cannot become monks, the requirements for ordination are not rigorous in that they do not demand a high level of intellectual ability, or previous educational attainment. Virtually any man is eligible to follow the 'way of the monk', whose chief aim, in theory at least, is to perfect his understanding of the *Dhamma*.[27]

THE MONKHOOD AS A CHANNEL OF MOBILITY

We have now located some of the possible obstacles to a Thai man's assuming the most meritorious role in the whole social inventory. The question must now be posed as to whether or not there are any factors which might make this role more attractive to some men than to others, on a fairly permanent basis. In the preceding paragraphs I did not discuss the factor of personal tastes as a deterrent to ordination, powerful though this may be: and similarly the question of individual temperament is beyond the scope of my examination of the more positive aspects of this issue; my rejecting 'personality' studies can at any rate be justified after the event, in that my observations showed that because of the leeway allowed in the interpretation of the *bhikkhus*' role the Thai *Sangha* accommodated men of very diverse types and capabilities. Instead I shall look to socio-economic factors to provide some solution to the question as to which men become permanent monks, although this is not to imply that these factors alone either determine or prohibit any man's becoming a monk, nor to ignore the possibility that personal or domestic crises might precipitate ordination,[28] or prolong an individual's stay in the *wat*. Nevertheless it remains true to say that under any circumstances the role of permanent monk offers special advantages to men from a particular social milieu.

As far as the 'temporary' monks are concerned, in Ayutthaya at least, my research showed that young men from all social backgrounds are equally likely to be ordained for a short time. Temporary *bhikkhus* were, with a few exceptions, young men who had, as yet, acquired relatively few social responsibilities. That is to say that older men who held vital positions in the national bureaucracy or as managers of family firms were unlikely to spend even the period of one *phansa* in the *wat*, although the sons of these pillars of the community and junior clerical or business staff were all to be found amongst the ranks of temporary monks.

[27] It is of course possible for a man to pose as a monk without having been ordained, and thus receive respect and support from the laity. See Appendix 1*b* for a case in point.
[28] See below, p. 156, the case of Khun Siri Imchai.

On the other hand, observable similarities existed between permanent monks in terms of their respective social circumstances.[29] As the earlier description of the position of the Buddhist *bhikkhu* in Thai society clearly showed, this role offers great advantages to any incumbent in terms of increased prestige. But one implication of the thoroughgoing institution-alization of the role of monk in the Thai context is that it presents other and more tangible benefits, making it particularly attractive to men on the lower rungs of the social ladder, namely to farmers and to members of the urban service classes. In the remaining paragraphs of the present chapter I shall analyze this situation more closely.

It may be recalled that in ideal terms, the primary purpose behind any man's renunciation of the lay world is that of improving his understanding of the Word of the Buddha as set out in the *Dhamma-pitaka*, and, as far as the *bhikkhus* of Ayutthaya were concerned, direct questioning as to their reasons for becoming ordained almost invariably provoked a response in these terms.[30] In Thailand today the study of the *Dhamma* implies, in effect, studying for the ecclesiastical examinations at the primary or secondary level; the elementary standard is known as the *Nak Tham* or 'Student of the Dhamma Course' in which there are three grades, and is followed by the more advanced studies for the Pali or *Barian* examinations (Grades 3–9). Both the prescribed texts and the paper for the qualifying examinations are issued by the Ministry of Education in Bangkok.

Both the *Nak Tham* and the *Barian* courses are taught in ecclesiastical schools to be found at some of the larger urban *wats*. In Ayutthaya for example there are three such institutions located at *Wat* Suwandaram, at *Wat* Phanan Choeng and at the only monastery in town belonging to the *Thammayut* (or *Thammayutika*) Sect, *Wat* Senasanaram.[31] The *bhikkhus* who instructed the monks and the novices studying at the various schools, were either residents of local monasteries, or alternatively had been specially sent from one of the Buddhist Universities in the capital. These three monastery schools made Ayutthaya into something of an ecclesiastical educational centre, attracting monks from other Provinces of Thailand where facilities were less developed, though the most serious students usually made their way to Bangkok.[32]

An obvious consequence of the fact that the best teaching facilities for *bhikkhus*, as indeed for laymen, are to be found in urban centres is that the

[29] Many of the permanent monks had originally intended to remain in the Order for a short time only.

[30] 62% of my informants phrased their answers to the question 'Why did you become ordained?' in these terms. See Appendix 2 for further reasons given.

[31] See Map B.

[32] See Appendix 2 for previous places of residence of Ayutthaya's monks.

largest numbers of permanent monks are concentrated at the monasteries in town, which either have their own schools or are at least accessible to those that do. However, the predominance of men from farming families in the *wats* of Ayutthaya suggests this causal sequence might equally well be reversed; that is to say that instead of stating that men who remain in the Order for a number of years tend to move into town to continue their studies, quite a strong case could be made for saying that, in some cases, the desire to move to town, in order to gain access to the educational or other benefits of urban living, has considerable influence on the decision to become ordained. But leaving aside the question as to the priority of their motivations for entering the *Sangha*, the fact remains that the monks in the monasteries of Ayutthaya had free access to a number of schools which gave instruction in both lay and ecclesiastical subjects. Furthermore there are additional or alternative benefits available to the urban *bhikkhu* in the form of titles and ecclesiastical offices which are rarely located at rural *wats*; indeed although most of the younger monks study fairly regularly many of those who are middle-aged or older have long since abandoned academic pursuits and divide their time between administrative affairs and the performance of merit-making ceremonies for laymen in the vicinity. Indeed, although one of the attractions of living in Ayutthaya is that educational facilities are relatively easily available, this does not mean that the town is a centre of learning in any but the most literal sense; most of the monks, like most laymen, are interested more in the form than in the substance of education.

In attempting to explain why permanent monks prefer to reside in the town rather than in the country one should not disregard those features of the urban environment which make living there preferable to village society, in theory at least, for the majority of Thais, and which can be enjoyed equally by the *bhikkhu* and the householder. Amongst these features can be counted not only the greater ease of communications and accessibility to the capital, and to all it offers in the way of books, newspapers, television and so on, but also the faster pace of life, inevitable where there is a denser concentration of people. Life in town is in general considered to be superior to life in the country, not only in terms of material comfort, but also in terms of relative levels of 'civilization', and few people in Ayutthaya were sufficiently sophisticated to express any yearnings or nostalgia for simple, golden days in the rice paddies.

The assertions made in previous paragraphs that one of the functions of the *Sangha* is that it provides a channel of mobility whereby a man can move out of rural into urban society, are based not only upon interviews, the collection of life-histories and biographies, within the monastic and lay communities, but also upon information obtained from a questionnaire survey, the response to which was however rather disappointing, due largely to the *bhikkhus'* understandable apathy, not I think their positive antipathy, towards filling in forms, and to their belief that I would somehow always be around to ask questions in person.[33]

The survey was begun in December 1966, that is to say, more than two months after the close of the Lenten season, and only two of my informants stated that they had been ordained temporarily. The completed questionnaires showed that of the remaining *bhikkhus* who can reasonably be regarded as permanent, over 68% come from farming families outside Ayutthaya or other District or Provincial areas, whilst the rest came from the lower ranks of urban society occupied by vendors, labourers, some junior civil servants and so on.[34]

Enquiry as to the previous educational status of the monks surveyed revealed the interesting fact that only fourteen of the ninety who completed their questionnaires had received any secondary education and that the majority of these had studied the advanced syllabus for only one or two years; of the 47% who reported having received formal primary education 72% had been ordained as novices on completing *Prathom* 4 which marks the limit of compulsory education provided freely by the State. A further 11% of the total sample had entered the *wat* as novices on a permanent basis some years after leaving primary school. In most cases such boys had spent the intervening period during their early teens in helping their families with the business of living, whether this involved giving a hand with the rice-farming or with some more urban activity. For all of these boys, whether they came from families in the town or in the country, their ordination enabled them to gain access to educational facilities otherwise unavailable to them, and nearly two-thirds of all the *bhikkhus* interviewed who had been novices (*nen*) for a number of years, had received Higher Ordination as a monk on reaching the age of twenty, whilst the remainder had followed the 'way of the world' for varying periods of time before returning to the society of monks. It should be remembered that ordination as a monk is not necessarily preceded by a period of service as a novice in the *wats* of Central Thailand, and indeed over 50% of my informants had never been novices on either a permanent or temporary basis.[35] Any Thai male is eligible

---

[33] See Appendix 2 for results in detail.

[34] The five monks who gave their occupation prior to ordination as 'civil servants' had variously been employed as a janitor at the Town Hall (1), a museum guard (1), a postman (1), and government chauffeurs (2). Officials of this rank (Grade 4) are barely differentiated in terms of income and life-style from urban service-workers.

[35] The situation in some Northern villages appears to be somewhat different (Moerman 1966, p. 139).

to become a *bhikku* on reaching the age of twenty, and indeed 46% of the monks interviewed had received Higher Ordination at this stage in their lives, whilst a further 11% had entered the *wat* for the first time in their late twenties. As was mentioned earlier there is a second point in a man's life-cycle when he is likely to become ordained, namely when he is freed of his social responsibilities in later life, and 27% of the monks surveyed were ordained in later middle-age or beyond.

An interesting point revealed by the survey was that whatever the age of ordination the trend was for men from farming settlements to be ordained locally and then to move to join a monastic community in town, and indeed 80% of my informants had lived in two or more *wats*; the place of ordination was almost always located near to their family home. It cannot be supposed that the elderly men who retired into the *Sangha* and moved into town were lured by the educational facilities available, or by the possibilities of achieving high ecclesiastical office. Indeed as was suggested earlier such monks might well not be interested in carving out a career for themselves in either academic or other spheres. It was simply that they found urban society more congenial than the social environment in their home villages.

Although the primary concern of the present chapter is with those men who remain in the *Sangha* as 'permanent' monks, my work amongst the lay members of Ayutthaya society throws new light on the function of the monkhood as a possible channel of mobility, in that it shows that a period of service in the monkhood may enable a man to re-enter lay life at a higher position on the socio-economic ladder than that which he originally renounced. This is to say that these *bhikkhus* from farming families who belong to urban monastic communities will rarely return to the rice-fields should they decide to de-robe, but stay on in town, typically entering the lower clerical ranks of the civil service. Indeed many of the laymen whom I came to know very well in their capacity as members of the monastery lay committee (*kammakan wat*)[36] were civil servants with this kind of background who had come to town as monks. Their service in the *Sangha* had equipped them with the education and with the contacts necessary to obtain a clerical post in the civil service. As laymen their familiarity with both the bureaucratic and the ecclesiastical machinery made them uniquely qualified to act as liaison officers between the *Sangha* and the civil service, as well as between the ordinary townspeople and the monastic community.

From the observer's point of view some men appear to manipulate the system quite consciously in that they enter the *Sangha* with the intention of

---

[36] *Kammakan wat* committee of laymen and monks who organize the practical affairs of the monastery, e.g. they make the arrangements for renting out fields belonging to the *wat*, cf. below chapter 4.

obtaining as good an education as possible in the monastic schools, and in the Buddhist Universities in Bangkok; an education which they realize will stand them in good stead when they return to lay life. Indeed I know of several cases of spectacular mobility being achieved in this way, and it can be no mere coincidence that many of the higher officials in civil service ministries in the capital were once monks who had completed Grades 8 or 9 of the *Barian* course of studies. [37] However, such mobility, whether or not it involves conscious exploitation of the system, is easily justified in that monkhood is not necessarily regarded as a permanent vocation and it is generally believed to be a better thing to leave the Order than to seem to pursue the 'way of the monk' *(thang phra)* whilst harbouring worldly thoughts. The frank pursuit of academic honours which, in a few monasteries in Bangkok, may precede de-robing is certainly considered deplorable both by laymen and the majority of monks.[38]

It should be stated here that although the monkhood provides a channel of mobility for some men, it is only one of several such routes existing in Thai society; and by no means all *bhikkhus* employ it in this way. There are other ways to find room at the top; through success in business, skilful operation of patron–client links, through the army, and so on. And on the other hand the majority of Thai monks evince no eagerness to shine in the *Sangha*, nor to use their ecclesiastical training to advantage in the lay world.

In the previous paragraphs I have to some extent located and identified the 'permanent' monks whose relationship with the lay society and with each other within the monastic community is central to this study. It has been shown that in Thailand most of these permanent *bhikkhus* are concentrated in urban centres, not only because the institutionalized *Dhamma* studies cannot properly be pursued elsewhere, but also by reason of the fact that important positions in the nation-wide ecclesiastical hierarchy tend to be attached to *wats* in the town. Naturally enough the presence of teachers and of *bhikkhus* eminent in other spheres continues to attract more men away from rural areas, which at any rate provide an uncongenial situation for monks, or indeed for laymen, who prefer a faster pace of living, or for those who desire, consciously or unconsciously, to build up some kind of personal following.

[37] In his article entitled 'The Buddhist Monkhood as an Avenue of Social Mobility in Traditional Thai Society' *(Journal of the Fine Arts Department, B.E. 2509 (1966),* 10th year, bk 1, p. 49), D. K. Wyatt writes 'there is some evidence to indicate that sometimes sons of provincial farmers entered government service in the capital. In many such cases such men moved into government positions through the system of religious education.' (See also chapter 5 below for specific example of such mobility from my own fieldwork.)

[38] See *Visakha Puja,* 1967, published by Buddhist Association of Thailand (p. 24 and passim).

Thus for the reasons described above, ordination on a fairly permanent basis, as opposed to a short term of service in the *wat*, offers more advantages to men from the lower socio-economic strata of society, namely to farmers and to members of the working classes in the town; this is not to say that all men in these occupational groups become ordained (the statistics show that this is clearly not so) but merely to suggest that for some individuals who are dissatisfied with this particular social status, to become ordained as a monk appears an attractive alternative. On the other hand entry into the *wat* on any basis other than a temporary one would appear to offer fewer advantages to men in the higher income families, as the latter had no representatives among the ranks of permanent monks in Ayutthaya during my period of research. There are of course no barriers to a wealthy man's becoming ordained to improve his knowledge of the Word of the Buddha, but very few appear to do so. There appears in practice to be a kind of religious division of labour in operation whereby the members of the *Sangha* are recruited from the lower levels of society, and the wealthier individuals tend to demonstrate their interest in religious affairs by presenting substantial donations of money and material goods to the *wat*; a feature of Thai society to be examined more closely when the merit-making activities of individual laymen are under review.

Although, permanent monks are present in the greatest number in urban areas it would be misleading to imply that these are only temporary *bhikkhus* living in rural *wats*, where 'usually the Abbot . . . and one or two other monks form a core of professionals' (Tambiah 1968, p. 58), the majority of men being ordained only temporarily.

Another point of interest is that the permanent or 'professional' monks in rural areas differ from their urban counterparts in their respective spheres of activity. As has already been stated, ecclesiastical schools and teachers are attached to some of the larger *wats* in town and all the monks with any pretensions to study are to be found living at or near these educational centres. Despite the fact that not all the *bhikkhus* living in Ayutthaya utilize the facilities for *Dhamma* studies which are available to them, and allowing for the possibility that the occupants of some village monasteries study at least the preliminary courses (*Nak Tham* 1–3) on their own, nevertheless, the general level of academic attainment is somewhat higher in town.

But a further point of difference lies in the fact that the range and scope of a *bhikkhu*'s 'pastoral' activities vary according to his social environment. A number of studies of village Thailand have made it very clear that the *bhikkhu* fulfils a wide variety of functions in the local community in that he not only performs merit-making ceremonies but may also act as an astrologer, doctor or money-lender, as well as giving advice on a wide variety of domestic and agricultural problems (Kaufman 1960, p. 113). Similarly, in his recent monograph *Buddhism and the Spirit Cults in North-East Thailand* (1970) Tambiah shows quite clearly that the village monk is given a much wider brief. It is also interesting incidentally that the minimal literacy acquired in the monkhood is essential to the enactment of the more important lay ritual roles (Tambiah 1970, p. 13).

The distinction between town and country monks in terms of their respective activities is not absolutely clear-cut in that a few of my informants in Ayutthaya did specialize in telling horoscopes and performing cures, but in general their sphere of influence tended to be more restricted. This is partly a consequence of the fact that some of the functions performed by village monks are peculiar to the rural environment; to take just one example, country *bhikkhus* may take part in 'animistic' or other non-Buddhist rituals connected with the agricultural cycle[39] (Tambiah 1968, p. 79).

Similarly the monk's role as healer and apothecary especially, in urban areas, has to some extent been usurped by the more widespread acceptance of the methods of *witthayasat* (science) whose practitioners, the doctors and nurses of Ayutthaya, are more accessible to the townsfolk. The *bhikkhu's* function as banker and money-lender has also been taken over by professionals, whilst it is in the very nature of the greater occupational diversity and specialization of the urban situation that few monks are qualified to give advice on occupational problems.

Nor were the monks of Ayutthaya generally invited to give their opinion on any domestic difficulties which might arise; this may be explicable by the fact that *bhikkhus* resident in urban monasteries are more isolated from the surrounding laity than their rural brothers not only in terms of spheres of action but also with regard to the degree of intimacy existing between them and the members of the local lay community. This is an inevitable consequence of the fact that most of the monks come from outside the town and are not necessarily familiar with the personal details of the lives of laymen in the immediate vicinity.[40]

The interaction between monk and layman in town thus tends to be more restricted in its scope. But there is compensation in the fact that the merit-making ceremonies (*ngan tham bun*) which form the chief basis for their interaction, are not only more frequent, given the larger community of

[39] As was mentioned in the introductory chapter, the monks of Ayutthaya also tend to be more dismissive of animistic practices than do their rural counterparts (see above p. 22).

[40] This is true of monks in any town, but the situation is possibly heightened in Ayutthaya which is known as a centre for ecclesiastical education.

householders, but are also less closely bound to the seasonal cycle. As is clear from the calendar of religious events attended by one lay informant, which is presented in chapter 5, there is in town a continuous round of religious ceremonies sponsored both by private individuals, and by the State on the occasion of Buddhist national holidays. In rural areas on the other hand the pattern of religious participation is largely determined by the pace of agricultural activities, for outside the Lenten season (*phansa*) all except the young or the very old and infirm are involved in these.

Furthermore, as will become clear from subsequent discussion, the *bhikkhus* in an urban area are involved in more activities directly pertaining to the monastic community and to the Buddhist *Sangha* as the Church of Thailand than are their fellows who live in smaller and more isolated village monasteries.

2
The monk and the lay community

Son, wife and father, mother, wealth
The things wealth brings, the ties of kin
Leaving these pleasures one and all
Fare lonely as a rhinoceros.

Verses from the *Patimokkha* translated by
Edward Conze (Conze 1959, p. 81)

Having defined very broadly the scope and limits of a Thai monk's activities, it is now necessary to analyze more specifically the concepts and notions entertained by various informants as to how these varied activities should be evaluated, and to discuss the implications of this evaluation for relations between the monk and the layman. As might be expected, the order in which these role-attributes are placed varies according to the mental sophistication and scriptural education of the informant concerned; which latter qualities would in themselves tend to have certain rather loose spatial correlates. One would expect for example that a monk from one of the more academic Bangkok monasteries would have a concept of his role more similar to the Theravada ideal with which he is familiar from his own reading than would a semi-literate monk in a remote rural village, who is besides subject to more pressures from the laity to develop his less orthodox extra-curricular talents, as was mentioned above in the preceding chapter. The average small-town *bhikkhu* falls somewhere between these two extremes. It should be understood that I have been talking not in terms of clear-cut distinctions but rather in terms of general trends in the ways in which the role of the monk is conceptualized by different people in different places.

A second main theme of this chapter concerns the maintenance and creation of ties between the *bhikkhu* and the lay community. Interaction with the lay community varies both qualitatively and quantitatively as between monks and, as will become clear, both parties in the monk–layman relationship must tread a narrow line between social obligations and partiality, being careful to honour the first and to avoid the second, at least in appearances.

In the preceding chapter I drew attention to some of the discrepancies which exist between the role of the Buddhist *bhikkhu* as it is defined in the *Patimokkha* code, and its social interpretation; discrepancies which are by

no means apparent to all monks or to all laymen, although a few philo-
sophically sophisticated members of both sectors of society are aware of the
hiatus between ideal and practice. Nevertheless such awareness does not
give rise to grave spiritual distress on the part of its bearers nor fill them
with any desire for reform of the situation: as Buddhists they are ever ready
to recognize the existence of 'different levels of awareness of the doctrine,
characteristic of the people who approach it at different times and in different
places' (Mendelson 1965, p. 217).

Subsequent paragraphs are devoted to a more detailed analysis of the
varied activities entailed in becoming a monk, in an attempt to show how
far it is possible, or indeed considered desirable, for a man to turn his back
on lay society when he enters the Thai *Sangha*. As many scholars have
already pointed out, a certain degree of structural tension is inherent in the
institutionalization of the ascetic way of life in that the religious mendicant's
abstinence from secular activity renders him permanently dependent for
material subsistence upon those who remain in the world.[1] And yet, as will
become apparent, few if any of my informants were conscious of the paradoxical nature of the situation whereby the *bhikkhus* who should renounce
the world in order to perfect their knowledge of the *Dhamma*, not only
relied upon the householder for 'daily bread' but also spent the best part of
their time in ministering to his spiritual needs.

For the purposes of analysis the monkish persona can be regarded as
having three different aspects, to be labelled here 'personal', 'pastoral', and
'monastic' according to their several orientations. The monastic activities
are those which take place between two or more monks, who may be
resident at the same monastery or merely brothers in the nation-wide society
of the Thai *Sangha*. The procedures pertaining to disciplinary affairs
(*Sanghakamma* or Acts of the Sangha) which thus derive their ultimate
authority from the Pali canon, and administrative matters sanctioned by the
Royal Edicts pertaining to the Buddhist *Sangha* and Laws of the Council
of Elders,[2] are alike subsumed under the single category of monastic
activities. The actions known as *Sanghakamma* which can be performed only
by fully ordained members of the Order consist of regular observances, such
as the fortnightly recital of the *Patimokkha* code which takes place in every
monastic community where there are at least four monks, and other more
occasional ceremonies such as that performed to reintegrate into *Sangha* any

---

[1] See Michael M. Ames on the Sinhalese situation (Ames 1964, p. 21 and passim)
and Gananath Obeyesekere in his article 'Theodicy, Sin and Salvation' (Obeyesekere
1968, pp. 7–39).

[2] See the *Phrarachabanyatkhanasong* (Royal Edicts pertaining to the Buddhist
Sangha), B.E. 2505 (1962) and the *Kot Mahatherasomakhom* (Laws of the Council of
Elders), Vols. 1–3, B.E. 2507 (1964).

bhikkhu, guilty of a second-class offence, who has completed the required term of solitary self-purification.[3]

The administrative processes which are an aspect of the centralization and indeed the nationalization of the Order of Buddhist Monks in Thailand are irrelevant to disciplinary concerns except in so far as the boundaries of their spheres of authority overlap with respect to certain major offences such as murder or theft. All cases of homicide are in fact the concern of the State authorities, as are other criminal acts which involve a member of the lay community, and although in theory such offences as an act of theft committed by a monk against another monk could be settled within the Order, it would appear that disputes of this nature are usually taken to court by the plaintiff, to the embarrassment of the judges, who are loth to bring discredit upon a *bhikkhu*.[4]

The Acts on the Administration of the Buddhist Order of Sangha also regulate the procedure for appointment to Ecclesiastical Office, a monastic activity to be discussed in the following chapter.

SELF-IMPROVEMENT AND ACADEMIC INTERESTS

Those activities which, ideally at least, are entailed in becoming a monk, namely the study of and meditation upon the Pali texts, form the 'personal' category of actions which are my immediate concern. According to Buddhist doctrine, study and meditation are progressive steps on the path to *Nirvana*, in that techniques of meditation are used to gain an insight into the teachings which have already been absorbed intellectually. In practical terms, however, these activities are personal in the sense that the decision as to what level to pursue them, if at all, rests with the individual monk though at a later stage other *bhikkhus* might co-operate with him as teachers of Pali or Sanskrit, or to give instruction in techniques of meditation.[5]

It is interesting that in the Thai context, or rather in the context of Ayutthaya society, *wiphasana-thura* (lit. insight-work, meditation), which was originally intended to represent a more advanced stage in the process

---

[3] See below, chapter 3. For a complete list of the monastic activities known as *Sanghakamma* (Acts of *Sangha*), see Dutt (1960, p. 122).

[4] During my period of fieldwork in Ayutthaya a monk who felt he had been wrongly passed over in the procedure for appointing a new abbot at his monastery, to replace the previous incumbent who had died, tried to bring a court case against the ecclesiastical officials at District and Sub-District levels who had chosen the new incumbent. As the decision of the officials in question was final the plaintiff was dismissed, but the chief judge of the law courts in Ayutthaya was pained by his unseemly behaviour and embarrassed by his having brought to the public notice affairs which were the private concern of the *Sangha*.

[5] Wells (1960, p. 159) discusses some of the techniques of meditation (*wiphasana-thura*) used by Thai monks.

of self-purification, is a less highly regarded activity than is the study of the Pali texts: which is to say that the latter pursuit, being more easily assessed in terms of academic degrees and certificates, is accorded a higher evaluation than *wiphasana-thura*, for success in which the evidence is less tangible.[6]

Less than one-third of my informants in Ayutthaya reported that they practised *wiphasana-thura*, and even these monks only meditated 'from time to time' or 'when they were free'. When questioned as to the techniques used they invariably replied in very vague terms; some said that one should concentrate on a single fixed point (*chut dieo*) in order to empty the mind of all distracting thoughts and make one's heart peaceful; others said that they reflected upon inevitable death, or upon the grace of the Buddha. Although most monks paid lip service to the idea that one should meditate in order to forget one's selfishness and greed (even though achievement of *Nirvana* was out of the question) nevertheless it was regarded as an activity more appropriate to nuns (*mae chi*),[7] to *bhikkhus* who were *saiyasat* (magical practitioners),[8] or to those monks who *doen thudong* (go on pilgrimages to Buddhist shrines).

The Thai word *thudong* is derived from the Pali term *dhutanga*, meaning Austere Practices, of which there are thirteen mentioned at various points throughout the *Sutta-pitaka*.[9] The word *thudong* is, however, most commonly used to refer to those monks who leave the monastery and go on foot to visit the various Buddhist shrines which are scattered throughout the country. During this time the *thudong bhikkhu* takes only one meal each day, eating whatever food is offered, without discrimination, and directly from the alms-bowl. At night he sleeps in the open, under a large umbrella-like shelter (*krot*) which is equipped with a mosquito-net and can be folded for carrying on the back during the day. It is usual for two or three monks to *doen thudong* together, though they should talk to each other as little as possible, proceeding in single file along the road during the day and separating at night when they pitch camp, so that each may meditate in solitude.

Despite the contention frequently made that only an exceptional individual

---

[6] A personal communication from Mrs Freda Wint, who has spent some time in North-Eastern Thailand, suggests that this may not be the case all over the country. Indeed the climate of opinion in Ayutthaya may to some extent be a reflection of the more complete institutionalization of the *Sangha* of Monks in Bangkok and the towns of the Central Region. See fn. 7 for new trends and attitudes towards meditation.

[7] There is some evidence of a trend towards extending the *bhikkhu*'s pastoral role, by encouraging the householder to take a more active part in religious activities. One manifestation of this new emphasis is that some monks are starting classes to teach laymen how to meditate, as it is felt to be easier for them than scriptural study. This ruling also applies to *mae chi* or nuns who are encouraged to join these meditation courses, some of which are set up by *bhikkhus* sent by the Department of Religious Affairs from the Buddhist Universities in Bangkok.

[8] See below, p. 74.   [9] See Khantipalo (1965, p. 10).

can sustain the loneliness and physical hardship involved in making such pilgrimages, which may involve making a journey of several hundred miles, punctuated by sedentary interludes of four or five days at each shrine on the itinerary, nevertheless most of my informants when questioned indignantly denied ever having gone on pilgrimage; only 2% of my monk informants admitted to such experiences and were willing to talk about it.[10] The remainder described the *dhutanga bhikkhu* as being concerned only with *wiphasana-thura*, an activity which was compared unfavourably with *kantha-thura*, their own chief concern. The Thai word *kantha-thura* is derived from a similar Pali term *gantha-dhura* which literally translated means 'Book-work or study', but most of its self-confessed exponents took it to refer to the administration of the affairs of the *wat* community, and to performing merit-making ceremonies for the householder. According to this usage a monk proficient in *kantha-thura* is one with the ability to 'build up the *wat*' (*sang wat*) both literally and figuratively in that he attracts new *bhikkhus* to the monastery, and at the same time wins the respect of the householders, which is made manifest in the form of sizeable donations. By comparison, the *dhutanga bhikkhu* is regarded as selfish and lacking in public spirit.

In his article on certain aspects of Theravada Buddhism, with special reference to Ceylon, Obeyesekere discusses the difficulties inherent in the condition of the monk who tries to 'escape from the society of the monastery by isolating himself from the world . . . as pious laymen are attracted by the special charisma' which surrounds these *bhikkhus* and pursue them with gifts of alms, attempt to build living quarters for them and so on (Obeyesekere 1968, p. 31).

Thai attitudes to monks who choose not to live in orthodox fashion in a monastery are rather ambivalent; whilst it is true that some monks who lead the life of a hermit, living in isolated caves and forests, are highly revered, the *thudong bhikkhu* whose way of life ideally corresponds most closely to the mendicant ideal of the early Buddhists is regarded with great suspicion; not belonging to lay society, nor being properly integrated into a monastic community, *dhutanga* monks are frequently regarded as being on a par with tramps, beggars and other kinds of social derelicts.[11] Laymen also

---

[10] The Abbot of *Wat* Tuk said that when he had *doen thudong* in the North-Eastern Region he had wandered in the forest for several days without food.

[11] The *thudong bhikkhus* of whom I speak leave the monastery only temporarily, most usually for a period of a few weeks in February or March. The phenomenon of monks who leave the *wat* on a more permanent basis to live a more isolated life in a forest or cave appears to be absent from Central Thailand although 'hermit' monks of this type are to be found in the remoter areas of the North-East Region and in the Southern Provinces of Thailand.

fear that monks who are seen wandering over the country and are thus not clearly attached to any particular *wat* may not have been properly ordained, and may be laymen who have falsely assumed the yellow robe.

According to traditional practice in Thailand those monks who intend to *doen thudong* leave their monasteries at the beginning of February and travel to pay their respects at one or more of the well-known places of pilgrimage (Wells 1960, p. 37). Laymen and women also go by car, train and coach on 'day-trips' to the various shrines, where they offer candles and incense sticks before the Buddha images and press small squares of gold leaf to their surfaces; some particularly pious householders visit the *thudong bhikkhus*, encamped in special enclosures in the vicinity of the shrines, and make merit by presenting them with food. The rest of the day is spent in picnicking, taking photographs of each other and in general generally having a good time.

Some thirty miles north of Ayutthaya there is a shrine known as Phraphutthabat (Footprint of the Buddha) which consists of a complex of buildings and *cetiyas*[12] built on a rocky hill-side around the 'footprint', a large shallow depression believed to resemble the imprint which might be left by a giant human foot, which is decorated with an elaborate relief design in gold. The *dhutanga* 'season' at Phraphutthabat in 1967 lasted from 9 to 24 February and on some days as many as 600 *bhikkhus* from all parts of Thailand were encamped there. An increasingly vigorous attempt has been made in recent years to regularize the activities of monks who choose to *doen thudong* and this movement was made manifest at Phraphutthabat by the establishment of a committee of senior ecclesiastical officials from Ayutthaya *Changwat* and the adjacent Provinces (*changwat*) of Angthong and Lopburi. The members of this committee, who themselves stayed in the living-quarters of the *wat* attached to the shrine, made arrangements for the *thudong* monks to encamp in certain specified areas, and checked that each new arrival had received permission to 'go on pilgrimage' from the Ecclesiastical Head of the *Amphoe* (District) where his monastery was situated. Proof of official approval took the form of the signature or stamp of the *Chao Khana Amphoe* (Ecclesiastical District Head) entered in the identity card, which is carried by every Thai monk. Each *dhutanga bhikkhu* was allowed to stay at the shrine for five days, to enjoy the offerings made by lay visitors before moving on to the next stopping-place, or in some cases returning to the *wat*. When I visited Phraphutthabat a young monk who had already spent the statutory period of five days encamped at the shrine was discovered trying to gain access for a second term, and was turned away in tears. Observations of monks at the 'Footprint', several of

[12] *Cetiya* or *stupa*. See p. 7, n. 3.

whom I talked with at length, show popular assessment of the *thudong bhikkhu* to be fairly accurate; or rather show that the shadow and the substance go hand-in-hand, in that the *dhutanga* role is not highly respected and consequently only those monks with little interest in earning the good opinion of society will assume it. The *thudong* monks at Phraphutthabat appeared to belong to one of two types, being either elderly men who had retired into the Order, or younger *bhikkhus* out on a spree; and many of them, far from leading an austere life, accepted lifts in cars or gifts of train tickets from the faithful.

It was clear that in Ayutthaya at least, meditation, the religious action which it is most difficult if not impossible for an outsider to assess in that its techniques are directed towards improving the inner spiritual state of the practitioner, is regarded as being the speciality of *bhikkhus* who themselves occupy a somewhat ambivalent position; either because they *doen thudong* and thus, temporarily at least, cannot be identified with a particular monastic community, or else because they specialize in certain unorthodox techniques of healing and astrology (*saiyasat*) about which I shall have more to say in the paragraphs dealing with pastoral affairs.[13]

The other activity which was earlier categorized as 'personal', namely the study of the *Dhamma*, is rather more amenable to institutionalization than is *wiphasana-thura*. As was remarked in chapter 1, study of the *Dhamma* means in the Thai context studying for the *Nak Tham* or for the *Barian* courses of examinations. *Nak Tham* (*Dhamma* Scholar or Student) studies were introduced at the beginning of the present century by the Abbot of *Wat* Baworniwet in Bangkok, who later became the Supreme Patriarch (Wells 1960, p. 14). It was intended that all monks should take this course, which is divided into three stages (Grades 1–3) with an examination at the end of each year of study. The syllabus, which includes instruction concerning the previous lives of the Buddha and the basic tenets of his teaching, as well as upon the rules of conduct set out in the *Vinaya-pitaka* (Monastic Code), is designed to inculcate a general Buddhist education rather than to produce scholars of a high standard of academic expertise.[14] The texts

[13] In speaking of Burmese monks Nash reports (1965, pp. 148–9) that 'as a monk proceeds in inner wisdom, in fuller understanding and in self-purification, there should be some manifestations in his daily life, and in his ability to handle the universe'. He lists ten 'marvellous powers ... earnests of progress' along the road to *Nirvana* to which monks may lay claim. In Thailand, on the other hand, any *bhikkhu* who possesses anything approaching 'marvellous powers' for healing or prophesy, is careful to state that these talents which he regards as magical (*saiyasat*) can be learnt from the relevant textbooks by any person monk or lay, and that they have no relation to his role as a Buddhist monk.

[14] See *Sangkhomsatporithat* (The Social Science Review), Special Edition no. 4, August 1966, pp. 53 and passim, for the complete syllabus of both the *Nak Tham* and *Barian* courses of ecclesiastical study.

prescribed are published by the Ministry of Education and the papers for the annual examinations are set and marked by the *bhikkhus* in the two Buddhist Universities in Bangkok.

In Ayutthaya, most of the younger monks seemed to study fairly regularly though not necessarily to any great effect; the fact of studying appeared to be more important than its fruits for many *bhikkhus*, whilst older monks or those who had official duties to perform usually renounced all academic pursuits. Approximately three-fifths of the monks whom I interviewed however, had passed one or more of the *Nak Tham* grades, although only one third of the candidates who were examined at *Wat* Monthop (Ayutthaya) in December 1967 were successful.[15] The examinations which were organized by the *Chao Khana Amphoe*, were held on three successive days and provided an excuse for *bhikkhus* from all over the District to get together and exchange news. Indeed many of those in regular attendance at *Wat* Monthop had not come to take the examination but merely to meet old friends and renew acquaintance.

The *Barian* course of more advanced studies (Grades 3–9) is attempted by comparatively few monks in Ayutthaya, and the teachers at the ecclesiastical schools of *Wat* Phanan Choeng and *Wat* Senasanaram are capable of teaching Grades 3 and 4 only, which means that any *bhikkhu* with serious academic intentions must go to Bangkok to receive instruction.

Students of the *Barian* course are required to learn sufficient Pali (and at the higher levels Sanskrit also) to be able to translate simple sentences into Thai, as well as to gain a real understanding of the texts and chants in general use. In addition to this a deeper understanding of the metaphysical issues debated in the Pali canon, and in the *Abhidhamma-pitaka* in particular, is required. In Ayutthaya academic monks are sufficiently few in number for their talents, and in some cases their precise academic status, to be fairly generally known: any *bhikkhu* who has passed even the lowest *Barian* grade is entitled to use the term *maha* (meaning 'Great') in front of his name, to write his scholastic status after his name (e.g. *Barian* 5) and to carry a particular fan which also indicates his academic rank.[16] During

---

[15] See Appendix 3 for results of *Nak Tham* and *Barian* examinations in Ayutthaya, 1967.

[16] His fan is used by a *bhikkhu* only on certain occasions: when he pronounces the Three Refuge formula or gives the Five Precepts to the laymen present, prior to a merit-making ceremony; when a recitation begins; when he expresses thanks in a formal manner; and at certain stages of the cremation ceremony (see Rajadhon 1961, p. 87). Some fans are presented by the King to monks who hold high positions in the ecclesiastical hierarchy, or to those with honorific titles; such fans, which are insignia of rank, may be used only in a Royal Ceremony (*phithi luang*) when the King or his deputy is present. All *bhikkhus* own at least one fan which has been presented to them by the *chao phap* on the occasion of their ordination.

my period of fieldwork there were only twenty *bhikkhus* in the whole of Ayutthaya District (i.e. the municipality and surrounding rural areas) who could use the title *maha*, and of this number, the two monks most highly qualified had passed *Barian* examination Grade 6.

Although certain monks were known to be 'clever' and well-educated in ecclesiastical terms, academic qualifications alone were neither necessary nor sufficient to earn the respect and support either of monks or of laymen, and only five of the monks who were office-holders in the National Church hierarchy had *Barian* grades.[17] As will become clear in subsequent chapters abbots, at least up to the provincial level, are appointed largely on the basis of their popularity with monks and with laymen; the *bhikkhus* who are most revered have personal charisma independent of their formal academic qualifications though it should be stressed that study of the texts, unlike meditation, is regarded as an honourable pursuit for any monk and like all educational pursuits highly respected by the Thais.

PASTORAL SERVICES

As far as the monks of Ayutthaya were concerned, however, the time and effort expended upon study or meditation was insignificant when compared with that which was devoted to pastoral activities of various kinds. These pastoral transactions which take place between *bhikkhu* and householder consist in essence of the monk's conferring merit upon the layman who in turn expresses his gratitude and respect by presenting offerings of money, food and other items traditionally included, such as a pair of candles and a lotus-bud.[18] The ascetic routine adopted by the individual who enters the Buddhist *Sangha* gives him a higher spiritual status which enables him to confer merit upon those still enmeshed in the sensory world.

Any *bhikkhu* can serve as a 'field of merit' for any layman and as the highest ethical evaluation is placed upon giving without thought for oneself it is believed to be more meritorious for a householder to present alms to a

[17] One young monk (25) who had been appointed Acting Abbot of *Wat* Nang Plum was felt by some informants to be unsuitable on the grounds of his tender years, although it was admitted that he was clever enough as he had passed *Barian* 5.

[18] Some pastoral transactions, that is to say those between a *saiyasat* monk and a householder, are not primarily concerned with the making of merit, although merit is a necessary by-product of any activity between monk and householder, wherein the latter presents an offering of some kind to the former. Those *bhikkhus* who are also *saiyasat* (magical practitioners) specialize in healing or in telling horoscopes. Although most *saiyasat* are *bhikkhus*, as these magical activities are traditionally associated with the monkly role, in Ayutthaya at least, very few monks were *saiyasat*. Consequently throughout this chapter, unless otherwise specified, the term pastoral activities refers to more orthodox transactions between monk and householder, whose manifest intention is to make merit.

monk with whom he has no personal ties, or to the monastic community as a whole, without discrimination, than to confine his charitable effort to those *bhikkhus* who are also his relatives or friends.

The ideal of impersonal giving is probably most perfectly realized in the act of presenting rice to the monk on his daily alms-round (*pai binthabat*). Each monastery has several traditional alms-routes and the residents of any *wat* may receive rice from any of the householders who live along one of the established ways. This transaction, which expresses most clearly the quintessential relationship between the layman and the 'homeless' mendicant, based as it is on the disparity in spiritual status which exists between the two parties, may have little or no personal content. Merit is automatically conferred by the monk's mute acceptance of alms; it would be inappropriate for him to thank the donors, both because the burden of gratitude is on their side for the opportunity given them to make merit, and also because the *bhikkhu* must appear indifferent to material benefits. The rules of conduct in the *Vinaya-pitaka* prescribe that he should keep his eyes downcast throughout: the twenty-eighth of the seventy-two minor rules of conduct (*charit*) reads 'I shall accept alms-food with attention on the bowl' (Ven. Nanamoli Thera 1966, p. 76). As will become apparent in the following section on the *wat* the lay donors of daily rice are in general unaware that from every *wat* in town there radiates a number of alms-routes, established 'in olden times'; and consequently householders may not even know to which monastic community the recipient of their offering belongs. In other cases however the relationship between the two parties may become more regularized, should the householder invite a monk who frequently passes his gate to call in each day, or if he should visit the abbot of a nearby monastery and request him to detail some member of the community to stop by the house every morning as he makes his alms-round. In Ayutthaya however, such arrangements appeared to be relatively rare and did not represent a lapse from the ideal of impersonal giving, in that no word was exchanged between the two parties, and as the daily provision of rice remained the sole basis of their association. No instances came to my notice of a monk's receiving daily rice exclusively from his kinsmen and in fact in an urban context such a situation is less likely to arise as the majority of permanent *bhikkhus* came from the rural areas outside the town, and had thus moved beyond the geographical limits within which daily interaction with closely related kin was feasible.[19] Nevertheless many of these professional monks had friends or relatives of some degree who occasionally

[19] Temporary monks on the other hand usually receive daily presentations of food from their proud mothers. See below chapter 5 for the case-history of the ordination of the three sons of Khun Siri Imchai.

invited them to take their morning meal in their homes, as well as requesting their services for the performance of life-crisis ceremonies from time to time.

The activity of *binthabat* (making the daily alms-round), as the term *bhikkhu* (meaning 'mendicant') indicates, is ideally an automatic entailment of the monkly role. Nevertheless it has in practice become such a routine activity that little emphasis is placed upon its performance and approximately one-third of the monks questioned rarely if ever took to the streets with their begging-bowls.[20] Some of this number were spared the chore of *binthabat* by the fact that the monastery in which they lived was sufficiently richly endowed to provide food for its residents, whilst others who held office in the ecclesiastical hierarchy or high honorific titles received a small monthly allowance from the King which was administered by the civil service Department of Religious Affairs. This allowance, known as *nittayaphat* (from the Pali *nissaya* meaning 'support', and *bhatta* which means 'boiled rice, food'), enables its recipients to buy, amongst other things, the food which they require.[21] This rather curious institution was justified by some *bhikkhus* to whom I spoke as freeing from the arduous and time-consuming duty of *binthabat* the most eminent monks in the community, who were on the whole fairly advanced in years, and had besides many official duties to perform; not the least of their burdens of office being to provide material support for novices and monastery boys entrusted to their special care by pious parents. According to other informants the *nittayaphat* allowance had an additional function in that by preventing local luminaries from making alms-rounds it made it easier for ordinary monks to collect sufficient food, as it also prevented the lay donors from following their mistaken, but natural, inclination to give rice to monks whom they most revered.

This second explanation, ingenious as it is, seems to me to have little relevance to the facts of the case, and as I have already pointed out, householders tend to offer rice to any *bhikkhu* who is passing by their home when the food is ready, and are not interested in the recipients' credentials, beyond the fact that he is a member of the *Sangha*. One monk, who held office at one of the larger *wats*, belittled the significance of *nittayaphat* for his own routine by stressing that the chief beneficiaries were in fact the laymen who thus need provide rice for fewer *bhikkhus*! He seemd to have forgotten that monks who make a daily alms-round provide members of the lay community with a valuable opportunity to increase their store of merit,

---

[20] Nor is the actual presentation of rice regarded as highly meritorious, perhaps because it involves only slight expenditure of time and money. Less than 30% of the laymen questioned gave rice regularly, though most gave from time to time. See below chapter 5, on the religious behaviour of the Thai laymen.

[21] See Appendix 4*b* for list of the *bhikkhus* in Ayutthaya who received *nittayaphat*.

though in fact as already mentioned a relatively small proportion of the householders regularly perform this routine act of charity.[22]

The merit-making ceremonies held at the critical turning points in the life-cycle of every individual are, on the other hand, generally regarded by both parties as representing a more significant aspect of pastoral relations: most *bhikkhus* in Ayutthaya felt that the performance of these rituals on the layman's behalf was central to their role, whilst for the householder the act of financing a *ngan tham bun* (merit-making ceremony) has important implications for both his spiritual and his social status. The most crucial, and hence the most meritorious of all the *ngan tham bun*, are generally felt to be the ordination ceremony (*ngan upasombot*) whereby a man crosses over from lay society into the society of monks, and the ceremony of cremation (*ngan phao sop*) which accomplishes the transfer of the deceased from this world to the next. Buddhist monks are however usually invited to recite *parittas*[23] or merit-making chants on other occasions, such as prior to the actual wedding ceremony which is a civil affair, or to celebrate the entry into a new house and the opening of a shop or school; a rare form of *ngan tham bun* is performed at a time of grievous illness, within the family or of epidemic proportions (Wells 1960, p. 207).

The merit-making rituals performed on the occasion of life-crises have been described in detail elsewhere, notably by Wells (1960) and Tambiah (1968 and 1970). The present discussion can thus be confined to those features of the *ngan tham bun* which are directly relevant to the examination of the relationship existing between the Buddhist *bhikkhu* and the lay community.

A layman who has decided to sponsor a merit-making ceremony invites (*nimon*)[24] a number of monks from one or from several *wats* to come to his house at a certain time on the appointed day.[25] A quorum of more than

[22] It is interesting that many monks in Bangkok for whom the alms-round has become functionally obsolete – either because their food is provided by the monastery, or bought from their own *nittayaphat* allowance, or simply because the *wat* is situated in a non-residential part of town – yet continue to perform the *binthabat* routine as a symbolic act; this practice serves as a reminder of the Buddha's total renunciation of the world, and of their own mendicant status. The monks of Ayutthaya have not attained this level of sophistication.

[23] The Pali term *paritta* means protection, removal, warding-off; both the ritual and the texts used during the ritual are termed *paritta*. The texts themselves are derived from the *Kuddaka-Nikaya* which is the fifth part of the *Sutta-pitaka* and is divided into sixteen distinct works. The first of these – the *Khuddaha-patha* – is further sub-divided into nine parts, seven of which are used in the *paritta* ritual. (See Banerji 1964, p. 45.) Thai monks use Ceylonese *parittas* and *sutras* from the Pali canon, and also many chants and responses of their own composition (Wells 1960, p. ii).

[24] The term *nimon* meaning 'to invite' is used only with respect to monks; the equivalent word for laymen is *choen* or *chuan*.

[25] Cremation ceremonies provide an exception to this as they are held in the *wat*.

four monks is necessary for the performance of any merit-making ceremony and to have a chapter of five, seven or nine monks recite the chants is generally regarded as auspicious, although an even number of *bhikkhus* is more appropriate for the blessing ritual held prior to the marriage ceremony proper.[26] In Thailand the texts recited by the monks, most of which come from the *Sutta-pitaka*, are included in a compilation known as the 'Royal Book of Chants' (Wells 1960, p. 268) and are also issued as smaller separate booklets by the Buddhist Universities and the printing presses of the Religious Affairs Department. When they first enter the *Sangha*, most monks spend a good part of their time in memorizing the few basic chants which may be used for most merit-making rituals.

During my stay in Ayutthaya I witnessed only one ceremony where the *bhikkhus* were required to use an unfamiliar text which they had clearly not memorized. This was on the occasion of the ritual for Blessing the Rice Seed held annually in Bangkok at the beginning of May, but new to the monks of Ayutthaya.[27] The ceremony which took place in the Ayutthaya Assembly Hall was organized by the civil servants in the division of Religious Affairs and presided over by the Deputy Governor of the Province: only a few high-ranking civil servants and their wives attended. The monks from *Wat* Senasanaram who had been invited to officiate kept hand-written copies of the chant semi-concealed on their laps.

At the close of all such ceremonies the lay host (*chao phap*) presents each monk who has taken part with a traditional offering which typically consists of three incense sticks, two candles and a lotus bud, items placed before images of the Buddha during the act of worship;[28] packets of tea and sugar, of washing powder and cigarettes, and other personal articles of everyday use as well as a small sum of money, usually between ten and thirty *baht* or a chit for that amount which can be cashed on application to the *waiyawachakon* or lay-bursar at the *wat* of the recipient. These presentations which are made to individual monks (*thuai thaiyathan*) and become the personal property (*khong suan tua*) of the recipient must be distinguished from offerings presented to the community as a whole (*thuai sangkhathan*)

Only a few monasteries have a permanent crematorium or *men*, although in some cases a temporary structure is erected for the occasion in the compound or *thi wat*. Nevertheless monks resident in a monastery with a *men* are more often invited to officiate at cremation ceremonies as it is customary for the layman to invite them whether or not he knows them personally (see below p. 66).

[26] See 'Merit-Making Ceremonies' (*Pithi Tham Bun*) by Phra Khru Sitthikankoson (Bangkok, B.E. 2504).

[27] See Wells (1960, p. 239) for a discussion of texts used, and a description of the ceremony.

[28] Wells (1960, p. 44) also mentions 'puffed rice' as being an essential article for acts of worship, but this does not seem to have been the practice in Ayutthaya.

which are theoretically more meritorious and belong to the *wat* as a corporation (*khong klang* or *khong wat*); the second category is reviewed in chapter 4 below.

It has already been remarked that any individual who becomes a Buddhist monk automatically assumes a special and privileged relationship towards all members of the lay community: by donning the saffron robe he does indeed leave society to the extent that, to all appearances, he has shed his previous social identity, and in a sense becomes the common property of the laity. His new position is made manifest in the fact that all householders treat him with deference and respect, and may well speak to him in the street or when he is travelling alone on a bus or by train, in circumstances where social or sexual constraint would prevent members of the lay community from striking up a conversation with each other.[29] This formal difference in spiritual status between the parties is similarly the basis of more institutionalized interaction; in the context of the alms-round transaction, for example, the personal content is minimal or wholly absent as the householder can make merit by providing food for any member of the *Sangha*. In theory this situation also appertains with respect to merit-making ceremonies and there is no reason why a layman should not invite unknown *bhikkhus* to make up the quorum necessary for the recitation; indeed invitations of a non-specific nature are thought to bring more merit to the lay host. Nevertheless most *bhikkhus* do receive invitations from kinsmen and from lay friends from time to time; although it is regarded as improper to support only monks who are also relatives or friends, equally it is disrespectful and a violation of rules of social behaviour not to invite (*nimon*) such members of one's family and acquaintance as have been ordained, to take part in the performance of one's life-crisis rituals: as indeed other relations and friends are invited (*choen*) to witness the ceremony, with the expectation that they will also contribute to the cost.[30]

The very act of entering the Order (*ngan upasombot*) requires the co-operation of a number of laymen – friends and kinsmen of the *nak* (ordinand) – which implies that all *bhikkhus* begin life in the *wat* with at least the beginnings of a 'parish', and after ordination these original links with the lay community may well be extended as more remote relations, and friends of friends request his services. Indeed it is a source of pride to have

[29] The elegant word for 'monkhood' in the sense of the status of monk (rather than the Order of Monks) is *samanaphet*: *samana*, meaning Buddhist monk, and *phet* meaning 'gender' or 'sex' as in *phet chai* – male sex, masculine gender.

[30] The ethical priority which is given to unselfish action is of course based on the Buddhist belief that one should renounce all *khamma* or volitional acts which bind the actor to the cycle of rebirth (*samsara*) and arise from the ignorance of the impermanence of all things, including that entity we call the Self. This connection was not made explicit by my informants.

a monk in the family, and to invite (*nimon*) friends or relations who are members of the *Sangha* to perform a merit-making ritual in one's house is both an obligation and a pleasure.[31]

These links with particular householders which can be termed 'prior' since they antedate the *bhikkhu*'s ordination may become increasingly attenuated the longer he remains in the Order; not only through the operation of natural processes whereby people die, marry or move away, but also because of the fact that for many monks the degree of role-commitment is directly correlated with the extent of their spatial separation from the natal home – given the fact that the role of permanent monk acts as a stepping-stone into an urban environment for many men from rural areas. Thus the prior relationships between a monk and a number of householders may be weakened because of geographical considerations; yet even where the parties are living at some distance apart, it is likely that these links will be reactivated from time to time – though this depends largely upon the wishes of the householder, as the monk can take no real initiative in these matters although his informal visiting may keep the links alive.

But the Buddhist *bhikkhu* does not perform pastoral services solely for people with whom he was associated before his ordination. The source of the other invitations he receives is largely determined by his place of residence, as he is likely to be invited by kinsmen of other monks living in the *wat* when the former need more *bhikkhus* to make up the required number, as well as by other laymen living in the environs of the monastery. According to a belief widely held in Ayutthaya any layman who intends to sponsor a merit-making ceremony in his home should invite both relatives and friends who have become monks and some of the *bhikkhus* living in the local *wat*;[32] not to invite the latter would in these terms be seen as a calculated slight resulting in loss of face (*khai na*) on both sides, in that the reputation of the monks would suffer from the implied insult to their capabilities and general worthiness, whilst the layman involved would be censured for his neglect or ignorance of proper social forms.

According to the usual procedure the prospective lay host approaches the abbot (*somphan* or *chao awat*) and asks him to delegate a certain number of

---

[31] It is quite customary to hold a ceremony known as the *Chalong Phra Mai* (Celebration of the New Monk) at his parents' home several days after he has entered the Order. This brings a great deal of merit for the new monk's father and mother (see Wells 1960, p. 150).

[32] From the layman's point of view the 'local *wat*' is the one with which he regards himself as being in some way associated, though he may visit it only infrequently. Nevertheless when he does attend Holy Day services, or when he needs *bhikkhus* to officiate at a *ngan tham bun*, it is to this monastery that he goes. He regards himself and is regarded as belonging to an entity centred upon the *wat* which is known as the *phuak wat ni*: 'supporters of this *wat*'.

bhikkhus to perform the ceremony on the appointed day; this collective and non-specific form of invitation is known as *kho song* (to ask for monks, to ask for a *Sangha*[33] or group of monks), and is felt to bring more merit than does the invitation of a specific monk (*nimon cho chong*), be he relative or friend. Nevertheless most householders who go to *kho song* at the local *wat* implicitly or explicitly include the abbot as representative of the community, in their invitation. In certain cases other considerations may overrule the factor of contiguity in deciding the direction of a layman's invitations: which is to say, for example, that monks in monasteries which offer special facilities for the conduct of cremation ceremonies, or which have as their abbot a particular popular *bhikkhu*, may be more frequent recipients of invitations of the *kho song* variety. But these factors rarely supersede the claims of the local *wat* altogether, and unless the latter is particularly run-down and disreputable any layman living in the vicinity also includes at least one or two of its residents on his guest list for the merit-making ceremony.

Interaction between a *bhikkhu* and a householder which originates in this way develops in some cases into a more permanent relationship, particularly if the monk remains in one *wat* over a long period and if the layman for his part does not change house. However there is no guarantee that links with laymen, which may be called contingent in that they post-date the ordination of one of the parties, will be enduring.[34] They are not conceptualized as permanent and their persistence depends upon the development of affective ties between the parties concerned, and more particularly upon the desire of the layman to continue the relationship by inviting the monk to officiate at successive *ngan tham bun*, and perhaps by himself paying informal visits to the *wat*.

As I implied above, the abbot of any monastic community tends to receive more invitations to officiate at merit-making rituals than do the other *bhikkhus*, as he represents the *wat* to the outside world and is thus the medium whereby a householder can 'ask for monks'. Moreover, links between abbot and laymen which arise in this way are more likely to endure as the incumbent of an abbotship in any monastery is unlikely to change his residence unless he receives promotion to a higher position in the ecclesiastical hierarchy of office.[35]

It might be imagined that the power of the abbot to choose certain of his subordinates to perform ceremonies at the layman's behest might give rise

[33] *Sangha* means literally 'herd, or congregation'.
[34] A special kind of contingent relationship is that which was formed when both parties were in the Order and has continued in an altered form, after one of the men has returned to lay life.
[35] See below, chapter 3.

to some dissension within the community and to competition for the privilege and consequent rewards of ministering to the laity; the abbot not only redirects the *kho song* made by householders but must also on many occasions appoint some other monk to attend a ceremony in his stead, because eminent *bhikkhus* – whether abbots or not – may receive a number of 'bookings' for the same day. Since it is regarded as equally important that the monk should show no more favouritism in accepting invitations than does the layman in making them, a popular abbot may have a number of conflicting appointments on any one day in which case he should give priority to the first-comer and, with regard to requests made later, direct other monks to attend in his place.[36] It is possible of course that the *bhikkhu* might give precedence to invitations made by relatives or close friends although I was not able to discover whether or not that was indeed the case, and it seemed more usual for the lay host not to fix the date for his merit-making ceremony until he had made sure that any *bhikkhu* whose presence he particularly desired was free to attend.

Before going on to examine the special nature of the relationship between an eminent monk and his public, let us make a brief digression to discuss the significance of the material rewards of pastoral service for the welfare of the recipients, and the consequent implications for the relations between members of any one monastic community. As I mentioned in the previous paragraph, the right of the abbot to delegate other *bhikkhus* to attend merit-making ceremonies, and thus to receive the traditional presentations, might appear to provide a potential source of friction within the monastery, but I saw no evidence of such competition and its absence can be explained in a variety of ways. In the first place, the overall ratio of monks to laymen is such that virtually all *bhikkhus* receive invitations to perform merit-making ceremonies, from time to time, on the basis of both prior and contingent ties. Furthermore, the abbot can only delegate pastoral duties to *bhikkhus* who are free at the time appointed for the ceremony concerned, which means in effect that he must choose the monks who receive fewer invitations on their own account than do their fellows.

With regard to the traditional presentations of money and material goods to the individual *bhikkhu* (*thuai thaiyathan*) at the conclusion of the *ngan tham bun*, it must be remembered that these offerings are not crucial

---

[36] One abbot who was seventy-two years old and held the position of *Chao Khana Changwat* (Ecclesiastical Provincial Head) in a Province adjacent to *Changwat* Ayutthaya left the *Sangha* as he said that he could no longer cope with the innumerable requests he received to perform merit-making ceremonies. He thus reversed the usual pattern according to which men retire into the Order in old age, when their social commitments are at an end. A monk who is highly revered may continue to receive invitations until, or even beyond, such time as his faculties desert him, as extreme old age might serve to enhance his personal charisma in the eyes of the laity.

to the very existence of the monk but should be regarded as extras in that, with a few exceptions, the Buddhist monk receives his daily food from households he passes on his alms-round. Furthermore, the presentations made in return for pastoral services are too small to give rise to serious income inequalities between monks, a factor which in itself lessens the likelihood of competition. The amount of money given (usually between ten and thirty *baht* per monk) is sufficient only for the purchase of newspapers and books, and in some cases supplementary food; the other items of groceries or ritual objects used in worship of the Buddha cannot be stored indefinitely, with the result that the monk who has more than sufficient for his own use normally gives the surplus to others in the *wat*. In fact, it was my impression that the prevailing ethic of *noblesse oblige* ensures the equitable distribution of these material goods; the more favoured a *bhikkhu* is in terms of presentation received, the more generous he is obliged to be; the lack of privacy both within the *wat* and with regard to the laity acts as a strong sanction against any monk's misuse of his personal property (*khong suan tua*). Thus the dilemma posed by the fact that the more revered the *bhikkhu* the more he is showered with worldly goods by the householder is to some extent resolved, in that he must maintain an attitude of indifference towards material possessions and wherever possible should give them away. Indeed eminent monks in particular must be seen to be generous if they are not to lose the lay support upon which their position is based.

This statement provides a cue for my taking up the main thread of the present argument once again in order to examine the relationship between members of the lay community and those monks who hold high office in the Buddhist *Sangha*. It is true to say that wide popular appeal is both a cause and a consequence of ecclesiastical eminence in that, up to the Provincial level at least, important ecclesiastical positions are bestowed upon those *bhikkhus* who are greatly respected by the laity, as well as by their fellow monks. Not unnaturally this official recognition results in even greater public support: as we have seen already any abbot, as representative of the whole monastic community, is invited (*nimon*) to officiate at merit-making ceremonies more frequently than his fellow residents, and those monks who possess very strong personal charisma attract support from a still wider and more varied public. As will become clear in succeeding chapters, by no means all the abbots of the *wats* in Ayutthaya enjoyed great popularity or renown, although the procedure for appointment to office marks an attempt to ensure that the successful candidate commands at least that minimal degree of respect necessary to enable him to perform his duties. On the other hand although not all abbots could be regarded as having charisma, all the monks in Ayutthaya who were possessed of this quality had been given official recognition in the form of honorific titles and ecclesiastical office; which is to say that their position in the society of the *Sangha* was to a great extent a reflection of their standing in the lay community.

With regard to their role performance the *bhikkhus* who enjoyed the most prestige in Ayutthaya appeared to belong to one of two main types which can be crudely categorized as 'active' and 'passive'.[37] The prime example of the second type is provided by the Ecclesiastical Provincial Head (*Chao Khana Changwat*) of the *Mahanikai* Sect who is also the Abbot of *Wat* Phanan Choeng in Ayutthaya. This monk, who was seventy-one years of age, had been born in a rural settlement outside the town; he was ordained as a novice at the age of fourteen in his local *wat* and had moved there to live at *Wat* Phanan Choeng where there is a school for monks and novices. He had remained in that monastery throughout his career and four years ago on the death of the previous abbot succeeded him to the title of *Chao Khana Changwat*, having occupied the post of Deputy or *Rong Chaokhana Changwat* for a good many years. The monk in question, who was referred to as Chao Khun Thep or Luang Pho *Wat* Choeng, had also been awarded the honorific title of *Phra Racha Khana Chan Thep* which made him the highest-ranking *bhikkhu* in Ayutthaya Province, although the academic achievements were negligible, for he had passed the examination for only the lowest grade of the elementary course of ecclesiastical studies, namely, *Nak Tham* 3.[38] Nor was he renowned particularly as a preacher or teacher of the *Dhamma* either to his fellow monks or on a popular level.

Nevertheless it was not difficult to discover the basis for his support in that there were current in Ayutthaya many stories which illustrated his admirable generosity and the simplicity of his ways, to the truth of which tales his practical example bore constant witness. His demeanour was calm and tranquil (*choei*), he was slow-moving and rarely spoke, and these characteristics do not seem to have merely been an aspect of his advanced age, as not even the oldest people to whom I spoke on the subject could remember his ever having been any different.

Unlike most Thai monks Chao Khun Thep was a vegetarian and took neither meat nor fish.[39] At the time of my fieldwork he was the only *bhikkhu*

[37] Kaufman (1960, p. 117) in writing about the appointment of the abbot of *Wat* Bangkhuad writes, 'The choice is usually between two distinct types; the verbose, glib monk, or the more reticent monk whose "forte" is control of the body, meditation, concentration.'

[38] Monks who have been awarded any of the *Phra Racha Khana* ranks are referred to as *Chao Khun* (My Lord) – see Appendix 4a for list of honorific titles. Any monk who is an abbot may also be identified by the name of his *wat* prefixed by the term *Luang Pho* or Reverend Father, e.g. *Luang Pho Wat* Choeng.

[39] The fact that Thai monks place a stricter interpretation on the rule against taking

in Ayutthaya *Amphoe* who regularly *chan che* (i.e. ate only vegetarian food), a practice which dated from a traumatic event which took place many years ago when, as a young monk, he paid a visit to his parents' home in the country. He had on the spur of the moment decided to take the boat out to his natal village to look up his friends and relations, but his mother was very flustered by his unexpected arrival, as she had no food prepared to present to him. Accordingly she netted some fish from the river and, without a second thought, killed them before the eyes of her son. The latter was so revolted by the thought that a living creature should be destroyed for his benefit that he vowed there and then that he would never eat flesh of any kind again. One implication of this abstinence was that householders who invited him to officiate at any merit-making ceremony had to prepare special dishes for his consumption at the meal which always follows merit-making ceremonies, and many laymen and women to whom I spoke took a special and self-important pleasure in the extra work thus involved in inviting him.

Another characteristic which merited Chao Khun Thep's being regarded as a *phu yai* (lit. Big Person, Elder) was his generosity, for he spent very little on himself and gave away a large part of the offerings made to him by the laity. He received numerous requests to perform merit-making rituals not only because he was well-known and respected but also because he was one of the eleven monks in Ayutthaya empowered to confer ordination (i.e. he was an *upacha*). During the period of my fieldwork he received on average eleven invitations each month, and considerably more than this in the months preceding the Lenten season; in May 1967 for example his services were requested on twenty-one separate occasions and he had twenty-eight such appointments in June, most of which were in connection with a *ngan upasombot* (ordination ceremony).

The *chao phap* (lay hosts) who invited him to officiate at their life-crisis rituals came from all parts of the town of Ayutthaya and a few lived in the neighbouring towns of Angthong and Lopburi. The majority of these laymen knew him by reputation and by sight as they had seen him performing other ceremonies in and around the town, but few if any of them appeared to be intimate with him, though some had spoken to him and even invited him to their homes on previous occasions. The abbot did not appear to regard any of these invitations as the outcome of established personal relationships, although approximately 45% of the *chao phap* in question had invited him on some earlier occasion, in the majority of cases

---

life than do the laity does not prevent them from eating meat. This prohibition (*ahimsa*) does prevent *bhikkhus* from tilling the ground lest they destroy organisms living in the soil. Some monks filter water used for drinking or bathing in an attempt to remove 'all living things' (Ven. Nanamoli Thera 1966, p. 60).

several years ago.[40] Part of the strength of the abbot's charisma indeed derived from the fact that unlike other people, he did not appear to be intimate with anyone – either *bhikkhu* or householder. His personal conduct seemed to indicate that he had to a large extent renounced all particular personal attachments, in that although he shed a diffused beneficent light on all who came into contact with him he expressed no partiality even towards his relatives.

However, during the year he twice visited his natal village to attend merit-making ceremonies sponsored by his kinsmen, by his half-brother and maternal uncle respectively, and on a third occasion performed several ordination ceremonies on the same day, in the *wat* of an adjacent rural settlement where a large number of candidates from the surrounding area had gathered together.[41] Furthermore in October 1966 he travelled to Bangkok to take part in a *suat chaeng* ceremony[42] sponsored by some rather distant relatives whom he had not met previously.

That so small a proportion of Chao Khun Thep's invitations came from people with whom he had some kind of prior link, either direct or by extension, was in part a function of his great age which meant that many friends and relatives who were his contemporaries had died; even the links between a *bhikkhu* and his kinsman are rarely inherited by the next gener-ation, and there is no guarantee that they will persist after the deaths of the householders, who originally took an interest in their monk-kinsman, although such ties may be more enduring if the monk is famous. And indeed the abbot's relatives in the capital who invited him to officiate at their ceremonies were in their early forties, that is to say three decades younger than Chao Khun Thep whom they could not have known prior to his ordination.

One of the burdens of office as Ecclesiastical Provincial Head was to officiate at ceremonies held to celebrate Buddhist national holidays sponsored by the State: one of the benefits of office was the receipt of the monthly *nittayaphat* allowance which, taken together with the money presented in return for his pastoral services to the laity, brought him an annual income of several thousand *baht* in cash alone, whilst he also received the usual groceries and ritual items as well as several sets of robes. During the year of

[40] Several of these invitations came from laymen who had previously spent some time as monks or novices in *Wat* Phanan Choeng.

[41] This procedure is often followed in rural areas where, because there are few monks eligible to confer ordination, an *upacha* is usually invited from the nearest town. He may ordain a great number of candidates on the same day, although only three *nak* can be ordained simultaneously. As, for some purposes, four monks can form a quorum or *Sangha* it is impossible for a quorum of *bhikkhus* to confer ordination upon more than three candidates at any one time.

[42] *Suat chaeng*: a pre-cremation ceremony (see Wells 1960, p. 273).

my fieldwork several laymen presented him with durable goods of greater value as a token of their respect rather than in return for specific services; these valuables included a vacuum flask (for storing iced water), an electric fan, a grandfather clock and a sofa. Some years earlier a man who had spent several years in *Wat* Phanan Choeng before returning to lay life, financed the construction of a handsome two-storey building fitted with teak floors and panelling, to provide new living quarters (*kuti*) for the abbot.

However, Chao Khun Thep's attitude to his material possessions was quite exemplary; several years previously he had inherited a share in the family paddy-fields which he had sold and had given the proceeds to help with the building of a school for lay children, just recently opened, in the compound of the *wat* (*thi wat*). Similarly, with regard to the offerings made to him by the laity he expressed no open pleasure or even interest; the electrical apparatus given to him was freely used by other members of the community; he never made use of his electric fan nor joined the crowd of younger monks and novices around the television set in his *kuti*. He kept only two sets of robes for his own use and had given others away to less favoured monks,[43] whilst baskets of fruit and other food presented to him were sent to the *wat* kitchens for consumption by the community at large.

Furthermore Chao Khun Thep appeared to spend very little of the money he received to satisfy his own modest needs; he ate little, took no newspaper, and rarely travelled; he liked to drink China tea, and occasionally chewed betel, habits which would have cost at the most a few pence per week, assuming that he bought these items himself.

One consequence of the reverence accorded him by the laity was that many parents requested that their sons be allowed to live under his care and guidance as novices or *dek wat* (monastery boys) and consequently Chao Khun Thep was sharing his *kuti* with five *dek wat* and six novices at the time of my residence in Ayutthaya. He provided for these boys not only advice and counsel, but also food, clothes and school equipment (pencils, note-books) purchased with his own money. Furthermore he shouldered a large part of the burden of expenditure on textbooks for the ecclesiastical school in the *wat* and regularly contributed to a Cremation Assurance Fund started at *Wat* Chin, situated in a facing position on the opposite bank of the river.[44]

Other students of Theravada Buddhist societies have drawn attention to the dilemma inherent in the situation whereby the monk and more especially

[43] According to the rules in the *Patimokka* code a monk should keep only one set of robes, but most Thai monks have two or more sets so that they can change them frequently for washing (see Ven. Nanamoli Thera 1966, p. 34 and passim).
[44] See Appendix 5 for a detailed account of Chao Khun Thep's annual income and expenditure, compared with those of Phra Sombat.

the eminent monk is presented with offerings of worldly goods with which he should have no truck. In Thailand, as I have already pointed out, it is in general not the homeless recluse, the forest-dwelling monk, who is most highly respected but the monk who is firmly integrated into the society of the *Sangha* and thus readily available to minister to the spiritual needs of the lay community. As the above case-history illustrates, the most revered *bhikkhus* are indeed offered substantial material support. But whilst they must accept such presentations, since their acceptance confers merit (*bun*) upon the donor, they must at the same time preserve their aloofness from these things of the world, and by so doing validate their claims to lay support. Indeed the *bhikkhu*'s renunciation of the world, partial though it is, is not a once-for-all event but a continuous process, as he is constantly presented with new opportunities to prove his disdain for secular pleasures, the more often the more highly he is revered.

Chao Khun Thep was perhaps the most respected of all the eminent monks in Ayutthaya of both the passive and active varieties. Though his knowledge of the scriptures appeared to be minimal his relationships with people and possessions most nearly approximated that of the *arahant*[45] or Enlightened person in that he showed little or no evidence of personal attachments. But the ideas of both monks and laymen concerning the *arahant* phenomenon were very vague and sketchy and many of them believed that *arahants* existed only at the time of the Buddha and in the years immediately following his decease. They revered the abbot so highly not because they were explicitly aware of his resemblance to this ascetic norm but – which is simply the other side of the coin – because his attitudes and conduct were felt to be most distant from their own, and most difficult to achieve.

All the eminent monks in Ayutthaya who were of this passive type were fairly advanced in years, although age alone does not provide a sufficient condition for eminence, and on the other hand, several elderly luminaries were far from passive; the abbot of *Wat* Phrayat provides a good contrast to Chao Khun Thep in his enactment of the monkly role. This *bhikkhu*, who was seventy-five years old, also came from the rice-fields and had been a member of the Buddhist *Sangha* for fifty-three years. As well as being head of the monastic community of *Wat* Phrayat the abbot (generally referred to as Luang Pho *Wat* Phrayat – Revered Father of *Wat* Phrayat) held the honorific title of *Phra Khru* (Grade 2) and was the Ecclesiastical Head of *Tambon Hantra* (*Chao Khana Tambon Hantra*). He had passed none of the ecclesiastical examinations, although he confessed to having made several

[45] An *arahant* is one who has achieved *Nirvana* or Enlightenment. See Obeyesekere (1968, p. 38) on the social function of ascetic renunciation.

unsuccessful attempts to obtain *Nak Tham* Grade 3, at the beginning of his career in the Order, before he became burdened with the responsibilities of office. Despite the fact that he had long since given up any interest in academic pursuits he regularly attended the annual ecclesiastical examinations at *Wat* Monthop to exchange news and gossip with other *bhikkhus*.

The abbot's popularity was in a sense of a more mundane kind than that enjoyed by Chao Khun Thep, in that it was a result of his approachability and friendliness, as well as of the belief that he could confer health and happiness by sprinkling sacralized water upon any person who applied to him. Because of his 'magical' (*saiyasat*)[46] talents he, also, was invited to the state-sponsored celebrations of Buddhist national holidays along with other senior ecclesiastical officials, and at the close of the recitation it was Luang Pho *Wat* Phrayat rather than any more senior abbot who sprinkled sacralized water upon the laity. In addition to this there was a great demand for his services from lay people who intended to sponsor a house-blessing ceremony, or a ritual to open a new shop or restaurant, and not infrequently people came from Bangkok to receive the abbot's blessing on their cars and coaches, for their future journeys on roads made hazardous by reckless and incompetent drivers.

Those *bhikkhus* who could give eloquent and amusing sermons belonged to another species of the genus active monk. In Ayutthaya several monks who were renowned for their skill in teaching and preaching were also well-educated in the sense that they had passed many grades of the ecclesiastical examinations; but academic qualifications were not in themselves sufficient to bring their bearer wide popular support even though they were sufficiently rare in Ayutthaya to result in some degree of popular renown. It was my impression that the link between intellectual and oratorial gifts was, where it existed, coincidental rather than causal, in that the type of monk who most enjoyed preaching to the laity was more likely than his fellows to be ambitious for academic and other honours.

The *bhikkhu* who combined scholarship with showmanship most effec-

---

[46] This example shows that monks who are revered by the laity for activities which are generally regarded as extraneous to the monkly role may receive official recognition in the form of ecclesiastical office. I have some doubts as to whether a *saiyasat* would ever be appointed to a more eminent position such as Ecclesiastical Provincial Head (*Chao Khana Changwat*), as it seems to me that the authorities in Bangkok who would be responsible for such an appointment are becoming increasingly careful of their image. They might be wary of conferring so high an honour on a monk with such unorthodox gifts. Evidence for this new trend is provided by Punyanubhab (1965, p. 173) who describes how the sacralizing of a bowl of water, an important part of any merit-making ceremony, was omitted from the ritual held in Bangkok to commemorate 'the twenty-fifth Buddhist Century' as this practice would be 'a source of undesirable remarks if seen by thoughtful Buddhists from all over the world'. See above, Introduction.

tively was the Deputy Abbot (*Rong Chao Awat*) of *Wat* Suwandararam, Ayutthaya. This monk, Chao Khun Sutthi, was forty-six years old and had entered the *Sangha* as a novice at the age of fourteen. He held the honorific rank of *Phra Racha Khana Chan Saman Barian* and had passed the *Barian* examination Grade 6 – an achievement equalled by only one other monk in Ayutthaya. Chao Khun Sutthi had however ceased his studies several years previously as he had become increasingly involved with parish duties and with the internal administrative affairs of the monastic community, the burden of which fell upon his shoulders as the abbot resembled Chao Khun Thep in the passive quality of his charisma.[47]

Chao Khun Sutthi was renowned for his witty and pointed sermons and received invitations from laymen in Bangkok and Chiengmai, as well as from other regions of Thailand. Indeed several Ayutthayans complained that he was rarely in town, and thus available only infrequently to perform merit-making ceremonies for the laymen of the locality. Chao Khun Sutthi to some extent represented a new kind of active monk in that he had been able to make use of educational facilities unavailable to older *bhikkhus*, for there has been only a gradual expansion of ecclesiastical education into the Provincial areas. Nevertheless, as was remarked above, the monk's academic standing was to a large extent irrelevant to his popularity in the town, and indeed the residents of *Wat* Senasanaram who placed greater emphasis on study than upon pastoral activities were comparatively unknown and unsung.

To make one final point about the importance of the age of a monk as a factor in attracting the retaining popular support: several of the older informants – both monk and lay – considered that Chao Khun Sutthi was at the age of forty-six still a little young to be a *phu yai* and that the appearance and demeanour rendering him worthy of that designation could only come with advancing years. But age, though a necessary qualification for real eminence, is not in itself sufficient to win the reverence and respect of the lay community.

In order to throw into clearer relief the special nature of the relationship between a famous monk and the lay community I shall now present for examination a description of the contrasting circumstances of a more ordinary member of the Thai *Sangha*. The monk in question, Phra Sombat, lived in the small and relatively obscure community of *Wat* Yanasen, Ayutthaya. Although he was in his mid-fifties he had spent only eight

---

[47] It is interesting to note that at each of the three larger *wats* in Ayutthaya one finds a passive and an active monk 'in harness' as abbot and deputy abbot respectively, which suggests that positions of supreme importance are more likely to go to *bhikkhus* of a more tranquil disposition.

phansa (Lenten seasons) in the *wat,* having resigned from his job as a train driver on the Royal Thai Railway. His home was in Bangkok, but he had chosen to live in *Wat* Yanasen both because it was 'peaceful' and because some of his kinsmen lived nearby.

During my period of fieldwork Phra Sombat received on average two invitations each month (June being a peak period during which he had eight appointments); this figure includes in almost equal proportions requests to officiate at merit-making ceremonies and invitations merely to take his eleven o'clock meal in the home of various relations in the locality. Of the invitations to perform merit-making ceremonies, all were of the *kho song* variety with one exception, which was provided by the specific request (*nimon chochong*) of one lay sponsor who was related by marriage to a kinsman of the monk. Unlike the other monks I have discussed, Phra Sombat had a great deal of time to spare for paying casual visits to friends in the monastic and the lay sections of Ayutthaya society. In his leisure hours he also read books on the history of Thailand and visited shrines and historic monuments throughout the country, always travelling by train as he was given free passage by virtue of his previous employment.

These contrasting case-histories of eminent and ordinary members of the Buddhist *Sangha* illustrate the varying extent to which a monk may retain specific personal ties with lay society. In a sense the more eminent and 'committed' the monk the less dependent he is on previous relationships with a number of householders, in that most of his pastoral services are bestowed upon unknown or little-known members of the lay community. This is not to imply that prior links are necessarily ruptured but merely to state that relationships formed on this basis comprise a smaller proportion of the total number of pastoral relationships with which he is involved. Similarly, more eminent *bhikkhus* rarely have time to spend on informal interaction; which is to say they tend not to make informal visits to relatives and friends, nor to receive invitations simply to take their morning meal with laymen, who themselves realize that such monks tend to work to a tight schedule, and are thus reluctant to impose (*kreng chai*) upon them.[48]

Other factors which affect the extent to which any monk retains his previous social affiliations are the geographical distance between his chosen *wat* and his natal area, and the length of time he has spent in the Order. The age at which he was ordained is particularly crucial with respect to the maintenance of prior links with non-related individuals, in that an elderly *bhikkhu* who entered the monastery as a novice is unlikely to have kept in touch with school-fellows and playmates of half a century ago.

---

[48] The Thai term *kreng chai* means 'to have consideration for, to be reluctant to impose upon' (see Mary R. Haas, *Thai-English Students' Dictionary* (1964)).

The monk and the lay community

As stated earlier, seniority in years, or lenten seasons spent in the *wat*, do not automatically bring a position of eminence, although most of the highly respected monks in Ayutthaya were fairly elderly and had spent many *phansa* in the *Sangha*; similarly not all 'famous' *bhikkhus* lived far away from their family homes, though it is true to say that if a man born in a small rural settlement takes up residence in the local *wat* it is unlikely that he wants or is able to attract widespread popular support.[49]

There have been two main threads running through the previous discussion; the first of which concerns the various activities associated with the monkly role, and the implications of the way in which these are evaluated for the standing of any *bhikkhu* both in the local community and in the society of the *Sangha*. It has I think been demonstrated fairly conclusively that the monk who is most highly regarded is not the solitary recluse dedicated to self-improvement but the *bhikkhu* who in a variety of ways ministers to the needs of lay society. It is important however that he should combine service to the world with a disdain for its fruits.

LINKS BETWEEN MONK AND LAYMEN

The discussion of the nature of the *bhikkhu*'s links with the lay community provided a second and closely interwoven theme in the foregoing paragraphs. It may be remembered that any man who becomes a member of the Buddhist *Sangha* automatically enters into a special relationship with the lay society he has left behind, in that he is able to confer merit upon them in return for the material support which it is their duty to provide. But each monk interacts with only a very few of these potential lay supporters and such interaction as takes place arises from *bhikkhu*-householder relationships which originate in one of several ways and are of varying degrees of permanence and stability. Fig. 2.1 represents an observer's model of possible variants in the relationship between a Buddhist monk and members of the lay community; the links which I term 'prior' are those with kinsmen and friends which were formed before the *bhikkhu*'s ordination and which have been carried over from lay life. Such ties may or may not be extended to more distant relatives and to friends of friends, after the individual in question has entered the Order, but their essential (prior) basis remains the same. These prior ties are relatively permanent and may be activated, by the individual layman, at intervals throughout the lives of the parties concerned. In between life-crisis rituals (*ngan tham bun*) which after all

[49] In chapter 3 I show how popular support is mobilized through the procedure for appointment to ecclesiastical office.

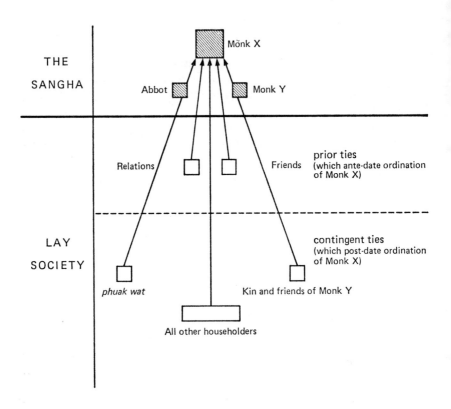

Fig. 2.1. Observer's model of possible monk–layman relationships in the context of merit-making ceremonies

Note: The length of the line between Monk X and the householder indicates the inevitability or potentiality of contact in each case.

happen relatively infrequently within any one household but provide the primary reason for interaction, such relationships may be maintained by the householder's making occasional visits to the *wat* or by his inviting the *bhikkhu* to take a meal at the house. The degree and frequency of this informal interaction is largely governed by geographic factors, although infrequent contact does not necessarily imply a breach of relations, and the householder who is to sponsor a merit-making ceremony normally places at the top of his guest-list relatives (*phi nong*) or friends (*phuan*) who have entered the *Sangha*, however distant their present place of residence may be.

Over and above these linkages which he carries over from lay life the monk forms contingent ties with a number of householders, ties which post-date his ordination and which are the inevitable concomitant of his being a Buddhist *bhikkhu*. The process of selection (over which the monk himself has no control) from the total universe of unrelated and unknown householders is largely a function of the *bhikkhu*'s place of residence, as laymen tend to invite (*nimon*) members of the local *wat* community to officiate at any ceremony; and also because any monk may receive indirect invitations from laymen who have specific ties with a fellow resident in the monastery. Thus contingent relationships are usually mediated through some other monk, either the abbot of the *wat* or some more junior member of the community although, as has been demonstrated very clearly, very eminent or famous monks receive direct invitations from householders whom they do not know and who may well live outside the immediate locality. However, contingent ties, whether they arise from accidental spatial relations or as a result of the popularity of the monk concerned, may in time come to resemble prior linkages as affective ties develop between the *bhikkhu* and the householder. To sum up, we may say that the number and identity of non-related laymen who request the services of any member of the *Sangha* vary according to the movement of the *bhikkhu* between monasteries and with the rise or decline in his personal charisma; such factors may also influence his relationships with kinsmen and long-standing friends from lay life, though these tend to remain more stable despite geographical mobility and the vicissitudes of fortune.

The monk's own classification of his relationships with householders in the context of merit-making ceremonies is slightly different from that illustrated by the observer's model and is presented in Fig. 2.2 The *bhikkhu* recognizes that some of the invitations he receives over any given period of time are specific (*cho chong*) and are the outcome of fairly established and permanent relationships existing between himself and the several hosts who may be relatives or friends; his links with people in the latter (*phuan*)

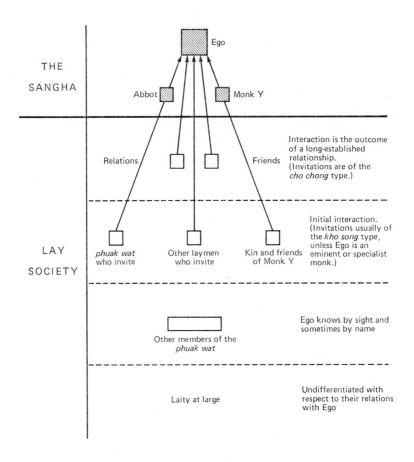

Fig. 2.2. Monk's classification of his relationships with laymen in the context of merit-making ceremonies

Note: Distance of layman from Ego indicates the degree of permanence and specificity in the monk–layman relationship.

category may, according to my classification, be of a prior kind, or alternatively may be contingent ties which have become more permanent over the years. The *bhikkhu* himself, if asked, can of course distinguish between old and new friends, but for him the major distinction is between *chao phap* whom he knows and those with whom he is not acquainted, whose initial invitation may or may not represent the beginning of a more stable relationship.

Those invitations which are of the non-specific or *kho song* variety come from householders who are unknown to the *bhikkhu* or at least from people who are insufficiently acquainted with him to make a specific request even though they may know him by sight. Interestingly enough, although it is more meritorious to invite a chapter of monks by the process known as *kho song* than to particularize (*cho chong*) it would be extremely discourteous to include in such a generalized invitation monks whom one knew at all well, which is to say to the extent that each party knows the name of the other and conversation has taken place on several occasions. Consequently a layman who wishes to invite several monks from the same *wat* requests their services individually if he knows them well.

As we have seen already, eminent monks receive invitations which fall half-way between these two types, in that they are direct and specific but frequently come from householders who are unknown to the *bhikkhu*. In such a case it is the reputation of the monk in question, rather than his relationship with the host, which is established and recognized; it is his own eminence which serves to single him out from his fellows in the *Sangha* and places him in a particular position as a 'public figure' with respect to the lay community.

Beyond this, the monk differentiates between householders with whom he has had no contact only along very broad lines. He recognizes some laymen as belonging to the *phuak wat ni* whether or not he has entered into interaction with them. Such people who are particularly affiliated to his *wat* are known to him by sight and sometimes by name. Other members of the lay community are undifferentiated with respect to their actual or potential relations with him in the context of merit-making activities. In some cases the *bhikkhu* may know of their allegiance to some other *wat* in town, though the majority are simply 'householders' categorized only according to their age and sex. Exceptions to this ruling are provided by lay-brokers who act as liaison officials between the householders and the monastic community in the context of merit-making activities. These laymen, to be discussed in subsequent chapters, can be regarded as the counterparts of the eminent members of the *Sangha* in that they may be widely known by name and reputation, and consequently are requested to act as brokers by both *bhikkhus* and laymen who are not intimately acquainted with them.

It must be remembered however that in the context of merit-making activities the monk initiates the relationship; nor does he regard laymen in the light of potential invitations and material rewards, as he receives his daily support from routine gifts of rice, or in some cases from the monastery itself.

The laymen represented in Fig. 2.3 do not act jointly with respect to the *bhikkhu* in the case and do not feel themselves to be related with respect to him. There is, in effect, no equivalent at the level of the individual monk to the *phuak wat ni*, a collection of people who recognize themselves, and are recognized, to be associated with a particular monastic community, even though they may rarely co-operate as a body with respect to that *wat*.

Several laymen who are related to a particular member of the *Sangha* may indeed share the expenses of a merit-making ceremoney to which he – along with a number of other monks – is invited, although the arrangements for the ceremony are normally made by the individual host acting on behalf of his own family household. Thus even laymen who are kinsmen of a particular *bhikkhu*, and who consequently from time to time share the expenses of a ritual in which he, as well as several other monks, takes part, do not regard themselves as forming a group in relation to the monk concerned.

In Fig. 2.3, in order to clarify this situation, I present the layman's view of his position with respect to the Order of Monks. Although all *bhikkhus* are equally eligible to minister to his spiritual needs, the householder who is preparing to sponsor a merit-making ceremony recognizes nevertheless that he is under an obligation to invite particular monks who are also relatives or friends, as well as having a more generalized obligation to invite a few members of his local *wat* community. Furthermore he may feel bound to invite one or more *bhikkhus* who are closely related to friends in the lay community. Beyond this he may also invite distinguished, fashionable or specialist monks whom he knows by reputation alone; if for example a householder is to hold an ordination ceremony he must invite a monk who is empowered to confer ordination upon the candidate (i.e. a monk who is an *upacha*) – as such officials are relatively few in number it frequently happens that the lay host requests the services of an *upacha* who is unknown to him. Similarly a householder who is moving into a new house may well invite a monk whose presence, like that of the abbot of *Wat* Phrayat, is felt to be particularly auspicious to officiate at the associated ritual of blessing. In the chapters dealing with the religious behaviour of the Thai layman I describe in detail a merit-making ceremony which can be seen in sociological terms as a kind of 'action-set' (Mayer 1966, p. 105) centred on the lay host,

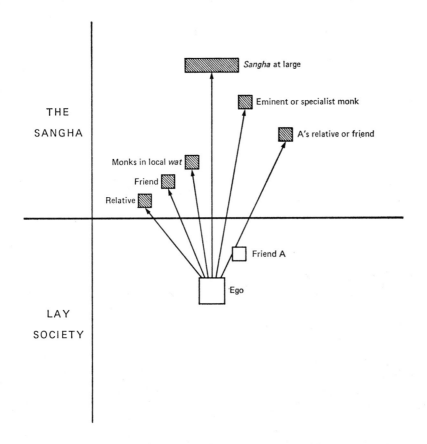

Fig. 2.3. Layman's view of the *Sangha* when inviting monks to perform a merit-making ceremony

Notes:

i. The length of the lines between Ego and various members of the *Sangha* indicates in each case the degree of obligation felt by the layman towards the monk in question.

ii. On some occasions it is necessary to invite an eminent or specialist monk, e.g. a monk who is an *upacha* must be invited to an ordination ceremony. The question of prior obligation is irrelevant in this case.

comprising both the monks who officiate at the ceremony and the laymen who attend.

It must be stressed once again in conclusion that the Buddhist monk performs his pastoral activities only by invitation and that he does not go out to bring his lay flock into the fold as does the Christian priest. The passivity of the *bhikkhu* in this respect can be explained by the fact that the primary purpose of his ordination is to begin the long task of self-improvement and not to bring the *Dhamma* to the unordained;[50] and indeed, as I have already mentioned, attending to the needs of the householder forms, in theory, a secondary and relatively unimportant aspect of the monkly role (Dutt 1957, p. 93).

Interestingly enough, in Thailand today increasing emphasis is being given by the national authorities to the function of the monks as priests and shepherds of the people. At the beginning of this century the *bhikkhu*'s role as a school-teacher was usurped by the introduction of state education to Thailand, and furthermore, as was pointed out in the previous chapter, the increasing economic complexity and specialization common to the urban situation restricts still further the monk's sphere of activities.[51]

However there have been recent moves by the government, working through the Department of Religion in the Ministry of Education, to train monks in community development for projects in underdeveloped areas of the country (Mulder 1969), and generally to refurbish their role in the community by establishing lay religious associations and teaching courses for householders which are run by the monks themselves (Wells 1960, p. 252).

These new trends and developments may have important implications for the future position of the Buddhist *bhikkhu* in Thai society.

Individual reaction to the monk's extension of his traditional role varies greatly both within and between the lay and the religious sections of society. Some people consider it most unsuitable that the *bhikkhus* should be actively involved in the practical affairs of the lay world, especially when the activities in question have overt political implications, as is the case with the community development projects in deprived, and therefore potentially disaffected areas. An alliance of this nature between the government and the *Sangha* was felt by these people to be to the credit of neither party. Some more cynical and perhaps more realistic observers view the desacralizing of the monk's role as a *sine qua non* of his retaining any kind of function in modern Thai society, which they see as becoming increasingly secularized

---

[50] See Kaufman (1960, p. 128) for a similar point.

[51] In an urban environment the greater acceptance of the methods of *witthayasat* as well as easier access to doctors and hospitals renders the activities of *saiyasat*, both monks and laymen, less important (see above, chapter 1).

and where many attributes of the monkly role have already been taken over by specialists. The choice presented to the monk would appear to be that of losing any real social function whilst maintaining a semi-divine status, or of increasing his involvement with the lay world at the cost of diminishing his special prestige.

3
The *wat* community

In friendship of the world anxiety is born
In household life distraction's dust springs
up
The state set free from home and
friendship's ties
That and only that is the recluse's aim.

Verses from the *Muni Sutta* (*Sutta-Nipata*
1, 12) translated by T. W. Rhys Davids
(Rhys Davids 1963 (Dover edition), p. 1)

In chapters 3 and 4 we shall be taking a closer look at some current anthropological clichés relating to the *wat*'s position as central to, even defining the boundaries of, the lay community. In so doing we shall see in what way the term monastery as a translation of the Thai word *wat* is inadequate or misleading, suggesting as it does to the reader who is more familiar with the tradition of Western monasticism, a closed and inward-looking community whose members are more concerned with their personal quest, and with each other, than in their relations with outsiders. Let us address ourselves in the first instance to this second issue.

The Thai monastery or *wat* is not only a place of residence for Buddhist monks, but also a church or religious meeting ground for the laity; its physical lay-out clearly reflects this dual function.

Within the monastic compound (*thi wat*) are situated both the living quarters (*kuti*) for the *bhikkhus*, and the more conspicuous and elaborately decorated public buildings, namely, the *wihan* (Pali: *vihara*) or preaching hall, and one or more *sala* (pavilions) where services are held, and sermons addressed to lay devotees (*ubasaka*). The *bot*, which is the most important edifice, being situated within the consecrated area marked by the *sima* (boundary stones), is used both for those activities relating to disciplinary affairs, which are the exclusive concern of the *Sangha*, and for other ceremonies, such as that marking an individual's entry into the Order, at which laymen and women are also present.

The information presented in the following paragraphs concerning the structure and internal organization of the *wat* community is based upon study of fifteen monasteries situated in the municipal area of Ayutthaya.[1]

[1] Each of these fifteen monasteries belonged to the *Mahanikai* Sect.

These monastic communities consisted of between five and twenty-nine permanent monks, and of varying numbers of novices (*nen*), monastery boys (*dek wat*) and, in a few cases, nuns (*mae chi*).[2]

The composition of any community to some extent reflects its orientation; as the statistics show, the two main teaching monasteries, *Wat* Suwandararam[3] and *Wat* Phanan Choeng, have a higher proportion of novices, as these boys are attracted by the study facilities offered. Furthermore these larger and more prosperous establishments, where food and accommodation are readily available, have a greater appeal for *dek wat*, whether they live there on a permanent or part-time basis. *Dek wat* of the former type are usually children of poor homes who are given food, board and some informal education by the monks, in return for performing domestic duties such as washing the robes of the monks, and keeping clean the compound, and the various buildings in the *wat*. The part-time or temporary *dek wat* are boys from outlying areas who attend school or college in Ayutthaya, and thus have lodgings in the *wat* only during term-time. After school hours they too perform chores for the *bhikkhus* and novices.

The general tenor of the community also has important implications for the kind of monks who choose to reside there. It is noticeable that there are few retired monks in the larger teaching monasteries in Ayutthaya, namely *Wat* Suwan and *Wat* Phanan Choeng, where approximately half the total number of *bhikkhus* are in their twenties or early thirties; the remaining older residents are permanent monks of long-standing who do not fall into the category 'retired'. Indeed the abbots of these *wats* have been known to refuse admission to men who wished to spend their declining years there, on the grounds that the living space available was needed for monks and novices, who intended to make use of the educational facilities provided. Several smaller monasteries had a similar policy: the community at *Wat* Salapun, for example, centred upon the abbot, who was highly educated in ecclesiastical terms, having passed *Barian* Grade 6; he felt quite strongly that *bhikkhus* who were not interested in studying would not be 'happy' there, and indeed suggested as much to unsuitable applicants.

On the other hand certain establishments are little more than hostels for old men, and are in consequence shunned by younger monks who, whether or not they have serious academic intentions, perfer to live in livelier communities.

Small groups of nuns (*mae chi*) had taken up residence at five of the fifteen *wats* with which I was most familiar. Although *mae chi* are said to have been ordained (*buat*) they are regarded as belonging to the lay sector of

[2] See Appendix 6 for statistical information.
[3] More commonly referred to as *Wat* Suwan by the inhabitants of Ayutthaya.

society, rather than to the religious, which is comprised of monks and novices. There is in fact no Order of nuns organized hierarchically on a nation-wide basis, although sometimes the nun who is the most senior, by age or by ordination, is referred to as the *hua na* or 'head' of the group at any one *wat*; her authority is of a purely informal and domestic kind and depends upon the willing co-operation of her juniors.

Nuns observe Eight Precepts, as against the Five Precepts observed by the ordinary layman; the three additional injunctions forbid them to take an evening meal, to sleep on a soft bed or couch (rather than upon matting laid down upon the floor) and to use jewellery or cosmetics with which to adorn themselves.[4] Those women who have been 'ordained' as nuns shave their heads and wear white robes similar in style to the monks' habit.

The group of nuns in residence at *Wat* Yai Chai Mongkhon was the only one which was of considerable size and to some extent integrated into the monastic community. Both these features can be explained by the fact that most of them had come to study with the abbot who was renowned as a teacher of meditation techniques (*wiphasana-thura*). The groups of *mae chi* at the other monasteries in my sample can only be said to belong to the community in so far as they have been given permission by the abbot concerned to build their living quarters in the compounds of the respective *wats*. All the nuns interviewed received donations of both money and food from their relatives as well as occasional gifts of surplus rice from the monks and novices in the *wat*.

As the figures given in the appendix show quite clearly, all the monastic communities studied experienced an influx of monks during the Lenten season (*phansa*), which lasts from mid-July until mid-October. During this period even those I have dubbed 'old men's hostels' (e.g. *Wat* Kluai) welcomed new residents, the majority being the younger relations of the regular inmates, coming to join the latter for the three months of *phansa*. The greatest relative increase occurs in rural monastic communities which might otherwise comprise only one or two permanent monks, but during the Lenten retreat in 1967 the numbers in even the larger urban monasteries in Ayutthaya almost doubled; at *Wat* Phanan Choeng for example the number of *bhikkhus* rose from twenty-nine to forty-five and at neighbouring *Wat* Suwan sixteen new monks joined the twenty-eight *bhikkhus* in permanent residence. In some Bangkok monasteries where the monks devote their entire time to academic pursuits and take little interest in the lay community, the number of residents may be unaffected by the onset of *phansa* but none of the *wats* in Ayutthaya is oriented exclusively to study in this way.

---

[4] Some members of the laity observe Eight Precepts as against the usual Five, for the duration of Holy Day (*Wan Phra*) only: see below, p. 107.

In urban areas the size of some monastic communities increases temporarily during the hot season (April–May) when many men take their annual holiday. The abbot of one monastery in Ayutthaya coined the phrase *phak ron buat* (ordination during the hot season holiday) to describe this phenomenon, and compared it with the more usual *phansa buat* (Lenten ordination) described above. Few of the men who become ordained during the hot season (*na ron*) stay in the *wat* for longer than two or three weeks.

During the Lenten season the number of novices also increases temporarily; some boys are ordained simply to make merit for senior relatives, both the living and the dead, whilst others become novices or monastery boys in order to accompany their elder brothers who have been ordained for a short time, 'according to custom or tradition' (*pen prapheni*). Similarly the general intensification of religious activity may be visible by a slight increase in the number of nuns during these months, as the statistics indicate.

Let us now examine the implications for the individual *bhikkhu* of belonging to a particular monastic community; what does affiliation to a monastery entail? The Acts on the Administration of the Buddhist Order of *Sangha*[5] in Thailand state that all monks 'must be attached to a monastery and have permanent residence', but the practical application of this ruling deserves further attention. Before his ordination, a man must obtain permission from the abbot of his chosen monastery to take up residence there. A number of factors may influence his choice; he may be attracted by the location of the *wat* or by the facilities for study or meditation which it offers; or on the other hand the presence of a particularly talented monk, or simply of a monk whom he knows already, may be decisive. It is quite usual to find in any urban *wat* a number of *bhikkhus* from the same or from neighbouring rural settlements. In any case it is customary, in requesting permission to take up residence in a monastery, for the suppliant to approach the abbot through a third person, either monk or layman, who will introduce him, and present his request. The abbot rarely refuses permission except in the kind of case already mentioned where it is felt that the applicant would be happier elsewhere; for example an elderly monk who applied to live at *Wat* Phanan Choeng was advised to try down the road at *Wat* Prasat where there were already several older men in residence, and where the tempo of life was somewhat slower.

Outside the Lenten period there is little or no pressure upon accommoda-

[5] See Acts on the Administration of the Buddhist Order of Sangha, B.E. 2445 (1902), Part IV, Art. 7, in a compilation published B.E. 2506 (1963) by the Mahamakuta Educational Council, The Buddhist University, Bangkok.

tion in any *wat*, and even during *phansa* it is usually possibly to find a space in the living quarters, or on the balcony outside, for another *bhikkhu*. It should be remembered that popular and populous monasteries are more likely to receive from the laity substantial sums of money, which can be used to construct any extensions necessary.

The residence of any monk is recorded, along with the signature of the abbot, in the identity card with which each *bhikkhu* is issued on his entry into the Order; subsequent changes of residence are also indicated by the written approval of the heads of the communities concerned.

Historians trace the development of the Buddhist cenobium from the practice, current among religious wanderers in India long before the coming of the Buddha, of going into retreat during the rainy season (Dutt 1957, p. 67). Furthermore it is believed that the Buddha himself specifically exhorted his followers not to wander abroad during the period lest they damage the new rice (Müller, vol. 13, p. 298).[6]

During the Lenten season in present-day Thailand a monk may not spend one night away from the *wat*, which is his official place of residence, unless he has obtained special permission from the abbot. Such permission is only given in extremely critical circumstances. The example always given by my informants was that of a monk whose father or mother, living at some distance away, becomes gravely ill during *phansa*. In such an instance the *bhikkhu* may be permitted to visit them provided that he returns to the *wat* after seven days and seven nights. Should any monk stay away from the monastery for longer than the time allowed, or without permission, he is said to have 'broken Lent' (*khat phansa*) and cannot count that season towards his seniority in the Order; nor may he receive a share of the *Kathin*[7] presentation taken to every *wat* by a group of householders at the end of the Lenten season. (Vajirananavarorasa 1963, p. 68.)

The practice of spending every night of the Buddhist Lent in one's own monastery (i.e. *cham phansa*, lit. to 'observe' or 'remember' Lent) seems to be observed quite strictly on the whole. One *bhikkhu* remarked that, during the year previous to my fieldwork, he had been forced to *khat phansa* because he had gone to the monks' hospital in Bangkok for treatment at that time. Another monk from the capital, who gave instruction on Buddhist 'morality' in provincial schools and colleges, regarded this restriction on his movement as most irksome and unnecessary. He said that he would return to Bangkok only once every seven days, to request permission for a further leave of absence.

---

[6] A minor injunction in the *Patimokkha* code reads as follows: 'In damaging plants there is a case entailing expiation' (Ven. Nanamoli Thera 1966, p. 48).

[7] See below, p. 113.

The wat *community*

It is during the period of *phansa* that every abbot in the country submits details as to the number of monks resident in his *wat*, their names and qualifications, to the Ecclesiastical District Head (*Chao Khana Amphoe*),[8] who in turn relays the information in tabulated form to the Department of Religious Affairs in the capital.

Outside the rainy season, however, there is considerable movement between *wats*, as *bhikkhus* pay visits to friends living in monasteries in other parts of the country, or spend some time in the monastery nearest their family home, in order to renew relationships with kinsmen and old friends. A few *bhikkhus* leave the monastic community altogether and go on pilgrimages (*doen thudong*) to visit shrines and monuments throughout the country.

But with respect to relationships within the monastic community, visiting monks are not differentiated from the permanent residents; they are similarly subject to the authority of the abbot in that *wat*, and are on the other hand, eligible to take part in Acts of Sangha (*Sanghakamma*) pertaining to monastic organization, provided that they are of the same sect as their hosts. In short, membership of a particular monastic community is of fairly minor significance for the ordinary monk, and for his relationships with his fellows in the *Sangha*; such criteria as relative age and seniority of ordination are of greater importance in structuring interaction between monks than is their affiliation to the same or different *wats*.

But some qualifications must be made with respect to the *bhikkhu* who is the abbot of a particular monastic community, and thus tends to have a stronger sense of identification with his *wat* than does the ordinary monk. It has been shown in the previous chapter that the abbot is seen as the representative of the whole *wat* community by the laymen outside, and may even be referred to by the name of that monastery. Furthermore, because his office is attached to a particular *wat*, an abbot automatically loses his position if he changes residence voluntarily.[9]

As concerns the abbot's relationships with his brothers in the *Sangha*, it must be noted that, except in the cases of higher ecclesiastical officials (e.g. *Chao Khana Tambon*, or *Chao Khana Amphoe*) the boundaries of his jurisdiction do not extend to monks in other *wats*; nor need his position in

---

[8] The *Chao Khana Amphoe* frequently acts as a liaison official between the central authorities in Bangkok and the local monastic community. In this respect his function is very similar to that of the *Nai Amphoe*, his civil counterpart.

[9] He may of course change residence if he is promoted to higher office in another *wat*. The previous abbot of *Wat* Nang Plum was appointed Deputy Ecclesiastical Provincial Head (*Rong Chao Khana Changwat*) and had to move to *Wat* Salapun to assume his position.

any way affect his relationships with monks not under his direct authority, as in outward appearance an abbot is indistinguishable from any ordinary *bhikkhu*. Consequently the abbot's relationship with non-office-holding residents of other *wats* are also conducted with reference to relative age and seniority of *phansa*, rather than with respect to the standing of the parties concerned in the official ecclesiastical hierarchy.

But what is the nature of the abbot's authority as head of the *wat*, the smallest unit of ecclesiastical administration, and how is this position achieved?

The minimum formal requirement for a monk to be appointed abbot is that he should have spent at least five Lenten seasons in the Order.[10] An equally important factor is that the *bhikkhus* in the *wat* and interested laymen in the vicinity should approve of the appointment, or at any rate, that they should have no overwhelming objections. During my period of field-work the position of abbot (*chao awat*) at one monastery became vacant on the death of the previous incumbent. After some weeks the monk who was the Ecclesiastical Head of the Sub-District (*Tambon*) in which the *wat* was situated, convened a meeting of the twelve other abbots in that area. At this assembly it was suggested that a younger monk already resident at *Wat* Khrutharam, the monastery concerned, should be appointed to fill the post. In the following days the abbots who lived nearest to *Wat* Khrutharam where the post was vacant, canvassed the opinions of *bhikkhus* in that monastery, and in their own establishments, with respect to this tentative decision. They also spoke to members of the lay community who were known to take an interest in religious affairs in the town and particularly to those who served on the Monastery Committee (*kammakan wat*) at *Wat* Khrutharam. When they had ascertained to their satisfaction that their candidate was not objectionable to any person, monk or layman, the *Chao Khana Tambon* went to discuss the matter with his immediate superior, the Ecclesiastical District Head (*Chao Khana Amphoe*). The latter knew and approved of the monk in question, and accordingly recommended his

---

[10] In Thailand great importance is attached to age seniority: the average age of the seventy-two abbots in *Amphoe* Ayutthaya was 56.3 years (Lenten seasons 26.1), as compared with the 42.25 years (Lenten seasons 14.3) of the ordinary monks in the same area. Nevertheless there were no formal age requirements for the appointment of abbots, although an abbot must be at least twenty-five years old, given the fact that he must have spent five Lenten seasons in the Order, which he may not enter until he has reached the age of twenty. Six of the seventy-two abbots mentioned above were under thirty years of age, and a further half-dozen were between thirty and forty years of age. The 50–60 years age-group was most strongly represented. But it was by no means automatic that the oldest monk in the *wat* was appointed its abbot when the post fell vacant. Furthermore, in approximately 50% of cases *bhikkhus* from other *wats* were brought in to assume this office.

appointment to the Ecclesiastical Provincial Head (*Chao Khana Changwat*) who in due course conferred it.[11]

This appointment is intended to be permanent unless the monk in question leaves the Order of his own volition or is compelled to disrobe. If an abbot wishes to abdicate his position he must request the permission of the authorities who appointed him in the first place. It is usual in such cases for the monk concerned to go and live in another *wat* and indeed the desire to change his place of residence may well be the cause of the *bhikkhu*'s retirement.

Once given, the appointment is rarely withdrawn, even from monks who prove unable to perform their duties because of age or ill-health, or from simple lack of interest. The general principle seems to be that inefficiency or negligence as opposed to out-and-out delinquency is tolerable; and, as was illustrated in chapter 1, even graver misdemeanours may be ignored for the sake of the reputations of all those involved.

If an abbot is merely inadequate, the normal reaction of the householders in the vicinity is to take their custom elsewhere, which is to say that they invite monks from other monasteries, and attend services at some other *wat* in the locality. The higher ecclesiastical authorities may be unwilling to initiate action for various reasons; as the Ecclesiastical District Head himself explained, if the abbot is old and feeble it would be inhumane to turn him out; both the *Sangha* and the victim would lose face by the action. Besides which, such a man may soon die and so provide a natural solution to the problem.

In other cases another monk is appointed as acting abbot (*phuraksakanthaen chao awat*)[12] where the *de jure* abbot cannot fulfil his obligation for one reason or another. Several of the *bhikkhus* who were first introduced to me as 'The Reverend Abbot' (*than chao awat*) later proved to be 'acting' on behalf of some aged monk still living in the *wat*, though rarely seen, who yet retained the name if not the substance of his position.

---

[11] See Appendix 8 for procedure of appointment to higher ecclesiastical office, viz. *Chao Khana Tambon, Chao Khana Amphoe, Chao Khana Changwat*. These positions are also conferred according to a similar process of recommendation to higher levels. The laity are not consulted at every stage, but in any case only abbots, to whom they have already given their approval, are eligible for higher office.

[12] The term *phuraksakanthaen chao awat* is also applied to 'probationary' abbots who have not fulfilled the formal requirements of having spent five Lenten seasons in the Order; or to the heads of communities which are still under the general guardianship of the previous abbot who has since moved to take up a higher post in another *wat*. For example, the abbot of *Wat* Nang Plum was promoted to be head of the community at *Wat* Salapun (see p. 91, n. 9) but he maintained an interest in the affairs of the former monastery where a younger resident – a talented twenty-five year old 'academic' *bhikkhu* – had been appointed as *phuraksakanthaen chao awat* (lit. the person taking care of affairs on behalf of (or instead of) the abbot).

Whether or not another monk was appointed *phuraksakanthaen chao awat* when the abbot was incapable of performing his duties appeared to me to be rather arbitrary. To give two brief examples: the abbot of one monastery appeared to divide his time fairly evenly between raising bantam hens and tinkering with numerous clocks he had collected. He allowed the buildings of the *wat* to disintegrate around him and it was widely reputed to be little more than a doss-house for tramps and vagrants in the area. Even the kinsmen of the two or three elderly monks living there shunned this monastery and no rites of any kind, neither Holy Day service nor merit-making ceremony, took place within its walls. Nevertheless no action was taken to replace the abbot and only on his death was a younger and more vigorous man appointed to the post.[13]

On the other hand at neighbouring *Wat* Yanasen a *bhikkhu* had been appointed as acting abbot to replace the real incumbent whose only defect seemed to be lack of interest. He moved, without apparent concern, from the living quarters reserved for the abbot, to a smaller *kuti* at the back of the *wat*.

It is difficult to see why these two cases were not treated in the same way. Both *wats* were small and relatively unimportant in the life of the town as a whole, and the availability of an appropriate substitute in each instance does not provide an adequate explanation. There were many monks more eligible for office than the first abbot of whom I spoke, and the monk appointed as acting abbot at *Wat* Yanasen was by no means of exceptional calibre, though amiable enough.

One factor in the case might be the different temperaments of the two Ecclesiastical Sub-District Heads involved; the *Chao Khana Tambon* of *Tambon* Thawasukri 2, where *Wat* Yanasen was situated, was a more forceful and outspoken character, more careful of the 'image' of the *Sangha* than was his counterpart in the adjacent sub-district. But this must remain on the level of mere speculation as it is susceptible to neither proof nor contradiction.

At larger and more important monasteries this situation is unlikely to arise, not merely because the procedure for appointment to the more important offices located at such communities is more rigorous,[14] but also because it is customary for the abbot to appoint a deputy from amongst the *bhikkhus* in that *wat* to assist him. Should the abbot become unable to perform his duties then they would be assumed by his deputy. As was mentioned in an earlier chapter, it is in any case quite common for the real

[13] The elderly 'cronies' of the deceased betook themselves to other monasteries on the arrival of the energetic new abbot.
[14] See Appendix 8 for procedure of appointment to higher ecclesiastical office.

business of running the *wat* to be undertaken by the deputy, whilst the abbot preserves his charisma by remaining aloof from these affairs.

The primary duty of the abbot is to govern the community of which he is the head. This means, as we have already seen, that he may grant or refuse permission to individual monks or novices to live in that *wat*, or to transfer their residence; he should moreover be informed if any *bhikkhu* intends to stay away from the *wat* for a long period of time, and may allow a monk to be absent from the monastery for a seven-day period during Lent, under special circumstances. Beyond this the abbot can delegate duties to his subordinates; he may charge a senior *bhikkhu* with the instruction of the newly ordained, or direct junior members of his community to follow a particular route on their daily begging-round (*binthabat*).

The abbot is also responsible for seeing that *Sanghakamma* pertaining to the conduct of the community are performed at the appropriate time. The most important of these is the service held on *Uposatha* day which falls on the fifteenth day of the waxing and waning moon (i.e. every lunar fortnight). On this occasion all the monks in the community collect in the *bot* to recite the *Patimokkha* code, after making a collective and generalized confession of their minor offences against the discipline.[15] The abbot should see that such offences are expiated according to the procedure laid down in the *Vinaya-pitaka*, and minor breaches of the peace within the community can be punished by the allotment of domestic chores such as sweeping the compound or cleansing the latrines.

It must be remembered with respect to *Sanghakamma* that these acts can only be performed by fully ordained *bhikkhus*, all of whom are however equally eligible, regardless of their position, or lack of position, in the ecclesiastical hierarchy. Nevertheless it is the duty of the abbot, as the officially appointed head of the community, to ensure that these procedures are observed regularly and according to the rules laid down in the Buddhist texts.

The abbot also acts as a link between his community and the higher ecclesiastical authorities; he is responsible for keeping his subordinates informed about ecclesiastical conferences or examinations which are arranged on a Provincial or District basis. Similarly it is his duty to relay information

[15] Offences against 4 of the 227 rules in the *Patimokka* are inexpiable: the *bhikkhu* who engages in sexual intercourse (1), steals (2), takes human life (3), or falsely claims superior powers of understanding of the *Dhamma* (4), should be expelled automatically from the Order. The only case of proven infringement of one of these major prohibitions which came to my notice concerned a case of murder in a Bangkok monastery. The police intervened and arrested a *bhikkhu* who was alleged to have stabbed a fellow monk 'eleven times'. Other offences against the Discipline can be expiated by confession alone, or by confession succeeded by a period of solitary self-purification. See Kaufman (1960, p. 136) and Wells (1960, p. 190).

in the other direction, which means amongst other things that he must make an annual report to the *Chao Khana Amphoe* concerning the size and the state of the community in the *wat*.

Although these formal rights and duties are entailed in his office, the extent to which an abbot enjoys real influence within his community depends upon his ability to retain the goodwill and respect of his subordinates; by abuse of his authority the *chao awat* can only alienate the monks, and the laymen who are his sources of support.[16] The fact that the authority structure within the *wat* is not more highly developed can be explained with reference to a number of factors; in the first place, as I have already pointed out, the hierarchy of ecclesiastical office which exists in Thailand is an aspect of the institutionalization of the *Sangha*, which is more important for relations between the *Sangha* and the state authorities than for interaction between monks. Indeed the internal affairs of the Order, as well as the personal conduct of its individual members, are regulated by the rules laid down in the *Vinaya-pitaka*.[17] Secondly, the absence of a more complex system of internal organization within the monastery can to some extent be explained by the fact that there is a great deal of movement not only into and out of the *Sangha* but also between monasteries on the part of more permanent monks. I do not want to give the false impression that all *bhikkhus* are in perpetual motion, as many of them stay in the same monastery for the duration of their career in the Order; nevertheless, it is true to say that movement is easy and frequent, and that although a monk must at all time be registered with a *wat* no importance is attached to having permanent residence in any one monastery.[18] The relative simplicity of the internal authority structure can in the third place be attributed partly to the fact that the majority of monastic communities are both small in size and outward-looking; the average Ayutthaya monastery housed between eight and ten permanent monks most of whom were more concerned with interaction between them-

[16] See Appendix 7 for duties of the abbot as laid down in the Acts on the Administration of the Buddhist Order of Sangha (1902).

[17] 'It does not occur to me', says the Lord in reply to Ananda, 'that I am the leader of the *Bhikku-Sangha* or that it owes allegiance to me.' He made this more explicit later by declaring in a brief exhortation shortly before his decease, that the bond of the *Sangha* must be the *Dhamma-Vinaya*, that is the community of faith and religious practice, not common allegiance to a person. It was evidently implied by his words that in the future polity of the *Sangha* there must be no ideal of individual leadership or personal guidance (Dutt 1957, pp. 62–3).

[18] 79% of my informants had lived in two or more monasteries. About one-third of this number had changed residence soon after their entry into the Order and had remained in that second monastery from then onwards. Office-holders are likely to have been resident in the neighbourhood, if not in the particular *wat* where they hold office, for a number of years if they have become sufficiently known and respected to have been appointed. But in formal terms only the monk appointed to be *Chao Khana Changwat* (Ecclesiastical Provincial Head) is asked to meet any residence requirements.

selves and members of the lay community than with relationships within the *wat*. Indeed in most monastic communities there is relatively little formal and purposive interaction between fellow residents.

But before going on to discuss the transactions which take place between monastery and the lay world I must briefly mention some minor variations on the simple authority structure outlined above. In some larger monasteries the residents are organized into groups or *khana* under the leadership of senior *bhikkhus* known as *chao khana* (Lord or leader of the group). This subdivision merely represents a duplication of certain facets of the abbot's authority which is necessary when the number of permanent monks is such that the personal leadership of one individual ceases to be effective. Although the abbot retains ultimate rights to permit or prohibit a *bhikkhu* from taking up residence there, in monasteries with *khana* the leaders of these group-ings are responsible for the behaviour of monks in their care and may, for example, grant leave of absence for a short time. The abbot allows new resi-dents, monks, novices, and temple boys to particular *khana*, each of which occupies a certain group of living quarters and may be designated by the name of the current *chao khana* or by some permanent name or number (e.g. South *Khana* or *Khana* 1, 2, etc). It is usual for members of the same *khana* to take the same route on their daily begging-round and to eat together afterwards.

In Bangkok the larger monasteries of both sects are organized in *khana* but it is interesting to see that even smaller communities of *Thammayutika* monks are usually subdivided in this way. This feature can be seen as just one aspect of the tighter organization of the monasteries of the smaller reform sect, related to their emphasis on a stricter interpretation of the *Dhamma* and *Vinaya*, which means amongst other things that *Thammayut bhikkhus* tend to be oriented towards study rather than to pastoral affairs. There is thus more constant interaction between monks within the com-munity which necessitates a more complex system of internal organization.

At *Wat* Senasanaram, the only *Thammayut* monastery in Ayutthaya, the 25–30 permanent monks were organized into five *khana*. The *chao khana*, chosen by the abbot, were all Pali scholars with *Barian* Grades 4 or 5, and had been in the Order for at least ten Lenten seasons. Only one other *wat* in town, namely *Wat* Prasat, had instituted *khana*, although there were usually no more than ten or eleven monks in residence. Several of my informants considered that the abbot's action in reorganizing the com-munity in this way was unnecessary and affected, as he was behaving as if he were the head of a much larger group of monks than was in fact the case. One or two people accused him of aping the pretensions of the *Tham-mayut* monastery down the road.

The word *khana* is also applied to informal groupings of some degree of permanency centred on particular monks within the *wat*. *Khana* of this second type come into being when young monks enter a monastery with the specific intention of studying with respected *bhikkhu*, and when parents entrust their sons as novices and monastery boys to his care. The personal excellence of such a monk may also be recognized by the abbot's directing him to act as *phi liang* or mentor to newly ordained members of the community, by instructing them in the 'way of the monk'.[19]

In many ways these groupings serve the same function from the individual's point of view as do *khana* more formally constituted, although there is no specific delegation of authority to the monks upon whom they are centred; that is to say that these informal *chao khana* are not empowered to grant leave of absence to their subordinates. As is the case with the true *khana*, however, members of these looser groupings usually live in adjacent *kuti* and take their meals at the same time.

Multiplex links typical of any patron–client relationship in Thai society exist between the nodal *bhikkhu* and his *luk sit* or pupils. Such relationships usually have a material aspect, which is to say that '*than achan*' (Revered Teacher) is expected to provide at least some of the daily food for the younger boys – the *nen* and *dek wat* – in his care; he may sponsor the ordination of promising boys as novices, or finance the higher ordination of eligible *nen*, and should assist junior *bhikkhus* by sharing with them the money, robes and other material gifts presented to him by the laity.

In return the *dek wat* and *nen*, and to a lesser extent the junior monks, perform various tasks and errands on his behalf; they should sweep his quarters and wash his robes, and may accompany him to the market, where they make the purchases for him and carry his parcels. The younger monks in his *khana* are usually chosen by their *achan* to represent him at merit-making ceremonies which he is unable to attend because he has two or more appointments at the same time. Finally, all pupils should from time to time present him with small gifts of tea and cigarettes to express their continuing respect. Such groupings are only referred to as *khana* when there are several of them, which is to say that their existence presupposes a monastery of some size where there are several *bhikkhus* of sufficient seniority to be *chao khana*. In the two larger monasteries in Ayutthaya, *Wats* Suwan and Phanan Choeng, there were *khana* of this type. In the latter case the existence of different *khana* appeared to indicate some underlying hostility between their respective leaders; hostility which seemed to be based more upon temperamental incompatibility than precise grievances.

[19] This usually involves instructing them in such practical matters as the correct way to don the robes, to carry the bowl on the alms-round and so on. The *phi liang* may also teach his pupils how to intone the Pali chants, the texts of which are memorized from books published by the Ministry of Education.

The popular abbot of a smaller monastery may have many boys entrusted to his care, and may also attract younger monks to live there, as was the case at *Wat* Salapun and at neighbouring *Wat* Na Phramen; but a monastic community with a single focus cannot be said to have *khana*. Similarly, *bhikkhus* within the *wat* who come from the same area do not constitute a *khana* unless they are organized in the way described above; the fact that Monk X came to live in a particular *wat* in town because Monk Y, from the same rural *amphoe*, was known to live there neither implies nor creates enduring ties.

In conclusion I must stress once again that the existence of *khana* groupings, formal or informal in nature, represents only a possible variation on the basic pattern of relationships within the community. In most monasteries the generalized authority relationships which exist between the abbot and the other residents provide the only formal organizational links. The residents are differentiated into two main categories, the religious and the lay, the latter consisting of *dek wat* and *mae chi*, and, in a few monasteries, of social derelicts, the poor or chronically sick who have taken refuge there.

The nuns or *mae chi*, though subject to the authority of the abbot as head of the community are, except in a few cases, outside the system properly speaking, and have little contact with the monks and novices in the *wat*.

In most monasteries the novices and boys are not attached to a particular monk in the way described above but form a kind of common pool, upon which any *bhikkhu* may draw should he need a boy's assistance on a shopping expedition or company for a long journey.

Between *bhikkhus*, the fully ordained members of the *Sangha*, considerations of relative age and seniority of *phansa* shape the patterns of interaction. The junior monk should defer to the more senior whilst the latter should give aid and counsel in all matters. In many cases only lip-service is paid to this ideal; that is to say a monk who is thirty-five years old, who has fifteen Lenten seasons behind him, and has passed *Barian* Grade 5, will greet an elderly man, recently retired into the Order, in a respectful way; he may seat himself at a lower level than the older *bhikkhu* in deference to age, but would be unlikely to ask his advice on ecclesiastical affairs. It should be noted that in Ayutthaya monasteries little formal instruction is given by senior to junior monks, as was traditionally the case, as those *bhikkhus* pursuing courses of ecclesiastical study attend the monastery schools at *Wat* Suwan and at *Wat* Phanan Choeng. The teachers at these institutions are monks from Bangkok or from the larger local *wats* who take classes of as many as sixty pupils from all the monasteries in town. This factor reduces the possibility of the formation of *khana* within the monasteries themselves.

4

The *wat* and its social matrix

*As a bee without harming the flower, its
colour or scent flies away, collecting only
the honey, even so should the sage wander
in the village.*

The Dhammapada verse 49, translated by
Narada Thera
(John Murray, London, 1959)

As its title indicates, the present chapter is specifically concerned with the
relationship between the monastic community and the householders who
contribute money and material goods, as well as time and labour, to its
support. Which is to say that we shall be exploring the reality behind some
of the phrases, familiar from anthropological studies of Theravada Buddhist
societies; phrases such as, 'The monks beg their food from the laity', or
'The monastery is the focal point of the lay community'.

In an earlier chapter I spoke of the *phuak wat*,[1] as a grouping or collectivity
of lay people owning a common allegiance to a particular monastery. It may
be recalled that the *bhikkhus* in any *wat* normally receive invitations to
perform merit-making ceremonies from laymen in the vicinity who are
regarded, and regard themselves, as belonging to the *phuak* of that *wat*.

In subsequent paragraphs, where I describe the transactions which take
place between the laity and the monastic community as a whole, the form
and function of the *phuak wat* is defined more clearly, as is its relationship
with other groupings and categories of people variously associated with the
same monastery. It will become apparent that there exists no simple one-
to-one relationship between a particular *wat* and a single unified 'parish' of
lay supporters, because each monastic community is the focus for a variety
of groupings of householders, which are mobilized on different occasions and
different purposes.

THE COLLECTION OF ALMS

An examination of the mechanisms for collecting alms may seem anomalous
in this context because only one monk and one householder are engaged in

[1] *Phuak* means 'group' or 'party'. See Mary R. Haas, *Thai–English Students' Dictionary* (1964).

the *binthabat* transaction. Nevertheless I have included it in the present chapter since the route taken by any *bhikkhu* on his alms-round, as well as his strictness in observing this practice, is to a large extent determined by his residence in a particular *wat*. Furthermore, this section includes a description of a number of extraordinary mechanisms which are set in motion from time to time to provide rice for the whole monastic community.

The sketch map (Map C) shows the begging-routes taken by *bhikkhus* from monasteries in the central area of Ayutthaya. In order to avoid an overabundance of detail several *wats* located in the district have been omitted from this plan. Nevertheless it is still quite clear from the information presented that *bhikkhus* from different monasteries may tread the same path on their morning rounds, and conversely that residents of the same *wat* usually take a number of different routes. This situation raises the question as to how decisions are made with respect to the routes taken by monks from any one community, and whether or not there is any degree of co-operation or collaboration between monasteries in settling their respective 'beats'.

Each of the fifteen abbots whom I interviewed declared that monks resident in his *wat* had 'always' followed the same begging-routes, which had been established 'in olden days' by some previous head of the community. Every monastery can thus be seen as the starting-point for one or more traditional circuits which normally remain unaltered. But because these ways are determined less by any theory of 'rightness' than by the conditions underfoot and the location of inhabited settlement, they are in fact liable to be changed from time to time. During my period of fieldwork, for example, some teachers from the Agricultural College, recently built in Ayutthaya, asked the abbot of the *wat* nearest to them, *Wat* Thammikarat, if he would detail some monks to pass by the college each day. The college was situated in an isolated area of town and was usually ignored by the *bhikkhus* going out to collect alms.

There was no evidence of 'demarcation disputes' taking place between communities with regard to their respective begging-routes. It appeared that even in the centre of town where monks and monasteries were most numerous, the lay population was sufficient to provide adequate support for all those *bhikkhus* who *pai binthabat* (went on alms-collecting rounds). Interestingly enough, the market area, Hua Ro, occupied almost exclusively by Chinese shopkeepers and restauranteurs, acted as an unofficial collecting-point for monks from many communities. Several informants remarked that they could rely upon having their bowls filled if they went to Hua Ro, partly because the Chinese gave generously, but also because many householders from outlying areas of town, neglected by the *bhikkhus*, took rice

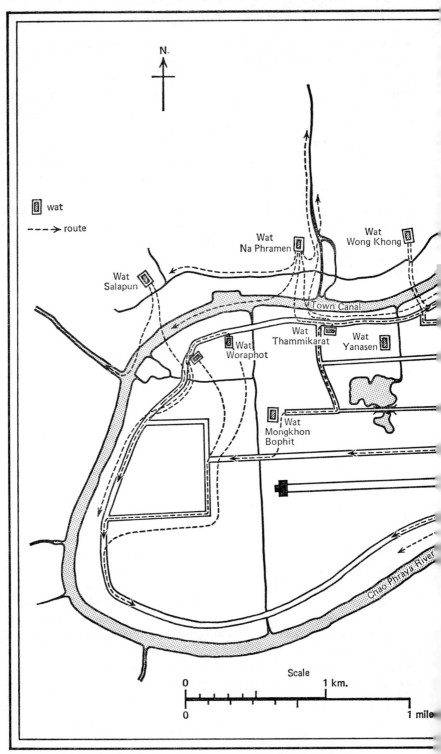

Map C   Alms-routes taken by monks from the monasteries studied

Note: No information for *Wats* Tuk, Senasanaram, Nang Plum

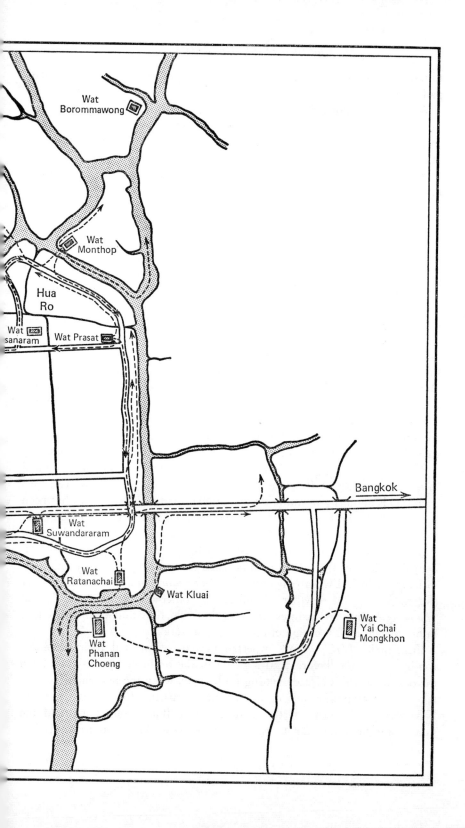

to the morning market with them, in order to present it to the monks who gathered there.

Within each monastic community the abbot should be responsible for directing each of his subordinates to take a particular begging-route, in every case bearing in mind the density of settlement, as well as the age and fitness of the *bhikkhu* concerned. Although several monks from the same monastery may be assigned to take the same track they may or may not *pai binthabat* together each morning, but it is usual for a newly ordained *bhikkhu* to accompany his mentor (*phi liang*) and for members of the same *khana* in any one *wat* to proceed together in single file along their allotted route.

A few examples will give the reader some idea of the variety of existing arrangements. For instance, the five or six *bhikkhus* in permanent residence at *Wat* Yanasen took the same route along the right-hand side of the road leading to Hua Ro, but each monk set out in his own time. The two youngest members of this community rose early and left the *wat* between 5 and 5.30 a.m. every day whilst most of their fellow residents did not begin their alms-rounds much before 6.30 a.m. On the other hand all the monks of *Wat* Salapun left their quarters at the same time around 5.30 a.m., whilst the residents of *Wat* Prasat *binthabat pen khana* (went in *khana* to collect alms). Each of the three *khana* took a separate route, although it was customary for all the monks to leave the compound simultaneously. In those monasteries where the abbots take a more active interest in governing the community, it is usual for the constituent monks to begin their begging-rounds at the same time, and, unless there are *khana*, to eat their meals seated together in front of the abbot's living quarters, rather than in their individual *kuti*, as is the case at *Wat* Yanasen. The head of the community can thus exercise his authority in minor organizational matters although, as has been shown already, he has very little real power. Many informants placed great value upon concerted action between *bhikkhus*, taking it as evidence of strong community spirit; by contrast they tended to disparage the independent behaviour of the monks at *Wat* Yanasen and elsewhere, as being antisocial and selfish. I was frequently told '*chan ruam kan di kwa*' – 'it is better (for monks) to eat together'. Similarly lay observers regarded the formal *khana* groupings as manifestations of individualism and competitiveness, rather than as aspects of tighter internal organization.

Incidentally *bhikkhus* are expected to have completed their *binthabat* routine some time before 7.30 a.m. when the ordinary business of life in the outside world is already getting under way, when the householders have taken their own morning meal, and are preparing for the day's work. Nevertheless, the head of the community at *Wat* Wongkhong told me that it was important not to *pai binthabat* too early, that is to say before the women of the various households had had time to prepare any food. Consequently, out of consideration for the exigencies of domestic life, he rarely left the monastery much before 7 a.m. But his general lack of enthusiasm for collecting alms provides a more likely explanation of his tardiness, in view of the fact that he preferred to have a light breakfast bought for him from the market by one of the novices, and later in the morning to take a *samlo* to a favourite shop near the railway station, for a more substantial meal of chicken noodles!

Several lay informants gave the difficulty of synchronizing their routine with that of the *bhikkhus* as the reason why they did not offer rice as frequently as they felt they ought. In fact, as was mentioned earlier, rather less than 30% of the householders questioned gave food to the monks every day.

Nevertheless the food contributions made by the laity are usually adequate to meet the needs of the town's monastic population. Most monasteries recognized that they could depend upon one or more households, situated along the routes traditionally followed by their respective residents, to give rice each day. The number of these *ban pracham* (lit. regular houses) claimed by each of the fifteen *wats* in my sample varied between one and fifty.[2] In a few instances this relationship had been initiated by the householder's requesting the abbot to detail any member of the community to pass by his home every morning, so that he might daily have the opportunity to make merit. But, more usually, the household whose members regularly presented food had, over the years, come to be recognized as *ban pracham* without this initial formality. Moreover such householders might, and usually did, give rice to any *bhikkhus* walking by, without discriminating or even distinguishing between them, and, at least with respect to the presentation of alms, did not identify themselves with any one *wat*. Indeed, in several instances, a single house was regarded as a *ban pracham* by two or more monasteries.[3]

But no community relies entirely upon these *ban pracham* for support and though the routes taken by the residents of any *wat* remain fairly constant, the actual distance covered may vary from day to day according to the degree of liberality shown by the laymen who live along the way. On a bad day a *bhikkhu* might have to walk for some distance before he collected

---

[2] I think it more likely that the larger figure refers to the number of houses situated along the begging-routes taken by the *bhikkhus* from the monastery concerned, but the abbot of this community insisted that this was not the case. See Appendix 6 for details.

[3] It was suggested by one layman that prominent monks might have their own *ban pracham* but I found no evidence for this in Ayutthaya. Nor did the arrangement whereby a lay sponsor or *upathak* provides a *bhikkhu* with a monthly allowance for food, books, clothing etc. appear to exist in my area of study. It is however quite common for monks in Bangkok to have a personal *upathak*.

an adequate amount, although most of them said that the combined offerings of four or five householders were sufficient for the day's needs. When a monk has 'accepted alms-food in proportion to (not overflowing from) the capacity of the bowl'[4] he replaces the lid and returns to the *wat* with the begging-bowl (*bat*) concealed under his outer robe – an attitude which indicates to other householders that he has already been given sufficient rice. One rather eminent monk said that, as he was responsible for feeding several novices (*nen*) and monastery boys (*dek wat*) who had been entrusted to his care, he had to walk further than his colleagues in order to collect adequate supplies. Frequently he was accompanied by a young *nen* who carried a *pinto* (multi-tiered enamel food-container) to accommodate the extra rice and relishes received.

The food collected by individual *bhikkhus* is usually 'pooled' on their return to the *wat*. Even in monasteries whose residents do not habitually eat together it is customary for younger and more active monks to share their food with the sick and aged amongst them. The latter may not have been able to *pai binthabat*, or, at least, may not have walked so far. It is usual for monastery boys and novices who do not *pai binthabat* to take the food which is left over when the senior members of the community have finished eating, although in some monasteries supplies are distributed along the lines of *khana* groupings, of formal or informal constitution.

On some days, however, the food supplies of the monastic community as a whole are insufficient for its members' needs. These occasions, though relatively rare, generally occur in the weeks preceding the Buddhist Lent, when the rains are already beginning to fall. Many *bhikkhus* are reluctant to risk being soaked as they make their daily begging-round, and similarly few householders are intrepid enough to brave an early morning downpour. Usually on such days, some of the laymen who live nearby (whether or not they are regular donors) take some food into the *wat* after the rain has stopped.

Several of these householders may belong to the *phuak wat* of that particular monastery and can thus be relied upon to provide support in a crisis though they do not necessarily belong to *ban pracham*. If the laity who are classed as *phuak wat* do not volunteer supplies, *dek wat* may be sent on behalf of the community to request presentation of food from them. As many of these boys come from the locality they may also apply to kinsmen and friends living in the town, whether or not they belong to the *phuak wat*. Few householders refuse such requests, and if several homes each send enough rice for one or two people, the community's needs are soon satisfied.

---

[4] This injunction is one of the 72 minor rules of conduct in the *Patimokkha*. See Ven. Nanamoli Thera (1966, p. 74).

It must be remembered that by Western standards, food in Thailand is extremely cheap.

When the food collected is insufficient, it is also quite common for *bhikkhus* to buy supplementary provisions for the community, with the money they have received for their performance of merit-making ceremonies. It may be recalled from the previous chapter that for the few monks who receive a regular food allowance (*nittayaphat*)[5] from the King, the buying of rice is not an emergency measure but a regular habit. Furthermore my observations showed that monks of some standing who did not receive *nittayaphat* rarely went out to collect alms. These *bhikkhus* could afford to purchase food from the market each day, or rather to have it bought on their behalf by a novice or monastery boy. The abbot of *Wat* Wongkhong was not entirely atypical.[6]

On the days when a *bhikkhu* is invited to officiate at a merit-making ceremony he does not need to collect alms as it is customary for the host (*chao phap*) to provide food for the monks just prior to their recitation of the texts, and to give them a second meal at the close of the ceremony. If the monk invited out is the head of *khana* it is usual for him to provide the *nen* and the *dek wat* attached to him with sufficient money for the purchase of rice on that day.[7]

Similarly, on those days when the householders attend services and ceremonies held at the *wat* it is unnecessary for the *bhikkhus* living there to *pai binthabat*. On the Buddhist Holy Day[8] (*Wan Phra*) for example, many lay people visit their local monastery to pay their respects to the Buddha image in the *bot*, and to present rice, dishes of curry and desserts to the monks.

On these occasions some of the householders who are especially devout spend the night in the monastery, usually sleeping on rush matting spread out on the floor of one of the *sala* (pavilion). For the duration of *Wan Phra* they undertake to observe three additional precepts, which prohibit them from taking an evening meal, from using jewellery or cosmetics to adorn their bodies, and from sleeping on a soft bed or couch.[9] These lay devotees (*ubasaka*) who represent a minority group are referred to as the *khon thi ma thu sin* (the people who come to observe the precepts) whilst the majority who return home in the afternoon when they have presented food, and

[5] See above, p. 61.

[6] Approximately two-thirds of all the monks questioned said that they went out on alms-rounds every day.

[7] This was Chao Khun Thep's practice. See above, chapter 2.

[8] Holy Day (*Wan Phra*) falls on the eighth and fifteenth days of the waxing and waning moon. On *Uposatha* day, the fifteenth day of each cycle (i.e. every lunar fortnight) the monks in every monastic community recite the *Patimokka* code.

[9] That is to say that for one day these laymen observe the Eight Precepts which are regularly observed by Thai nuns.

listened to the sermon given by one of the monks, are known as the *khon thi ma tham bun* (the people who come to make merit).[10]

The figures given in the appendix show however, that outside the Lenten season there were no services for *Wan Phra* at six of the fifteen monasteries studied, which means that most of the monks in residence there do *pai binthabat* on these days. It was customary at those monasteries where house-holders did go to make merit for the begging-bowls of the monks, and some other containers, to be placed in rows on the floor of one of the *sala* so that the lay donors might place a little of the food they had brought into each one. On such days the *bhikkhus* normally eat together – even where that is not the usual practice – in full view of the laity, who take their own meal at the *wat* when the monks have finished.

For the three months of *phansa* (Buddhist Lent) special arrangements for the provision of food are made at most monasteries in Ayutthaya. During this period there is a general intensification of interest in making merit, a trend which is manifest in the sudden influx of monks and novices into the Order, and in the larger congregations which gather at the *wat* on Holy Day. Fewer rituals are held in the homes of the householders during this period, and the *bhikkhus* devote more of their time, in theory at least, to *Dhamma* studies, and to the instruction of the newly ordained.

At most urban *wats* the people who belong to the *phuak wat* are organized to provide *kaeng wian*[11] (curry in rotation) during *phansa*. This means that each household, or in some cases a group of households, undertakes to pro-vide food for the monastic community on two or three days during the rainy season. It is usual for members of the monastery committee (*kammakan wat*) to work out a rota on the first day of Lent, a national holiday, when householders go to their local monastery to present food to the residents.

Most of my informants stated that *kaeng wian* groups were established for the duration of the Lenten season, because the increase in the number of *bhikkhus* and novices might otherwise place too great a strain on the re-sources of the laity. But this explanation is hardly adequate in that the for-mation of *kaeng wian* groups does not create more support but merely organizes those householders who are already willing to donate. Moreover the friends and relatives of monks ordained for a short time (*chua khrao*),

[10] It is of course meritorious to observe three additional precepts on *Wan Phra* but in this instance as in many others the expression *tham bun* or 'to make merit' means to provide material support, to make gifts etc. The householders who are said to *tham bun* are those who only give food to the monks. The others who make merit by ob-serving Eight Precepts usually give food as well. See Appendix 6 for figures.

[11] *Kaeng*: curry, curried food; *wian*: to circle, to turn. This temporary arrangement for the provision of food bears a certain resemblance to practices followed throughout the year in some Northern villages (de Young 1955, pp 115–16).

and in particular the proud mothers of these young men, usually take it upon themselves to provide special rations for the new *bhikkhu*.[12]

The real function of *kaeng wian* appears to be that its provision frees the monk from the necessity to beg for his food, and thus allows him to remain in the *wat* and to concentrate on monastic affairs. It may be recalled that the monk is forbidden to travel very far from his place of residence during this period. Furthermore, in practical terms the provision of 'curry in rotation' compensates the *bhikkhus* for those meals which are taken in the home of the laity at other times of the year, and also for the sums of money received in return for their performance of merit-making rituals outside Lent. As has been shown already, this personal money is frequently used to buy food, to supplement or substitute for donations from the laity. It is interesting to see that *kaeng wian* groups are never formed at rural *wats* where the new monks are all local boys and can rely on their respective families for the provision of food; this further supports my contention that where the *kaeng wian* mechanism comes into operation, it is largely for the benefit of permanent monks whose parish activities, providing both money and food, are in abeyance during Lent. In urban monasteries it is these permanent *bhikkhus* who are unlikely to have close friends or relatives amongst the local populace, as most of them come from rural settlements outside the town.

Some exceptions to most of the generalizations made so far with regard to the sources of monastic food supplies, are provided by four of the larger urban monasteries included in my sample. The *bhikkhus* residing at *Wats* Suwan and Phanan Choeng, at *Wat* Borommawong and at *Wat* Yai Chai Mongkhon rarely go on begging-rounds at any time of the year; nor are *kaeng wian* groups established at these monasteries during *phansa*. Both these anomalies can be explained by the fact that at each of these monasteries a charitable fund known as *munithi*[13] has been established to provide food for the community throughout the year.

It might well be asked what features these four monasteries have in common, which would serve to explain their possession of *munithi*. The case of *Wat* Borommawong can be considered first of all, as a *munithi* fund is clearly necessary for the survival of its residents.

This monastery was built at some time in the seventeenth century by an aristocratic Ayutthaya family. The founders' descendants moved to Bangkok

---

[12] One of my informants wanted his son, who was to be ordained temporarily, to live at *Wat* Salapun as the abbot there was very learned. His wife however, protested that the monastery was too far away for her to go there each day with food for the boy. Consequently when Lent came the new monk was ordained at the *wat* nearest his home and remained there for the whole of the Lenten season.

[13] *Munithi*: foundation, charitable trust.

several generations ago and the area around the *wat* has long been deserted. Until quite recently *Wat* Borommawong had fallen into disuse, as it was virtually impossible for *bhikkhus* living there to collect sufficient food by the practice of *binthabat*.

In 1964 however, the present head of the founding family rallied his friends and relatives to the support of the monastery with the result that the sum of 79,582 *baht*[14] was presented as *munithi* at the time of the annual *kathin* ceremony, which takes place at the end of the Buddhist Lent.[15]

The ecclesiastical authorities appointed an able and respected monk as head of the community, and a number of other *bhikkhus*, some of whom were his pupils (*luk sit*), came to take up residence there. Some of the money presented has been invested in government bonds, whilst a proportion of the remainder is taken from the bank each month in order to buy food for the community.

The need for such a charitable fund is perhaps less clear cut in the case of *Wat* Suwan and of *Wat* Phanan Choeng. The former monastery is in possession of *munithi* amounting to 20,000 *baht*, approximately 80 *baht* of which is spent each day on buying provisions for the monks, novices and other members of the community. *Wat* Suwan is situated in a densely populated area and many of the 28 *bhikkhus* and a few of the older novices do *pai binthabat* each day. The food thus collected was said to be sufficient only for the first meal taken by the community; the rice, and relishes for the second repast, beginning at 11 o'clock, were purchased with money from the *munithi* fund.

Wat Phanan Choeng, like *Wat* Suwan, is a large and famous monastery, which provides educational facilities sufficiently good to attract monks and novices from other regions to study there. This monastery is however built on an island where there are few houses, and the small number of monks and novices who do go out to collect alms must go by boat, or take the ferry across the river to the main part of town. The *munithi* fund at *Wat* Phanan Choeng amounted to 120,000 *baht*, of which 100 *baht* was expended each day on the purchase of food for the community.[16]

It might be recalled that in other smaller monasteries the *bhikkhus* use their own personal money to buy supplementary food when the amount collected from the householders is insufficient. As many of the monks in

[14] Roughly £1,592 according to exchange rates at the time of writing, i.e. 50 *baht* to £1 sterling.

[15] *Kathin*, see below, p. 113.

[16] On the basis of their previous experience the monks at these *wats* expected that the *munithi* would be replenished from time to time by new donations from the laity. In most cases this money was deposited with a bank at an interest rate of $3\frac{1}{4}\%$–4% p.a. Unlike some monasteries in Bangkok the richer *wats* in Ayutthaya did not invest their capital in more productive ways.

both *Wat* Suwan and *Wat* Phanan Choeng are, in ecclesiastical terms, well-off, by virtue of their official positions in the Church and because of their pastoral services to the lay community, it might seem unnecessary and unfair for such monasteries to be presented with *munithi*.

The possession of those funds was justified by the beneficiaries in the monasteries concerned on a number of grounds; in the first place it was pointed out, with justification, that monasteries which offer educational facilities tend to have a higher proportion of novices to monks than is the case in ordinary *wats*;[17] novices (*nen*) are virtually 'non-producers' in that they do not for the most part *pai binthabat* and never perform merit-making ceremonies, which as we have seen, provide a small but steady personal income for most *bhikkhus*. Another point to be borne in mind is that at these larger monasteries there are generally more *dek wat* who also expect to be provided with their daily rice. Whilst these informants agreed that many eminent monks belonged to these communities they also claimed that the laity were so exigent that some of these luminaries were hardly ever in residence, and thus did not have the time to look after the children entrusted to them by the householders. If it were not for the *munithi* the burden of supporting all these *nen* and *dek wat* would fall upon themselves, the junior members of the community.[18] As things were they were freed from the need to *pai binthabat* every day, and could give themselves to academic pursuits. But this seems however to provide a rationalization rather than a valid explanation for the possession of a *munithi* fund in view of the fact that alms-collecting is not a very time-consuming occupation and also because the *bhikkhus* in question seemed to be far from neglectful of pastoral interests.

Whether one regards the *munithi* funds established at *Wat* Suwan and at *Wat* Phanan Choeng respectively as providing for a real need, or as constituting a luxury item – a collective allowance which frees the monks from the chore of collecting alms – depends to some extent on whether one is a beneficiary. The fact remains nevertheless that, in each case, the private individuals who contributed considered the fund's creation justified. The charitable funds at both monasteries had been established some years previously and I could not obtain much information as to the identity of the donors other than that, in the two cases, they had been 'rich people from Bangkok'. But the fact that these householders came from the capital is in itself revealing, as it does suggest that the local people may have been unable to provide adequate support. Indeed the denser concentration of monks in Ayutthaya – which is a centre for ecclesiastical education – might have meant that the townspeople would not be able to support all the *bhikkhus*

[17] See Appendix 6 for comparative figures.
[18] This is not necessarily so. See above, p. 107.

were it not for the fact that *munithi* funds had been established at some of the larger *wats*. It is necessary, in other words, to consider the function of *munithi* for relations between the monastic and lay sectors of society, as well as for its beneficiaries.

In one or two rare cases a monastic community may lose the day-to-day support of lay people in the vicinity because of the real or alleged misdemeanours of one or more of its members. In such cases also the community must rely on personal friends and acquaintances of the monks to provide support.

It is clear from the preceding paragraphs that food can be provided for a monastic community by the laity in a variety of ways, leaving aside for the time being those occasions on which the *bhikkhus* use their own money to purchase supplies. In the normal course of events the monks collect alms-food from some of the people who live along the routes traditional to that monastery. The map of these begging-circuits, studded with *ban pracham*, exists only in the mind of the abbot of the monastery concerned, and in the minds of a few senior monks who know which paths are regularly taken by their fellows. Clearly, then, the householders who live along the various routes taken by the *bhikkhus* from any one monastery do not form a group with respect to that *wat*, nor with respect to any individual *bhikkhu*. In most cases the layman does not know to which monastery the monk to whom he presents rice is attached. Moreover, in the *binthabat* transaction each donor enacts this primary aspect of his role as Buddhist householder independently of others, although as we shall see presently the entire household of which he is a member is believed to benefit from the merit thus acquired.

In other instances the relationship between the lay donor and the monastic community to which food is presented is more specific. This is true of those occasions when people from the *phuak wat* provide supplementary rice if the supplies collected were inadequate, or when some of them present food to the community on Holy Day (*Wan Phra*). This same collectivity of people who recognize common allegiance to a particular *wat* is perhaps most fully mobilized for the provision of *kaeng wian* during the months of the Lenten retreat. It should be noted that even on these occasions when there is some rudimentary co-operation between different members of the *phuak wat*, the household, usually represented by one or more of its senior members, is still the basic merit-making unit. Each household takes its turn to provide *kaeng* (*wian*) for the monks, whilst on the other occasions mentioned, although a number of households present food at the same time, supplies are only pooled when placed in the begging-bowls of the monks.

Finally, the monastic community can be provided with food by the establishment of *munithi,* or a charitable fund. Where it is necessary or desirable, people from outside the immediate locality can support a monastery by means of this institution. As was suggested earlier, there is no reason why the local people should not themselves establish *munithi,* yet if they were both willing and able to do so there would by definition be no need, as the function of *munithi* is to enable the monks to purchase food when ordinary sources of supply are inadequate, for one reason or another. The organizer of a group of householders who combine to contribute to such a fund usually stands in a particular relationship to the monastery itself, or is alternatively a friend of the abbot or one of the other residents.

CEREMONIAL CONTRIBUTIONS

The donations of money and material goods which are offered to the monastery by various members of the lay population provide the subject matter for the present section. The object of presenting this material is, in the first place, to clarify still further the nature of the relationship between the monastic community and the householders who offer their support. In the second place, by examining the use to which these donations are put I shall attempt to assess whether or not the layman derives any benefit, of an other than transcendental kind, from the money he spends in support of the monastery, or indeed of the *Sangha* as a whole.

The *kathin* presentation, which is made annually at the close of *phansa,* constitutes one of the major contributions received by any monastic community. The practice of offering *kathin* in Theravada Buddhist countries at the present time consists in essence of giving new robes to the *bhikkhus* who are coming out of retreat at the end of the rainy season. However, the three sets of robes customarily presented are usually accompanied by gifts of durable goods, furniture, crockery, altar tables and so on, and by a sum of money which varies in size according to the capacity of the contributors. Both the money and the goods presented at the ceremony known as *Thot Kathin*[19] become the property of the monastic community as a whole (*khong song* or *khong wat*) but the monastic community allots it to individual monks by the procedure of *Kran Kathin* (lit. 'to spread out robes') (Wells 1960, p. 171). As only the *bhikkhus* within a particular *wat* are concerned with the allocation of robes the ritual of *Kran Kathin* need not detain us here where we are discussing the monasteries' external relationships.

Householders wishing to *Thot Kathin* must do so during the next lunar

[19] *Thot Kathin* means literally 'to lay down a wooden frame on which to cut cloth'. For origin and meaning of this ceremony see Wells (1960, p. 105) and Dutt (1960, p. 157).

month after the end of the Buddhist Lent (*phansa*), that is to say, between the full moons of October and November. *Kathin* robes can only be taken to a monastery where there are at least five monks, all of whom have 'observed lent' (*cham phansa*) by spending the entire season at that *wat*. Every monastery receives a *kathin* presentation each year provided that there is a sufficient number of eligible monks in residence, but each monastic community may only receive one such offering in any one year.

The layman who intends to mobilize a group of householders to offer *kathin* visits the abbot of the monastery of his choice at some time towards the end of *phansa*. An appointment is then made for the presentation of *kathin* at some future date during the stipulated month, provided that the privilege has not already been granted to another group.

Any one of a variety of reasons may determine an individual's choice of the *wat* to which he will lead a *kathin*-bearing group. This lay leader or *chao phap* may make his decision on the basis of his acquaintance or kinship with one of the *bhikkhus* resident in the monastery. To take one example, one of my best lay informants, Khun Siri Imchai, organized a group to take a *kathin* presentation to a *wat* in Chiengmai (Northern Thailand) whose abbot was fairly distantly related to Khun Siri's wife. Many laymen who have, over the years, moved away from the area in which they were born decide that it would be a good idea to *Thot Kathin* at the local monastery in their home town or natal village. It is, for example, quite common for members of a civil service department to take *kathin* robes to a monastery which is situated near to the parental home of the head of that department. The latter may have been ordained there as a novice or as a monk at some time during his life. For the occasion of the presentation of *kathin* it is likely that he will be referred to as the *chao phap*, although it is more probable that one of his subordinates has performed the real work of group organization.

As was shown in the previous section, the *chao phap* of such an expedition may belong to the founding family of the recipient *wat*.[20] On the other hand the leader of a *kathin*-bearing group may know the monastery of his choice by reputation only.

Kathin presentations are categorized as 'royal' (*luang*) or 'commoner' (*rat*) according to the status of the monastery concerned. Royal *wats* are those which were built by the Monarch or a member of the royal family, or by a high-ranking official. These foundations are generally larger and better endowed with material resources of various kinds; namely with money, monuments and land. Furthermore important ecclesiastical offices are most often located in *wat luang*; *Wat* Suwan and *Wat* Phanan Choeng,

[20] See above, p. 110 for presentation of *kathin* at *Wat* Borommawong by the head of the founding family.

which have been mentioned at various points throughout the text are both royal foundations. Monasteries which are labelled 'commoner' may however be promoted to royal status if they are obviously 'booming' which is to say that there are in residence large numbers of permanent monks who stand high in the opinion of the laity. Conversely royal *wats* which have become deserted or have fallen into disrepute and disrepair are deprived of their rank. Although there is inevitably some time-lag before a change of circumstances, for good or ill, is given official recognition, the terms *luang* and *rat* are reasonable indices of current condition.[21]

Only the King of Thailand or a person appointed to represent him has the right to *Thot Kathin* at any of the 149 *wat luang* in the country. But any other householder can request his permission, through the official channels of the Department of Religious Affairs, Bangkok, to make a *kathin* presentation to one of these monasteries. Although this procedure appeared to be a mere formality, in that permission was rarely if ever refused, it is likely that only private individuals of wealthy and high-ranking families or people who were heads of civil service departments would make such a request; it is these individuals who have the contacts and the self-confidence needed in applying for royal permission, as well as the financial wherewithal to make a presentation appropriate to the status of any *wat luang*.

The data collected concerning the leadership of groups bringing *kathin* to the five royal monasteries I studied bears out this contention; in two instances the *chao phap* were members of aristocratic Bangkok families appointed by the King to represent him; the leader of the expedition to a third *wat luang* was a member of an old Ayutthaya family who had obtained royal permission for the presentation, whilst the fourth and fifth were senior officials in the Department of Fine Arts and the Ministry of Education respectively. The latter was in fact the Minister of Education himself, as well as a descendent of the founder of the royal *wat* in question.

It is not usual for a monastery to receive the *kathin* presentation from people whom it regards as belonging to its *phuak wat*.[22] However it is sometimes the case at smaller and more obscure urban monasteries that no other individual or group has requested permission to offer robes. As it is felt to be essential that every monastery should receive the annual gift of *kathin*, those householders who are associated with a particular *wat* usually rally round to make the presentation if no other offer is forthcoming. At the close of the Lenten season in 1967, for example, the laymen who

[21] See *Phrarachabanyat Khanasong*, Sect. 5 for the conditions governing the status of monasteries.

[22] Partly because the practice of *Thot Kathin* is expected to provide an excuse for an excursion. Some laymen may join two or more such expeditions because it is such fun (*na sanuk mak*).

lived in and around the compound of *Wat* Kluai combined with other householders who felt that they belonged to the *phuak wat* and made a *kathin* presentation of 2,000 *baht*[23] (approx. £40 sterling).

As the figures in the appendix show, the smaller donations tend to go to the smaller *wats* but there are several notable instances of unimportant monasteries receiving substantial sums of money from the presentation of *kathin*. In each of these cases the contacts or the charisma of the individual abbot, rather than the standing of the monastery itself, was instrumental in attracting a larger offering than might have been expected. The Abbot of *Wat* Woraphot, for example, was related to the Director of the Yellow Bus Company in Bangkok who organized the *kathin* group which brought 24,173 *baht* (approx. £483) to this relatively insignificant *wat*. The head of the community at *Wat* Tuk, where 40,000 *baht* (approx. £800) was presented at the time of *kathin* was known to be very capable in 'building up the monastery' (*sang wat*); he attracted many monks to live in his *wat* and travelled far and wide to renew acquaintances from lay life, and to look up householders whom he had once known as monks, in order to raise funds for restoring the monastery buildings. His enthusiasm was such that he was even to be seen clambering about the scaffolding on the roof of the *bot* which was under repair.

On the other hand, some royal foundations received relatively small sums of money. One monk living at *Wat* Suwan which received a *kathin* presentation of only 11,000 *baht* (approx. £220), explained this disappointingly small offering with reference to the fact that the King, on some occasions, appointed as his representative an individual of suitable family background, who might yet be either unwilling or unable to make a generous contribution.

The *kathin* presentations offered to different *wats* also vary in terms of the material goods included. The householders who *Thot Kathin* at *Wat* Kluai, for example, omitted even to take the robes, simply presenting the monetary offering and a considerable quantity of food to be consumed at the close of the ceremony. In contrast to this, the presentation made to *Wat* Phanan Choeng comprised not only the three sets of robes traditionally given and a large sum of money, but also several sets of gilded altar tables, a great deal of expensive crockery, and three electric fans for the use of the community.

The lay *chao phap* might choose to *Thot Kathin* at a particular *wat* for any one of the large variety of reasons given, which is to say that the

[23] In country areas *kathin* presentation may be taken by people in one village to the *wat* in a neighbouring settlement on the understanding that the favour will be returned at a later date (Wells 1960, p. 106).

interaction between the monastic community and a group of householders in this context might be based on the ties of kinship or acquaintance existing between one of the *bhikkhus* and the *chao phap*, or some other member of the group; on the other hand, their interaction might simply be a consequence of the fame and reputation of the monastery concerned. It has also been implied that the members of any *kathin*-bearing group might be related to one another in a variety of ways; the householders recruited to any such expedition may be relatives or friends of the *chao phap* or his co-workers and colleagues in an office, school, or business firm. More usually the links between members of this 'action-set' formed for the purpose of *Thot Kathin* are 'derived from many social fields' (Mayer 1966, p. 108), in that the party includes the relations, friends and colleagues of the *chao phap*, as well as the families and friends of his friends, which is to say that in Mayer's terms it 'contains paths of linkages'.

Lay groupings similarly constituted make direct contributions of money and material goods to the *wat* on other occasions. The offerings given as *pha pa* (Wilderness Robes) may be virtually indistinguishable from a *kathin* presentation except that the amount of money given is usually smaller. The offering of *pha pa* may furthermore be made at any time of year and unlike the *kathin* presentation it is optional and is generally felt to require both fewer formal preparations and smaller expenditure. Another difference lies in the fact that although as is always the case with *kathin* presentations the initiative in taking *pha pa* to a monastery usually rests with the householders, it sometimes happens that an abbot suggests to a layman whom he knows well, that a *pha pa* presentation would not be unwelcome.

Other fairs and ceremonies are organized directly by the *wat*, often with a view to raising funds for a specific programme of building or restoration. An annual event at many monasteries is the *Thet Mahachat* or recitation of some of the stories relating to the previous lives of the Buddha. On this occasion certain chapters from those tales known as the *Jataka*[24] are recited by *bhikkhus* who are particularly skilled in this art.

Some weeks prior to this ceremony, printed invitation cards are distributed by the *bhikkhus* and members of the monastery lay committee (*kammakan wat*) amongst their relatives and friends. The invitation card issued by *Wat Prasat* in February 1967 requested the recipient to come to the monastery at 8 a.m. on the appointed day, the second day of the month, in order to present rice to the monks who would not go on the alms-round on that day. The *bhikkhus* from several neighbouring *wats* were also invited to *Wat Prasat* to receive donations of food from the laymen. At 9 a.m. the recitation

[24] The *Jataka* form part of the fifth *Nikaya* (or collection of works) in the *Sutta-pitaka* (Banerji 1964, p. 61).

in the Pali language was due to begin, to be followed in the afternoon by a repeat of the same stanzas in Thai. The faithful were invited to 'sponsor' one or more stanzas of the *Jataka* tale to be recited and to contribute generously to the costs of completing the *bot* which had already been under construction for several years.

Prior to the day of the ceremony, the householders who had decided to sponsor the recitation of one or more stanzas presented a certain sum of money to the abbot or to a member of *kammakan Wat* Prasat. These contributions varied in size from 10 to 100 *baht* or more depending upon the affluence of the donor. Some of this money was used to buy soft drinks to be served to the monks and to the laity during the ceremony, to purchase flowers and fairy lights to adorn the *sala* where the recitation was to take place and to hire a band of musicians. The name of each contributor, and the size of the contribution, was recorded by the *waiyawachakon* (lay bursar or steward) and broadcast over the loudspeaker on the day of the ceremony. The money which had not been spent was attached to the branches of a 'tree' made from strips of bamboo which was planted in a bucket placed in the centre of the *sala* (pavilion). People who·had not received invitations, whether living in the vicinity of the *wat* or elsewhere in town, drifted in to listen to the recitation and chat with friends and acquaintances they found there. Most of them presented a sum of money to the *waiyawachakon* who sat near to the 'tree', affixing new donations to its branches and recording the particulars in his book.

This *Thet Mahachat* celebration at *Wat* Prasat realized 5,885 *baht*, most of which was used in the construction of the *bot* whose estimated total cost was 800,000 *baht*. The monastery had been trying to raise the money for this project over several years.

As is I think clear from the foregoing paragraphs, the congregation who came to listen to the recitation and to make some monetary contribution was very wide and varied. People in the locality who were known to have an interest in the *wat* (i.e. *phuak wat*) were included, as were householders who recognized an allegiance to a particular monk, rather than to the monastery as a whole. Furthermore many townspeople who had no particular interest in the *wat* or in its *bhikkhus* dropped in to pass the time of day, and in most cases made some contribution. The householders who give their support to the *wat* on such occasions can in sociological terms be regarded as an action-set centred upon the monastery concerned. The individual householder can of course donate money, donate goods, or even land to the *wat* at any time of year, but this appears to happen only infrequently. Informants in Ayutthaya could remember only a few occasions in recent years when wealthy individuals had made substantial presentations to one of the local monasteries. Some two or three years earlier a rich property-owner had given the sum of 3,000 *baht* (approx. £60) to *Wat* Phanan Choeng on the understanding that it was to be used to build new living quarters for the abbot. The donor had previously spent several years as a *bhikkhu* in the same monastery. During my period of fieldwork an elderly spinster living near *Wat* Ratanachai left 1,000 *baht* (approx. £20) to the monastery in her will with the stipulation that the money was to be used to provide food for the dogs which lived and fought in the compound of the *wat*.

In some cases, the benefactor's specifications as to the future use of the money he has given goes against the best interests of the recipient monastery. One abbot complained that rich lay donors always wanted to have a pavilion constructed in their name. Consequently the compound, particularly at those monasteries which fronted the main road, might become congested with ornate and conspicuous pavilions which were rarely used, whilst at the rear of the *wat* the monks' living quarters fell into disrepair about their ears.

In a few cases newly ordained monks present their worldly goods to the monastery rather than distributing them amongst their relatives. But this again is a rather uncommon practice and informants could provide me with only a few examples. The most notable of these concerned the present abbot of *Wat* Phanan Choeng, who, when he was ordained as a *bhikkhu* fifty years ago, presented the monastery with the right to twenty *rai* of paddy land.

In the majority of cases, as we have seen in a previous chapter, the individual becomes ordained before he has acquired an important stake in the material world, so that distribution of his goods presents no real problem. And even when the ordinand is wealthy it is usual for him to hand it over to his kinsmen when he enters the Order, rather than to the monastery.

In conclusion to the present section it can be added that most of the durable goods presented by laymen to individual monks (i.e. *thuai thaiyathan*) become the property of the monastery (*khong wat*) when a *bhikkhu* dies or leaves the Order. In some cases a man who is about to re-enter lay society gives those articles which symbolize monkhood – his robes, his begging-bowl and so on – to a fellow member of the *Sangha*. Alternatively, if these articles are not distributed in this way they automatically become the property of the *wat* where their owner has been living, and can be used by any member of that community at the abbot's discretion. Similarly, any larger and more valuable objects which the monk has received from the lay community are usually presented to the *wat* should the *bhikkhu* in question decide to disrobe. Although there are no legal sanctions behind this, it is felt to be both inappropriate and unlucky for a man to retain such objects after he has resumed his lay status. This unofficial ruling does not however apply to books, pens and other small articles bought by the *bhikkhu* with the money he received for his pastoral services. These items he may take with him when he leaves the *wat* without fearing that illness or some other misfortune will befall him.

The laws of Thailand state that on the death of a *bhikkhu* 'all his possessions become the property of the monastery which is his domicile unless he has disposed of them during his lifetime or by will'.[25] This refers only to those possessions acquired by the deceased during his service in the *Sangha*. It appears to be very rare if not unknown for a monk to give any of his possessions to laymen during his lifetime, though he may of course share them with fellow members of the *Sangha*.

In one or two cases, prominent monks gave money to help their poor lay relations and were praised for fulfilling their part of the obligation for mutual aid which exists between kinsmen. But had a monk given away a television set, an electric fan, or some other valuable object presented to him by a householder, there would probably have been an outcry against both the donor and the recipient, even though, in theory, the initial transaction would have been successfully accomplished by the monk's accepting the presentation, and conferring merit upon the layman who made it.

It appears furthermore that, though the monk can bequeath any of his possessions to other monks or to lay friends and relatives, very few *bhikkhus* avail themselves of this facility. Consequently possessions of all kinds – both those which are termed the Eight Requisites, and other more valuable goods – become the property of his monastery on the death of the monk. Thus these durable goods are transferred indirectly from the lay community to the *wat*, by being first presented to individual *bhikkhus*. Some of the larger monasteries which house the most eminent monks acquire, by this means, considerable quantities of valuable goods, as well as a store of robes, alms-bowls and other paraphernalia of everyday use. In the *kuti* of the Deputy Abbot of *Wat* Suwan many pieces of Chinese porcelain were displayed in two large cabinets inlaid with mother-of-pearl. Both the cabinets and their contents had belonged to a previous abbot, long since deceased.

---

[25] See The Civil and Commercial Code of Thailand, VI, Sect. 1623. This ruling first became law in 1935, although the practice whereby *bhikkhus* could make wills was first introduced during the reign of Rama V (1868–1910). See Lingat (1957, p. 461), for a discussion of the development of the laws relating to the disposal of property belonging to the *bhikkhus*.

MONASTERY ESTATES

The money received as rent from land owned by the *wat* provides another source of income for some monastic communities. With a few notable exceptions however, the proceeds from the lease of its property are less important for the support of the monastery than are those direct contributions made by the laity, which were described in the preceding section of the present chapter. Only in a few instances is the land-holding of any one monastery significantly larger in size than that of most peasant cultivators in the Region.[26] One reason why more householders do not make merit by giving land to the *wat* may be because it is considered inappropriate that *bhikkhus,* who are themselves forbidden to engage in cultivation, should yet become the owners of great estates (Wells 1960, p. 30). Furthermore, as there has throughout the country's history been no scarcity of land in Thailand, it may well be that because it is less highly valued there than in most other societies it is not regarded as a particularly meritorious gift.

Most monasteries do not make a great deal of money from their estates, and so conform quite closely to the ideal of the *wat* as a lenient landlord. Indeed this is an attitude which they can well afford to adopt when they can depend on receiving direct donations from the householders at certain points throughout the year. As the statistics given in the appendix show quite clearly, the estates belonging to some monasteries yield no rent at all; in some cases this is due to the generosity of the *wat* concerned in allowing the land to be freely used, whilst in other instances the holdings are un-occupied. This second factor may be explained with reference to the general abundance of land and also with respect to the fact that laymen tend not to give their best rice-lands to the *wat,* but to present plots which are more isolated or less fertile than the rest. This trend can in turn be attributed to certain features of this situation already mentioned, namely, that land is not regarded by most householders as a particularly meritorious gift, nor seen to be an important source of income by the majority of *wats.*

Each monastery is situated within a compound or *thi wat,* which can vary in size between communities from one or two to several tens of *rai.*[27] Any householder who intends to build a monastery must first present to the Department of Religious Affairs a piece of land of sufficient area to accommodate the monastery buildings. Hereafter, this land cannot be sold or transferred other than by an Act of Parliament, and in the event that the *wat* becomes deserted (*rang*) both the buildings and the land revert to the

[26] The average peasant cultivator in the Central Region farms approximately 26 *rai* of paddy land (Wijeyewardene 1967, p. 78); 1 *rai* = 0.4 acre.
[27] See Appendix 9.

121

State, and continue to be administered by Department of Religious Affairs.[28] Very few of the monks in Ayutthaya knew the name of the founder of the *wat* in which they lived and could thus say nothing about the source of the *thi wat*, other than that the compound had been presented to the *Sangha* 'in olden days' (*nai samai boran*).

At most monasteries in Ayutthaya laymen have been permitted to build their homes on the perimeter of the *thi wat*, although even where the *wat* is situated in a more crowded area in the centre of town the dwellings of the layman never directly adjoin the monastery buildings. The layman who wishes to take up residence in the compound of any *wat* usually makes his initial approach to the *waiyawachakon* of that establishment, or to some other member of the *kammakan wat*. If his request is approved the applicant is then presented to the abbot of the monastery concerned who must give his formal consent to the agreement.

Several of the monasteries studied allowed people to build quite freely upon *thi wat* on the understanding that they would make some contribution of money, food or labour on the occasions when the monastery chose to sponsor a ceremony or fair. The householders who live in the compound of *Wat* Tuk for example, pay no rent, but support the community when the need arises and contribute to the costs of water and electricity used by the monks. At neighbouring *Wat* Woraphot there is an arrangement whereby the owner of a private school which stands in the *thi wat* pays no rent, though the teachers there are expected to reheat the rice, collected earlier by the *bhikkhus*, for the eleven o'clock meal and to provide supplementary food when supplies are insufficient.

One or two monasteries however, do augment their income by renting out parts of the monastery compound to lay tenants, although it must be noted that their rates tend to be somewhat lower than those charged by lay landlords. The average monthly rental for a town-house in the Central Region is 85 *baht* (approx. £1.70),[29] which compares unfavourably with the 50 *baht* (approx. £1) per month paid by the tenants of the shophouses at *Wat* Prasat, and the 50 *baht* per annum charge made by *Wat* Yanasen.

In fact the former monastery, *Wat* Prasat, realized 31,200 *baht* per annum (approx. £624) from the buildings erected on the *thi wat*, and many of my informants censured the abbot for being extortionate, although, as was remarked above, the rent he charged was very reasonable by general standards. The financial policy of this monastery was compared unfavourably with that of *Wat* Senasanaram which also owned an area of land in

---

[28] See *Phrarachabanyatkhanasong*, Sect. 5 for details.
[29] Statistics from 'Household Expenditure Survey (Central Region)' B.E. 2506 (1963), published by the National Statistical Office, Bangkok.

the centre of town. This area was potentially more valuable, being greater in extent, nevertheless the householders living on this land paid no rent at all – or paid merely a token sum of a few *satangs* each year.[30] It was interesting to see that in terms of buildings and possessions *Wat* Senasanaram was clearly the richer of the two, although unlike *Wat* Prasat it was never described, disapprovingly, as being particularly wealthy. The distinction clearly lies in whether a monastery is thought of as making money out of the householders, or merely as receiving offerings from them; the second is considered essentially more appropriate to any monastic community. Whether or not the relationship between the people living on the *thi wat* and the monastery has an important financial aspect, these householders are inevitably regarded as belonging to that collectivity of laymen and women which is known as the *phuak wat*. This means that individual householders invite at least some members of that community to officiate at the merit-making ceremonies which they must sponsor from time to time, and that at any rate during *phansa*, they attend the occasional Holy Day service held there. It is also to be expected that some of these people who live close by the *wat* will put in an appearance at any ceremony which is held there, whether or not they are directly involved. Several householders may supply additional food, as well as helping to prepare and present the meal which it is customary to provide at the close of the ceremony.

Some monasteries, though by no means all of them, own additional areas of land outside the *thi wat*. These holdings, which are known as *thi thoranisong* (monastery estate), usually consist of rice-fields which have at various times been presented to the *wat* by devoted householders, or more rarely, by laymen on entry into the Order. Very few laymen make donations of land to the monastery even when they can afford to, as they prefer to present money or durable goods of some kind. During my period of fieldwork one monastery, *Wat* Na Phramen, received a bequest of 80 *rai* of paddy land on the death of an elderly spinster who had long been associated with the *wat*.

Unless the land had been presented within living memory, most of the abbots were ignorant of the source of the *thi thoranisong* belonging to their respective *wats*. In some cases the name of the donor was preserved in the crumbling ledgers of the Division of Ecclesiastical Property in the Department of Religious Affairs in Bangkok. In theory the abbot of every monastery must give details of such donations when he submits his annual report on the state of the monastic community to the ecclesiastical authorities, but, as I found to my cost, the words '*ma tae boran*' (acquired in olden days) were inscribed more often than was any more precise information.

[30] 100 *satangs* = 1 *baht*.

The prospective tenant of *thoranisong* fields belonging to any monastery usually enlists the aid of the *waiyawachakon* or of another member of the *kammakan wat*, in requesting formal permission from the abbot to begin cultivation. It should be noted that any householder can apply to become the tenant of any monastery, whether or not he has any previous links with that community.[31] In the cases I investigated the householders' choice was governed by the suitability of the land available rather than by other more personal considerations.

The annual rent charged by monasteries in Ayutthaya for the use of *thi thoranisong* varies between 30 and 50 *baht* per *rai*. These rates seem quite reasonable when compared with the yearly rental of between 60 and 90 *baht* per *rai* charged by lay landlords in the area.

It is usual for the *waiyawachakon* or for some other member of the monastery lay committee to collect the rent from the tenants of any one monastery. But monasteries are felt to be more lenient than other landlords, in that they are more prepared to waive their dues should any householder who has suffered some misfortune have difficulty in paying them. In fact, in several instances described to me, the tenants presumed upon the goodwill or inertia of the *bhikkhus* by neglecting to pay their rent, although they had no reasonable excuse. In each case, as the miscreants had rightly calculated, the monks involved felt that it would be improper and undignified to urge the *kammakan wat* to pursue the matter on their behalf. As most monasteries receive adequate support in the form of direct contributions made by the laity, it is not really necessary for them to make their land-holdings into a 'going concern', and indeed a few of them allowed members of the laity to cultivate *thoranisong* fields without charge. Nevertheless the estates of several monasteries remained unoccupied, or were used only in part. This circumstance can be explained with reference to the fact mentioned earlier that laymen rarely present their choicest fields to the wat; the two *rai* of paddy land belonging to *Wat* Prasat were poorly watered and situated a long way from any settlement, and several of the plots of land owned by *Wat* Suwan were regarded as uncultivable. There is thus little or no competition for the rights to work the fields belonging to most monasteries, despite the fact that these may be acquired for a rent which is usually no more than nominal.

As they have been donated by different householders at different times the fields which collectively comprise the *thi thoranisong* of any one *wat* may be scattered over a wide area. Moreover rice-lands which belong to a monastery in town are necessarily situated at some distance away, which

---

[31] This also applies to people living on the *thi wat*. In most cases they have no previous links with the *bhikkhus* in the monastery concerned.

means that the tenants of the *thi thoranisong* are not regarded as belonging to the *phuak wat* because they interact with the monastic community only relatively rarely. Their relationship with the monastery may be of a purely economic nature, although it is usual for individual householders to make occasional visits to the abbot to pay their respects. I heard of only one occasion when the people living on a monastery estate took concerted action with respect to the monastery which owned that land. This incident occurred at *Wat* Kluai where the tenants of its estate formed a group to make the *kathin* presentation at the close of the Lenten season. This situation was made possible by the fact that the monastery estate consisted of a single block of rice-fields situated quite near to the *wat* which stood on the outskirts of Ayutthaya.

The monastic revenue estate or *thi kalapana* comprises the third and final category of monastic land-holding. However the area known as *thi kalapana* does not belong to the monastery outright, as the lay owner does not relinquish his rights in this land but merely pledges to present to the *wat* a certain percentage of the proceeds from the sale of crops produced there. It is quite common for land of *thi kalapana* status to be bequeathed to the monastery on the death of its owner – that is to say that these fields become *thi thoranisong* – although this transfer is by no means automatic. During his lifetime the householder may ratify the original agreement made when he presents a share of the profits to the monastery after harvest, or, alternatively, at his discretion the relationship may be discontinued.

In his community study of a Thai village, Kaufman reports that the abbot of the monastery concerned hired labourers or engaged tenants to cultivate the *thi kalapana* (Kaufman 1960, p. 111), but in Ayutthaya it seemed to be the practice that fields under pledge were worked by the donors themselves, or by labourers whom they hired. The monasteries concerned were required to take no action beyond the pleasurable one of accepting a percentage of the proceeds – usually between 20% and 50% – from the sale of the crop.

Of the fifteen monasteries studied only *Wat* Suwan and *Wat* Phanan Choeng could claim any *kalapana* holdings. In both cases the figures given in the appendix represent pledges made by several farmers. All of the men to whom I spoke were people of some substance who had decided to make merit by giving a share of their profits to a famous *wat*; two of the four men who had pledged some land as *thi kalapana* to *Wat* Phanan Choeng had previously been ordained there on a temporary basis. On the other hand, none of the five lay owners of *kalapana* fields at *Wat* Suwan had had any previous connection with that monastery, and they had simply chosen to offer their support on the basis of the community's reputation.

All of these farmers lived at some distance from the monastery to which they had volunteered to donate a portion of their annual income and consequently none of them were regarded as belonging to the *phuak wat* there. Although most of these individuals called on the abbot occasionally to pay their respects, it seemed that at no time did all the owners of *thi kalapana* at any one *wat* take joint action with respect to its community of monks.

In economic terms the *wat* can be seen as acting as a centre for redistribution of property in a rather limited sense. It has already been shown that many monasteries allow the areas of land donated by wealthier members of the community to be used freely by other householders, or alternatively that they rent out their estates at a lower rate than is customary. Similarly, some of the valuables – the sets of altars, vases, crockery and so on – which typically form part of a *kathin* or *pha pa* presentation, are stored in the monastery and used by the community when the occasion arises, but may also be borrowed by any layman who needs additional equipment for a merit-making ritual to be held in his own home. The terms *khong wat* (*wat* property) or *khong klang* (common property) when applied to these articles not only indicate that they belong to the monastic community as a whole rather than to the individual *bhikkhu*, but also carry the implication that householders should be allowed to use them on request. Indeed it is only very rarely that the abbot of any community withholds his permission, as failure to provide the laity with 'reasonable facilities for merit-making'[32] can only result in a decline in lay support for himself and for the monastery.

But as the statistics given in the appendix show quite clearly, the larger part of the monetary income of any monastery is spent on its upkeep.[33] The most significant expenditures at most of the *wats* in Ayutthaya went towards the costs of constructing new buildings and maintaining the older ones. Smaller but more regular disbursements were made for water and electricity charges; the amounts spent by different monasteries varied between 500 (£10) and 100 (£2) *baht* per month for each commodity, depending upon the size of the community in question.

It should be remembered that laymen do not expect to receive any economic return for the financial support which they may give in various ways to a number of monasteries over a period of time.[34] From the observer's point of view, it can be seen that as a whole the lay sector of society does stand to benefit even in economic terms, for the support it gives to the numerous monasteries in Thailand; the *wat* not only serves as a

[32] See Appendix 7 where duties of the abbot are set down.
[33] See Appendix 9.
[34] With the exception of the direct contractual relationship which exists between a rent-paying tenant and land-holding monastery. In this instance the householder does receive a direct economic return for the money he gives to the *wat*.

storage point for merit-making facilities – both human and otherwise – but also provides a place of retirement for elderly men and a home for *dek wat* from poor families, as well as a hostel for country boys studying in town. Moreover at a few monasteries, laymen who are without home and kin, or those who are chronically sick, have taken up permanent residence in the public pavilions or *sala*, and any householder passing through a strange town can rest for the night in one of the local *wats*.[35] Furthermore, as the monkhood provides a means for social advancement in Thai society the householder who offers his support to the *Sangha* and its property is at the same time helping to hold open an important channel of social mobility.

But, for the individual layman the immediate reward for his merit-making activities lies in the emotional satisfactions to be derived from the approbation and admiration for his action, which is shown by his fellows in society. Indeed the householder's acquisition of merit is verified by these feelings of euphoria and self-satisfaction; interestingly enough the term *bun* or merit is equated by informants with happiness or *khwam suk*.[36] Because they provide a means whereby the layman can demonstrate not only his commitment to Buddhist values, but also his worldly success, merit-making activities must be regarded as a significant mode of conspicuous consumption for the Thais. It is true that some religious expenditures are obligatory in the sense that the ritual performed by the *bhikkhus* is an essential part of certain universally experienced changes of status. The ceremonies of cremation (*ngan phao sop*) and of ordination (*ngan buat*) are generally regarded as the most vital of all life-crisis rituals and few people enter into the civil contract of marriage without first being blessed by a chapter of monks. But for most householders, to hold a simple merit-making ceremony, with the minimum number of monks required, is inadequate whatever the occasion may be. It is generally felt to be better not to hold a ceremony at all if it is not to be on a lavish scale, and consequently *ngan* may be postponed for several years until the family and their friends can put on a show of sufficient magnificence. Several informants remarked that there is no point in holding a small ceremony, as it would cause you to be remembered primarily for your stinginess rather than for your punctiliousness in observing the occasion without delay – a circumstance to which little value is attached.

But the spending-patterns of the wealthier and more westernized members of Thai society are beginning to diverge more and more from this traditional model. The householders from higher-income groups tend to

---

[35] This applies largely to male householders, although in some cases nuns or *mae chi* may accommodate female travellers.
[36] See Tambiah (1968, p. 51 and passim).

spend more money on the acquisition of luxury goods such as cars, refrigerators and television sets, and at the same time to use a comparatively insignificant amount of money for religious expenditures.[37] In Ayutthaya for example, laymen from the professional classes sponsored relatively small life-crisis rituals and neglected altogether those optional activities, such as visiting Buddhist shrines and attending monastery fairs, which provided a major source of entertainment for their humbler fellows.

It is obvious that these changes in the pattern of consumption have some important implications for the future development of the Buddhist *Sangha*, and indeed in Bangkok the relationship between the monastic and the lay sectors of society has already undergone some significant modifications. In the capital there is both a greater concentration of monks than elsewhere in Thailand and a diminution of the general interest in religious affairs. The latter circumstance can be attributed both to the presence of so many people who are non-Thai and non-Buddhist, and to the fact that metropolitan Thais are on the whole more sophisticated than their fellow countrymen. Because of this combination of circumstances it is quite common for a monk in Bangkok to be supported on a permanent basis by one lay sponsor or *upathak* who provides him with an allowance for food, robes, travel and educational requirements, and for any other needs he might have. A *bhikkhu* who is supported by an *upathak* has no need to *pai binthabat* (collect alms) nor need he spend any time on pastoral services. Indeed many Bangkok monks are oriented almost exclusively to study and have little or no contact with lay society, other than with their personal sponsor.

Furthermore, owing to the general decline in lay support many *wats* in the capital must rationalize their economic activities in order to make a profit from their estates. This is none too arduous a task in booming Bangkok where the price of land is rising with great rapidity. In such a situation the *wat* may become more self-contained from an economic point of view, in that the community is independent of day-to-day support from the householders. From the social point of view, as was remarked above, the monastery may also become more 'closed' in that its residents have fewer contacts with lay society.

I must make it clear that this situation does not obtain in all the monasteries in the capital, nor are all the *bhikkhus* in Bangkok supported by individual *upathak*. But these new developments are interesting in that they can be seen as a direct response to the increasingly general lack of enthusiasm for spending lavishly to support the *Sangha*; an attitude which is correlated with the growing interest in Western ways and material culture. The changes in the patterns of consumption which are already discernible in the upper

[37] See below, chapter 5.

reaches of Ayutthaya society are discussed at length below in chapter 5, which is devoted to an analysis of the role of the Buddhist householder in Thai society.

A *wat* committee (*kammakan wat*) consisting of several laymen, the abbot and one or more junior *bhikkhus*, had been established at most of the Ayutthaya monasteries studied. As its constitution suggests, the *kammakan wat* provides a link between the *wat* and the wider lay community. It may be recalled from a previous section of the present chapter that the lay members of *kammakan Wat* Prasat distributed amongst their relatives and friends the invitations for the *Thet Mahachat* which was to be performed by *bhikkhus* resident in that monastery. Furthermore, at many urban *wats* the householders who belong to the *kammakan wat* mobilize that collectivity of people which is known as the *phuak wat* to provide *kaeng wian* for the monastic community during the Lenten retreat. These lay committee members also facilitate communication between the two sectors of society in the other direction, in that they may introduce to the abbot of the monastery concerned householders who are prospective tenants of the *thi wat* or *thi thoranisong*. Similarly a person on the *kammakan wat* may, on behalf of some other layman, negotiate the loan of ritual equipment belonging to the *wat* for use at a *ngan tham bun* (merit-making ceremony) to be held in the home.[38]

The establishment of a *wat* committee provides a partial solution to some of the problems inherent in the institutionalization of the *Sangha*, in that its lay members handle the financial affairs of the monastery, from which the *bhikkhus* should remain aloof. In a sense the *kammakan wat* serves a similar function for the monastic community as does the *dek wat* for the individual monk: the boy accompanies the *bhikkhu* on shopping expeditions and makes purchases on his behalf; the lay members of the *wat* committee negotiate with the builders concerning any work of construction or restoration which is necessary, collect rent from the tenants of the monastery lands, and take the proceeds from fund-raising fairs to the bank where the *wat* has opened an account.

From time to time a monastery may have dealings with the local officials of the civil service. During my fieldwork for example, the community at *Wat* Phanan Choeng asked to borrow 500 chairs from the Town Hall to seat the monks expected to attend the three-day triennial conference which

---

[38] Members of the *kammakan wat* who have spent several years in the Order often arrange ceremonies on behalf of their fellow laymen who are less familiar with religious affairs.

was held there in March 1967. Furthermore, a request was made for the officials in the Division of Religious Affairs at the Town Hall to publicize the occasion by pinning up a few posters in the market place. It was hoped by this means to attract the attention of the householders, who would then donate both money and food to support this dramatic influx of monks, between five and six hundred in number, from other parts of *Changwat* Ayutthaya and from the adjacent Provinces of Angthong and Lopburi.

It is clear that a townsman who has contacts in both the *Sangha* and the civil service, as well as some knowledge of the ritual procedures proper to each institution, can play a vital part on any monastery committee, and many of the most active members of *kammakan wat* in Ayutthaya do indeed combine these qualifications. Khun Siri Imchai, my chief informant and a member of *kammakan Wat* Nang Plum, spent twelve years of his life in the Order before re-entering lay life as a clerk in the Division of Religious Affairs in the Ayutthaya Town Hall. As I shall presently show, Khun Siri played a very active part in organizing the religious life of the town, both in his official capacity and as a private citizen.

The existence of a monastery committee also acts as a sanction against the *wat*'s misuse of the money and goods presented by the laity. In one case which came to my notice, the abbot of one Ayutthaya monastery began to refuse to lend to any layman the ritual equipment belonging to that *wat*. He justified his action by saying that as these articles were *khong wat* they should not be loaned to householders and that they would in future be used only at ceremonies held within th*e wat*. The lay members of the monastery committee tried to dissuade him from his purpose, and when they met with no success they decided to have nothing further to do with that community. After a few days however, the erring abbot realized that without their assistance he was virtually powerless to take any action, as he could not himself take over the management of the monastery's financial affairs without incurring even greater public opprobrium. Consequently the abbot dispatched a *dek wat* with an invitation to the *de facto* leader of the committee to visit him again. The latter complied, and finally an agreement was reached by which laymen might again be able to borrow the disputed *khong wat* on request from the abbot.

From the other point of view it can be seen that the inclusion of two or more *bhikkhus* on the *kammakan wat* acts as a check on any layman who, having volunteered his services to the *wat*, then decided to appropriate some of its property to himself.[39] According to Thai law at the present time, at

[39] Some years ago a layman who had been embezzling the funds of a small Ayutthaya monastery poisoned the new abbot who asked to see the accounts, as he was afraid of being exposed. He had had virtually complete control of the monastery's finances as the previous abbot had taken no interest in these affairs.

least two monks must put their signatures to any cheque or other document relating to the affairs of their *wat*.

The abbot or in some cases the acting-abbot (*phuraksakan thaen chao awat*) becomes the chairman of the *kammakan wat* automatically, but the use which is made of this position varies very much between individuals; some passive abbots remain mere figureheads, simply giving their formal ratification to decisions made by the others in the meeting, whilst other chairmen initiate action and lead the debates.

One of the ways in which an abbot can wield his authority is by co-opting members of the lay community on to the monastery committee, although in many instances it appeared that householders had come forward to volunteer their services and had thus become members of the *wat* committee. The length of their service on the committee varies very much between members as it is not usual for a new abbot to change the composition of the *kammakan* entirely, though he may invite additional members to join the group. At some monasteries one lay member of the committee is known as the *waiyawachakon*[40] or steward. Ideally this appointment is made by the abbot with the approval of the ecclesiastical officers at *Tambon* and *Amphoe* levels, and should be reported to the *Nai Amphoe* (District Officer) whose responsibility it is to inform the Provincial Governor and the officials in the Department of Religious Affairs in Bangkok. In practice however, the individual known as the *waiyawachakon* may simply be the recognized leader of the laymen on the committee and may have received no official appointment. His signature is to be found on most documents relating to affairs at the *wat*, and it is he who collects the *nittayaphat* (food allowance) granted to any of the *bhikkhus* in that monastery from the Division of Religious Affairs in the Town Hall. Furthermore, the *waiyawachakon* acts as intermediary between the householder and the monk when the former wishes to present a sum of money to the latter in return for his performance of merit-making ritual. It is customary for the layman to entrust this money to the *waiyawachakon* who, in turn, gives a written statement to the intended recipient informing him that he may apply to the steward for the stipulated sum, or alternatively that he may ask the latter to purchase for him any articles required up to that amount.

At four of the fifteen monasteries studied there was no *waiyawachakon* and no permanently constituted *kammakan wat*. In each case the abbot simply sought the services of laymen in the vicinity as the need arose, so that the constitution of the group of lay helpers might change somewhat from occasion to occasion. Indeed this situation may arise even at those

40 From the Pali word *Veyyavacca-kara* meaning 'one who serves'. See the *Kot Mahatherasamakhom*, Vol. 3, Part 1, Sect. 8, for conditions of eligibility.

monasteries where a committee has been appointed, as there are a number of 'floating' helpers who give their assistance at several *wats* from time to time. Siri Imchai, for example, was a regular member of the committee at *Wat* Nang Plum, in whose compound he had built his house. But he took an active interest in the religious life of the town and liked to help the abbot of *Wat* Yanasen, who was a distant affine, to negotiate any business he might have at the Town Hall, or to make the arrangements for a ceremony or fair to be held in the *wat*. He also lent his services to the abbots of *Wat* Borommawong and of *Wat* Suwan, both of whom he had befriended whilst he was himself in the Order, and he gave occasional assistance to the *bhikkhus* at *Wat* Phanan Choeng, with whom he had first come into contact through his work in the Department of Religious Affairs.

Most abbots, when questioned about the eligibility of the householders who had been included on the *kammakan wat*, replied that these people

TABLE 4.1 The composition of the Monastery Committee (*kammakan wat*) at *Wat* Nang Plum, Ayutthaya

Chairman: Phrasunthonthamkoson, Abbot of *Wat* Salapun, and previously Abbot of *Wat* Nang Plum which is still under his care

Vice-Chairman: Phrakhru phiphithawiharakan, Acting-Abbot (*phuraksa kanthaen chao awat*) at *Wat* Nang Plum

Two other monks from *Wat* Nang Plum

Lay members of *kammakan Wat* Nang Plum

Name & age	Occupation	Length of previous service in the Order of Monks	Lived in this wat as a monk
1 Khun Somnuk Suphanuan (62)	Property-owner	1 Lenten season	Yes
2 Khun Thai Tharisen (67)	School teacher (civil servant Gd. 3), semi-retired	8 Lenten seasons	No
3 Khun Siri Imchai (65)	Civil servant Gd. 3, semi-retired	12 Lenten seasons	No
4 Khun Chewanyen Saelim (51) (Chinese woman)	Ice-lollipop vendor & owner of grocery store	—	—
5 Khun Chua Sae Chao (52) (Chinese)	Owner of hardware & grocery store	—	—
6 Khun Phrasoet Assawong (46)	Civil servant Gd. 3	1 Lenten season	No
7 Khun Thong Sae Ung (57) (Chinese)	Hotelier and restauranteur	—	—
8 Khun Chuan Klinmahon (46) (Indian Muslim)	Owner of a haulage business	—	—

had 'good hearts' (*chai di*) and that they showed an interest in the affairs of the monastic community. As was mentioned earlier, many of these individuals were, or had been, employed in the lower ranks of the civil service. Several, Khun Siri Imchai amongst them, came from rural areas, and had acquired some education during their years in the *Sangha* before returning to lay life as junior officials in the national bureaucracy. Their links with the civil service and with the monastic community, combined with the respected position they occupied in the town, made these householders particularly suited to serve on the *kammakan wat*.

A period of service in the Buddhist *Sangha* is not a necessary pre-condition for membership of the monastery committee, but it is not surprising that some men who have been monks at some time in their lives should express a continuing interest in monastic affairs by becoming members of the *kammakan wat*. But, as is shown in Table 4.1, some committee members have very different antecedents and qualifications. This can be explained with reference to the fact that by serving on the *wat* committee a householder can demonstrate that he is a good citizen and that he is thoroughly committed to prevailing social norms and values. The *kammakan Wat* Nang Plum provides us with four extreme examples in Khun Chuan Klinmahon and the three committee members who belong to the Chinese community in Ayutthaya. None of these people professed to be Theravada Buddhists; Khun Chuan was a follower of Islam whilst the Chinese members practised Mahayana Buddhism freely mixed with Taoist and Confucian elements. Nevertheless, each of these individuals wished to participate in the life of the community and had thus offered his services to the local monastery. These offers had no doubt been accepted with alacrity by the abbot of *Wat* Nang Plum, not only because the people who made them were known to be of good character, but also because each had shown, in his chosen line of business, that he knew how to handle money.[41]

The lay members of the *kammakan wat* naturally belong to that collectivity of people who identify themselves, and are identified, as supporters of that monastery (*phuak wat*). In the majority of cases, as is true for *Wat* Nang Plum, these householders live in the vicinity of the *wat* so that they are in fairly frequent contact with the *bhikkhus* who can thus assess the suitability of actual and potential committee members, and can moreover be judged by them in their turn.

However, none of the people who make up *kammakan Wat* Phanan Choeng live very close to that monastery, which is situated in a poor and

---

[41] Kaufman (1960, p. 112) makes a similar point about the members of *kammakan wat* Bangkhuat when he writes 'Because of their wealth it is reasoned that not only are they less likely to steal, but that they are likely to make larger contributions.'

sparsely populated area of town. The householders who live close by the *wat* belong to the urban service classes, being employed as vendors, labourers, *samlo*-drivers and so on, which is to say that they are the kind of people who neither volunteer their services to the committee, nor receive requests from the abbot to join this body. As can be seen from Table 4.2, three of the five laymen on the committee at *Wat* Phanan Choeng have spent some time as *bhikkhus* in that monastery, which as a famous teaching centre attracts men from other regions of the country, as well as from all parts of Ayutthaya itself. It appeared that in the case of Maha Sawat, Khun Thep and Khun Uan it was the factor of old association, rather than of contiguity, which formed the basis for their continuing allegiance to that *wat*.

TABLE 4.2   The composition of the Monastery Committee (*kammakan wat*) at *Wat* Phanan Choeng, Ayutthaya

Chairman: Phrathepwongsachan, Abbot
Vice-Chairmen:
  Phrakhru Chan, Deputy Abbot
  Phramaha Kaew
  Phrakhru Lap
  Phra Maen
Lay members of *kammakan Wat* Phanan Choeng

Name & age	Occupation	Length of previous service in the Order of Monks	Lived in this wat as a monk
1 *Maha Sawat (62)	Civil servant Gd. 3 (retired)	10 Lenten seasons	Yes
2 Khun Thep Lengcharoen (48)	Civil servant Gd. 2	3 Lenten seasons	Yes
3 Khun Uan Kantabut (53)	Ferry-boat owner	5 Lenten seasons	Yes
4 Khun Phrachuap Santhirak (64)	Property-owner	—	—
5 Khun Chamnan Thaiphiphat	Doctor	1 Lenten season	No

* This man retained his monkly title after his return to lay life. The prefix *Maha* indicates that he had passed at least *Barian* Grade 3.

The two remaining members of the committee were both well-known figures in Ayutthaya society, and it seems that their services were requested for this reason. Both the *bhikkhus* and the laymen concerned thought it quite natural and highly appropriate that these two prominent citizens should belong to the *kammakan* of a most prominent *wat*.

Given the fact that the Thais place a great deal of emphasis on age seniority it is understandable that the householders who serve on monastery committees should be at least of middle-age. The fact that women are very poorly represented on the *kammakan wat* in Ayutthaya can be explained with reference to the belief that it is not fitting for female householders to work in close conjunction with the *bhikkhus*, and indeed it is stated in the Laws of the Council of Elders that a woman may not become a *waiyawachakon*.[42] A few women do serve as ordinary members of the monastery committee but as they tend to be less highly educated, and, allegedly, more naturally stupid than their male counterparts, they are felt to be unfitted for the 'paper-work' which committee membership may entail. With a few notable exceptions, some of them Chinese, women play a negligible part in the public life of Ayutthaya, although they have a significant role to play in supporting the *bhikkhus* with daily alms, and in attending services at the *wats* in town.

In none of the cases I investigated did the *kammakan wat* hold regular meetings as a matter of procedure. Individual members frequently called at the monastery concerned to chat to the abbot and to the other *bhikkhus*. On such an occasion either party might suggest that a meeting be convened to discuss business pertaining to the monastery estates, or to a projected ceremony or fair to be sponsored by the *wat*. The message could then be relayed to the other members of the committee in their homes. It was usual for meetings of the *kammakan wat* to take place in the *kuti* belonging to the abbot of the monastery in the early evening, between 4.30 and 6.00 p.m., when those householders who were civil servants had finished their day's work.

In concluding the present section let me briefly describe one such meeting which I attended at *Wat* Phanan Choeng on the evening of 7 February 1967 (B.E. 2510). I had been invited to accompany Khun Wachana Bunsanong, the manageress of the Thai City Bank, Ayutthaya, as she had made an appointment to meet the *kammakan Wat* Phanan Choeng at 4.30 in the afternoon. The purpose of her errand was to take charge of the proceeds from a fair held in the *wat* on the two previous days, in celebration of the Chinese New Year.

The committee of five laymen and two monks were seated on the verandah of a building situated behind the *bot* where they usually transacted their business. The Abbot himself was not present and as usual his Deputy Phra Khru Chan took charge of the proceedings; Phra Maen, a much more junior *bhikkhu*, operated the abacus. With frequent pauses for drinking iced-coffee or Coca-Cola the assembled company eventually counted the money and packed it into bags and holdalls which were borne away by Khun Wachana's attendant clerks. Before she left, the manageress presented Phra

[42] See above, fn. 40, for reference.

Khru Chan with a receipt for the deposit slip signed by himself, by Phra Maen and Maha Sawat.

As I have described in the previous sections of this rather long and discursive chapter each *wat* receives support in the form of money, of food, and of practical assistance in administrative affairs, from the lay community. In deciding which monastery he will support on any particular occasion the individual householder takes into consideration a number of different factors; for some purposes he directs his attention to the nearest *wat*, or to one whose reputation and standing appeal to him, whereas in other instances the fact of kinship or acquaintance with one of the *bhikkhus* in a monastic community is decisive in directing the layman's charitable effort. Furthermore his relationship with another layman who is already associated with a particular monastery can draw an individual into either a permanent or a more fleeting association with a *wat*. It may be remembered that the party which takes a *kathin* presentation to any monastery is typically an action-set centred on the organizer or *chao phap*, which is to say that many members of the expedition are involved by reason of their relationship with its leader rather than because they have any previous connection with the monastic community in question.

The householders who appear to the observer to form the matrix of supporters at one *wat* are classified, in Fig. 4.1, according to the nature of their association with that community. It should be remembered that these labels refer to several kinds of sociological entity; for example the householders who live along the alms-routes taken by monks from a particular monastery are not aware of themselves as forming a unit with respect to rice-giving or any other activity. Similarly those farmers who severally pledge an area of land as *thi kalapana* to the same *wat* do not form a group on this basis. But some of the sociological groupings under discussion do exhibit a greater degree of internal cohesiveness; for example the householders who belong to the *phuak wat* of any monastery are aware of themselves as being related to one another with regard to that community. In sociological terms the *phuak wat* may best be regarded as a collectivity, which is according to Merton's definition 'an entity without a recognizable structure ... whose members have certain interests or modes of behaviour in common which may at any time lead them to form themselves into definite groups' (Merton 1957, p. 229). Essentially it is the factor of contiguity which forms the basis for this collectivity, although as was explained in the previous section members of the *wat* committee are automatically

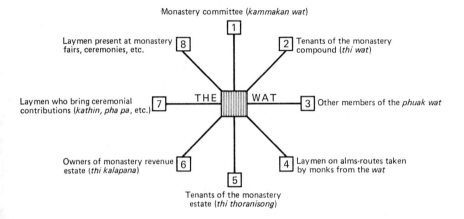

Fig. 4.1. Observer's model of relationships existing between *wat* and lay community

Notes:

i. The lay groupings are arranged numerically according to the probable constancy and regularity of their interaction with the *wat*.

Grouping 4 might alternatively be placed first as some of these laymen are in contact with monks from the *wat* each day, but more laymen from groupings 1, 2 and 3 interact more regularly with the monastic community by reason of their physical proximity. (See Fig. 4.2 for alternative arrangement.)

ii. The laymen making up grouping 7 may have had no previous contact with the *wat* and might never visit it again. It is unlikely that the same grouping will be organized to make a contribution to the same monastery in the future although individual lay members may be in contact with that community again.

iii. The gathering which comes together at a fair or ceremony in the *wat* (grouping 8) is unlikely to be exactly reproduced again.

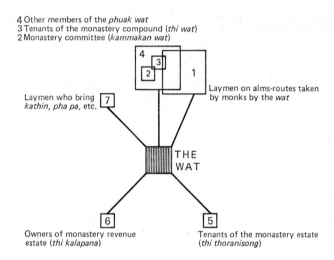

4 Other members of the *phuak wat*
3 Tenants of the monastery compound (*thi wat*)
2 Monastery committee (*kammakan wat*)

Laymen who bring 7 *kathin, pha pa,* etc.

Laymen on alms-routes taken by monks by the *wat*

THE WAT

6 Owners of monastery revenue estate (*thi kalapana*)

5 Tenants of the monastery estate (*thi thoranisong*)

Fig. 4.2. *Wat*'s model of the relationships existing between itself and the lay community

Notes:
i. The lay groupings are arranged numerically according to the probable constancy and regularity of their interaction with the *wat*.
ii. The arrangement of these groupings also indicates the most likely areas of overlap between them.

regarded as belonging to the *phuak wat* even when they come from outside the immediate locality.[43] As was explained earlier, membership of the *phuak wat* may form the basis for the organization of a *kaeng wian* group which provides food for the monastic community during Lent.

Certain of these sociological groupings invariably overlap in that membership of one of them automatically entails belonging to another. Fig. 4.2 which represents the monastery's view of the householders with whom it is associated shows the most likely areas of overlap. It can be seen that tenants of the *thi wat* (monastery compound) as well as members of the *kammakan wat* are regarded as belonging to the broader collectivity of the *phuak wat*. It is also probable that some of the householders who give alms to the *bhikkhus* from any community live sufficiently close to be included in the grouping *phuak wat*. An individual layman who is associated with one monastery in a variety of ways is identified by the *bhikkhus* with respect to that position which involves the most frequent interaction between the two parties, which is to say that a householder who lives in the compound and belongs to the *kammakan wat* is distinguished as being a member of the committee, rather than by virtue of his residence on the *thi wat*, or because he belongs to the wider grouping of the *phuak wat*.[44]

These groupings may also overlap in the sense that a number of householders who stand towards a monastery in a relationship of permanent association may be mobilized to make occasional monetary contributions although this is outside the scope of their normal interaction. On p. 125 above, I cited a case in which the tenants of the *thi thoranisong* presented *kathin* robes to the monastery which owned the land. It is interesting to see that the extent to which the groupings centred on any one *wat* overlap in this fashion varies according to the size and the reputation of the establishment concerned, in that larger and more famous monasteries such as *Wat* Phanan Choeng receive support from a wider area, in both social and geographical terms.

The fairs and ceremonies which are sponsored by a *wat* with a view to raising funds cannot very easily be incorporated into this model, in that the people who support these functions may belong to one or more of the groupings under discussion, or alternatively, may have no previous connection with the community in question.

---

[43] When a layman's home is equidistant from two or more monasteries, personal considerations such as preferring one abbot to another determine his *phuak wat* membership.

[44] It was my impression that in most cases the monks in any one monastery might not be able to list all members of the *phuak wat* by name but that they quickly recognized them by sight when they encountered them. Conversely they were quick to spot an unfamiliar face in any gathering at the *wat*.

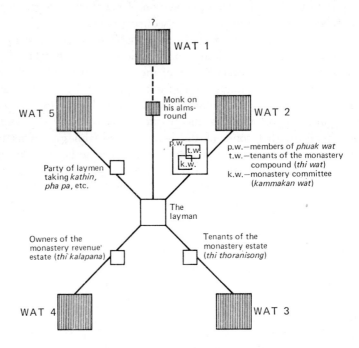

Fig. 4.3. Layman's model of relationships existing between himself and a number of monastic communities

Notes:

i. The numerical arrangement of the monasteries according to the regularity with which the layman interacts with each of them is again open to discussion. It should be remembered that even though monks pass by his house each day the layman need not, and with a few exceptions, does not give rice every morning. Furthermore, it is quite probable that he does not know where the monks in question come from.

ii. The layman can occupy a number of different positions with respect to a single *wat*, e.g. he may contribute to *kathin* presentation taken to *Wat* 2, to a number of whose residents he gives rice regularly or only occasionally.

iii. On the other hand, it is unlikely that certain aspects of the layman's role as Buddhist householder will be combined with respect to a single *wat*. It would, for instance, be unusual for a layman living in the compound (*thi wat*) of an urban monastery to form part of the monastery estate (*thi thoranisong*) of that, or indeed of any other *wat*.

Fig. 4.3 completes the picture by presenting this situation from the point of view of the individual layman. As is clear from this model, the householder can be associated with a number of monasteries in a variety of ways although it is likely that he recognizes a firmer allegiance to the nearest of these communities. The links he has with this *wat* are activated quite frequently if he also belongs to the monastery committee, or if he lives on or near the compound of the *wat*. Otherwise his interaction with the community of *bhikkhus* might be limited to occasional attendance at the Holy Day services, or to the provision of *kaeng wian* on a few days during the Lenten retreat.

As I have already pointed out, the groupings of laymen with whom the individual householder is associated with respect to any monastery vary very much in terms of the degree of cohesiveness they possess. It should be noted that from the householder's point of view no grouping of laymen is interposed between himself and the *bhikkhu* to whom he presents alms. The holders of *thi kalapana* appear to form the most diffuse of these lay groupings, as although in this context the individual layman is aware of himself as being one of a number of individuals making similar contributions to a particular monastery, he need have no personal knowledge of his fellow donors.

From the observer's point of view it appears that the lay groupings centred on any one *wat* must inevitably overlap with those for which another monastery provides the focus, since each householder is associated with a number of monastic communities in different ways. To take one final example, it is unlikely that the people who live on the *thoranisong* fields belonging to an urban monastery regard themselves, or are regarded, as members of the *phuak wat* if the land is situated at some distance from the town. In such cases it is usual for the householders concerned to recognize a stronger allegiance towards the nearest rural monastery, despite the fact of their continuing economic ties with another establishment.

5
The role of the Buddhist layman

> *The ceremony of* Dharma, *on the contrary, is very fruitful. It consists in proper treatment of slaves and servants, reverence to teachers, restraint of violence toward living creatures, and liberality to priests and ascetics. These and like actions are called the ceremonies of* Dharma.
>
> *Other ceremonies are of doubtful value. They may achieve their purpose, or they may not. Moreover the purposes for which they are performed are limited to this world.*
>
> *The ceremony of* Dharma, *on the other hand, is not limited to time. Even if it does not achieve its object in this world, it produces unlimited merit in the next world. But if it produces its object in this world, it achieves both effects: the purpose desired in this world and unlimited merit in the next.*
>
> Taken from Rock Edict no. IX in *The Edicts of Asoka* edited and translated by N. A. Nikam and Richard McKeon (1966)

No originality can be claimed for the idea that religious commitment varies as between individuals, though students of Thai society have so far tended to take at its face value the frequently expressed belief that to be Thai is to respect the Buddha, and have assumed that differential religious commitment is completely expressed by the division of society into monk and lay sectors. In the present chapter on the other hand I shall discuss the observable differences in role-playing which exist between Buddhist laymen, to see how far if at all they can be correlated with disparities in income and life-style. The effects of personal inclination are properly speaking beyond the scope of this study but my extensive use of case material in the present chapter will enable me to show in a necessarily rather impressionistic manner some of the ways in which factors of temperament and personality may affect a layman's interpretation of his role.

The role of the Buddhist layman

ROLE NORMS AND BEHAVIOUR

A Buddhist is, by definition, a person who reveres the Triple Gem of the *Buddha*, his *Dhamma* and the *Sangha* of monks. Before any merit-making ceremony begins both the monks and the laymen present recite in Pali the formula of the Three Refuges, which expresses their belief that the Buddha, his teachings and the *bhikkhus* who study and preserve the latter, can overcome the suffering which is inherent in this material world.[1]

The Buddhist layman, moreover, is expected to conform as closely as possible to certain moral injunctions known as the Five Precepts, which require: abstinence from the destruction of life (1); abstinence from taking what is not given (2); abstinence from fornication (3); abstinence from speaking falsely (4); and abstinence from spirituous, strong and maddening liquors which are the cause of sloth (5) (Obeyesekere 1968, p. 27). It might be recalled from previous discussion that these proscriptions are to be found in a more stringent form in the *Patimokkha* which provides a most comprehensive code of conduct for members of the Buddhist *Sangha*. The 227 ascetic rules of which this code is comprised are intended to facilitate the *bhikkhu*'s quest for Salvation by removing him from the mundane world of the householder. The Five Precepts on the other hand are intended to provide some kind of control over the drives and desires of those individuals who remain in lay society, and have thus no hope of achieving *Nirvana*.

It is customary, prior to any merit-making ceremony, for the lay leader of the congregation (*makhanayok*)[2] to request the Five Precepts from the most senior monk present. The congregation of householders then repeats in unison after the monk the Pali formulae stating their adherence to the Precepts, outlined above.[3] All the laymen to whom I spoke subscribed to these religious proscriptions in this formal sense whilst at the same time recognizing that it was impossible in the course of normal life to fulfil all or any of these injunctions to the letter. The fact that he agrees to abstain from taking life, for example, does not prevent a Buddhist householder from killing a snake or a mad dog, nor the rodents and vermin which infest his gardens and paddy fields. Similarly, the villagers I knew appeared to feel no compunction about taking the life of a chicken or a pig in order to provide food for the family. In fact, as far as most laymen were concerned, although they might from time to time express their abhorrence of destroying any form of life, the first precept was interpreted as being a prohibition against

---

[1] See Wells (1960, pp. 52–3).
[2] From the Pali *magga*, meaning 'a path' and *nayok*, meaning 'a leader': *magga nayok*.
[3] Wells (1960, pp. 53–4).

taking human life, a delict which naturally falls within the boundaries of secular jurisdiction.[4] The four remaining precepts are also susceptible to a fairly liberal interpretation, the fourth and fifth being most consistently contravened: few if any of my lay informants for example, practised total abstinence from alcohol, although even those who were habitually intemperate recognized that from moral, social, and medical points of view, it was both deplorable and foolish to drink too much.

In summary then, the Five Precepts provide very general guidelines for social action, and like all similar codes can be quoted or ignored as is expedient. It is felt however, that one should attempt to observe them as closely as is practically possible in order to avoid acquiring demerit or *bap*, although a positive increment of merit (*bun*) is achieved by other means.

It is generally stated that the most meritorious action a layman can perform is to enter the Buddhist monkhood – although many of my informants were careful to make it clear that the quality of any action depended to a large extent upon the intentions and ability of the individual actor. Which is to say that it is better to be a good layman than an indifferent monk; a man should not persist in following the arduous 'way of the monk' if he cannot meet the standards required.

The act of becoming ordained however, is regarded as being a merit-making activity of a special order, and somewhat different in kind from the other religious activities appropriate to the householder.[5] Leaving aside for the moment this renunciation of lay society, it can be said that for the layman the primary referent of the phrase *tham bun* (to make merit) is to give support to members of the *Sangha*, individually or as a collectivity. In theory it is more meritorious to make an offering to a number of *bhikkhus* (*thuai sangkhathan*) than to an individual monk. It is felt that in giving to monks whom one knows there is a strong element of self-interest which runs contrary to the doctrinal emphasis on the extinction of attachments, although by no means all laymen nor every monk could provide the philosophical basis for the higher evaluation accorded to non-specific and impersonal gift-giving. Moreover, this ideal is modified in practice in that householders must also honour their obligations to kinsmen and friends in

---

[4] In Thailand most butchers are of Chinese or Indian stock, but, as the commercial and business sector is largely monopolized by individuals from these minority groups it is not possible to attribute the absence of Thai butchers to the influence of the Buddhist injunction against taking life.

[5] This may serve to explain why this action was evaluated in different ways by the villagers interviewed by Kaufman (1960, p. 183) and Tambiah (1968, p. 69) respectively. My own experience would suggest that to rank merit-making activities in this way is to some extent to falsify the issue, in that in each case my informants stated that the quality of the action was affected by the intentions of the actor as well as by its own pragmatic value for the community.

the *Sangha* by inviting them to perform Buddhist rituals, in return for which service the monks are presented with traditional offerings of money and goods.

In ideal terms, the most meritorious act of charity a layman can perform is to give money to the Order of Monks for the construction of a monastery. But it is clear that very few individuals have the financial resources adequate for such donations, although most laymen contribute smaller sums from time to time as part of a *kathin* or *pha pa* presentation, which may be used for building or restoration by the recipient *wat*. Several informants remarked that to build a new *wat* at the present time was both a foolish and an ostentatious gesture, as there were already so many monasteries in the country which were falling into disrepair. Consequently it would be both more meritorious and more sensible for a rich man (*setthi*) to use his money for the benefit of the community by building a school or a hospital. Indeed when they were asked to grade the religious activities of the Buddhist householder with respect to the amount of merit to be derived in each case, both monks and laymen declared this to be impossible, because the results of these actions depended not only upon the purity of the actors' intentions but also upon the usefulness of the act itself. Consequently, I cannot feel myself able to follow the example set by Kaufman (1960, p. 183) and Tambiah (1968, p. 69) in constructing from informants' responses an ideal scale of merit-making activities, graded according to the amount of merit received in each case.

In practical terms, the most significant merit-making activity for the average layman to undertake is the sponsorship of *ngan tham bun* which are held at critical turning-points in the individual life-cycle. The arrangement of a merit-making ceremony does, as we shall see, require considerable expenditure of both money and time. The host (*chao phap*) must invite the requisite number of *bhikkhus* and he must also ensure that the necessary ritual equipment is on hand. He is responsible for seeing that the altar and the Buddha image are installed in the room chosen for the ceremony; that the monks are provided with a dais where they will sit to recite the chants; and that individual presentations of money and goods are prepared for them at the close of the ceremony.[6] Furthermore the *chao phap* must compose a list of lay guests who will be expected to make some contribution to costs of the *ngan*; on the day of the ritual these householders will in their turn expect to be provided with seating and refreshments, and in some cases with

[6] In the case of cremation ceremonies held in the *wat* the monks themselves may arrange and decorate the *sala* (pavilion) where the ritual is to take place. It is usual for them to make some charge for this service, varying from a few to several hundred *baht* according to the degree of display – in terms of flowers, lights etc. – required by the host.

entertainment in the form of a *liké*[7] or film, to be shown in the evening after the *bhikkhus* have returned to their monasteries. Despite the fact that some laymen save money for several years before sponsoring a merit-making ceremony, this is a religious observance which, unlike the building of a *wat*, is felt to be within everyone's scope. Indeed, as these *ngan* are held in association with life-crises it is inevitable that every individual should spend some money on his own ceremonies, or on those of his friends and relatives. In addition, the presentations of *kathin* or *pha pa* which are made to the *wat* at certain times of the year, provide less important, though more regular, opportunities for the layman to add to his accumulation of merit.[8]

It is generally true to say that to give support to the *Sangha* in a ceremonial context is felt to be more meritorious than the act of presenting alms to the *bhikkhus* or their begging-rounds. It might be remembered that very few of my lay informants in Ayutthaya gave rice to the monks every morning. I would agree with Nash (1965, p. 115) that this offering which most perfectly expresses the relationship of interdependence between the mendicant *bhikkhu* and the householder is felt to be a routine aspect of the layman's role, which, like the recitation of the Five Precepts or the Three Refuges formula, serves to keep the actors' 'merit-balance in an almost "steady-state"'.

On the other hand, those activities which result in a positive increment of merit are those requiring a greater effort on the part of the individual actor, and which also, incidentally, involve some degree of publicity and display. The publicity factor may help to explain why the custom of observing three additional Precepts on Holy Day (*Wan Phra*) is not regarded as one of the most important ways of improving one's spiritual credit; although it must also be taken into consideration that this mode of merit-making is by and large the prerogative of the aged, who have the time to spend the whole day in the *wat*.

Although the householder's merit-making activities primarily involve supporting the monkhood in one of the ways described above, it is believed that he also acquires merit by honouring his obligations to give material assistance to friends and relatives in the lay community. Each layman contributes to the costs of *ngan tham bun* sponsored by his kinsmen and acquaintances, on the understanding that the favour will be returned in due course, but similar acts of generosity which take place outside a religious context are also felt to bring merit to the benefactor. With respect to these transactions between householders, it is interesting to see that the acquisition of merit is felt to be a by-product of socially correct action, whereas in any

---

[7] *Liké*: traditional Thai drama, musical folk drama.
[8] See above, p. 113 for details.

charitable gesture which involves the *Sangha* of monks, *bun* provides the incentive and primary motivation.

Considerations of age and sex affect the way in which a member of the lay community performs the role of Buddhist householder. There is a tendency for lay men in any village or town to take the most active part in the religious life of that community, as they have a greater knowledge of the *Sangha* and its ways, than have the women. It is moreover, permissible for men to enjoy friendly relationships with members of the *Sangha* and to work in close conjunction with them. As the previous chapter showed quite clearly, most monastery committees (*kammakan wat*) are entirely composed of male householders. Fieldwork in the lay community of Ayutthaya showed that the laymen most actively concerned with the organization of *ngan tham bun*, with *kathin* and *pha pa* presentations, and so on, were male heads of households. The head of the family is usually responsible for providing a significant part of the family income, as well as for taking decisions concerning major expenditures of the household's resources. It is also one of his duties to organize life-crisis rituals for children who are living at home, even though some of them may be already married and are themselves earning a regular wage.[9] Because he has not yet retired from work the head of such a family group owns in addition extra-familial obligations towards friends, colleagues, and business associates, which means amongst other things that he must contribute to the costs of merit-making ceremonies sponsored by these individuals.

On the other hand, older men who are in retirement from work are unlikely to be actively involved in the arrangement of merit-making ceremonies, either public or private. It is usual for them to live in the household of one of their married children, who attends to the family's religious affairs on behalf of the whole group. The merit-making activities of elderly householders, both male and female, typically take the form of attending services at the *wat*, and in the case of the particularly devout, of obeying three additional Precepts for the duration of Holy Day (*Wan Phra*).[10]

Unless they are both wealthy and unmarried, female members of the lay community are unlikely to take a direct interest in the sponsorship and arrangement of merit-making rituals.[11] The women of the household are however responsible for providing the meals which are given both to the

---

[9] There exists incidentally a rather vague and unformulated belief that all people who live under the same roof share in the merit made by one of their number.

[10] See above, p. 107

[11] Several of the most generous donations received by the monastic community during my stay in Ayutthaya were made by elderly spinsters of independent means. Many of these women had few close relations, and thus spent little money on fulfilling familial obligations.

monks and to the lay guests at the close of any religious ritual. It is also the womenfolk who prepare alms-food for the *bhikkhus* on their begging-rounds, and present it to them, although the head of the household may decide how much food they should give and on what occasions.[12] In the traditional Thai situation fewer women have their own career and thus a lay woman of any age tends to have more time and leisure than do most laymen to spend in attending services in the *wat*. Thus, married women, girls, and a few old men make up the congregation at the monastery on *Wan Phra*, which may fall on a working day in the middle of the week.[13]

FINANCIAL STATUS AND RELIGIOUS EXPENDITURE

The way in which a layman enacts those aspects of the householder's role which are most appropriate to his status depends not only upon his temperament and personal inclinations, but also upon his income and consequent life-style. This statement applies particularly to the male heads of family households whom I have described as taking the most prominent part in the organization of religious rituals, and in subsequent paragraphs I hope to illustrate my point by describing the religious expenditures and activities of two such householders during the year 1966 to 1967. The socio-economic circumstances of the two citizens concerned, and the extent to which each is integrated into the life of the town, differ very greatly. Both of these factors have an important effect on the way in which Khun Thep Damkham, and Khun Siri Imchai respectively, perform the householder's role.

According to their general orientation the lay inhabitants of Ayutthaya can be divided roughly into two categories, namely into the 'conservative' or traditionalist, and the 'progressive'. Most of the progressive and sophisticated members of the community belong to the town's professional class, which is comprised of doctors, lawyers and bank managers and of other senior officials in government offices. The majority of these people have been educated at university or college in Bangkok, a circumstance which in itself implies a wealthier than average family background. The members of the professional classes who were known to me maintained a close interest in the capital and its Western ways and were only minimally involved in Ayutthaya society. Several of them commuted daily from Bangkok by car, whilst others spent only the weekdays in Ayutthaya and returned to the metropolis on Friday night. Most of the higher civil service officials felt that this spell of duty in the provinces, though an inevitable stage in a man's

---

[12] See below, p. 154, the case-history of Khun Thep Damkhan.
[13] *Wan Phra* falls on the eighth and fifteenth days of the waxing and waning moon.

career, should be terminated at the earliest possible time, by promotion to a higher position in Bangkok. These men relied on their subordinates, who came from Ayutthaya itself, to provide them with some knowledge of the local situation and to liaise with the rest of the community on their behalf.

There was a tendency for individuals from the higher income groups to scorn the less orthodox elements of practical religion; I attended several ordination ceremonies sponsored by wealthy families and in no case was the ritual of *upasombot* preceded by the Brahministic ritual of 'calling the *khwan* (*tham khwan*)' (Wells 1960, p. 137). Furthermore, my observations showed that the more progressive layman tended to assume that science (*witthayasat*) was more efficacious than magic (*saiyasat*) in the treatment of illness or disease, and that he would visit with some embarrassment and as a last resort a monk who specialized in magical practices.

Other optional religious observances, such as visiting shrines or attending monastery fairs, similarly made a smaller appeal to those more sophisticated laymen who sought more exciting forms of entertainment in the cinemas and night clubs of Bangkok.[14]

It can be seen that the larger salaries earned by these individuals placed new economic opportunities within their grasp. Much of their wealth was spent, not on merit-making activities, a traditional form of display, but in acquiring expensive durable goods, such as cars, television and stereo-sets from Japan and the West. Moreover, because they were in general less integrated into the life of the local community these prominent citizens owed fewer obligations to contribute to *ngan tham bun* sponsored by their fellows, although most of them felt it their duty to assist their clients and subordinates.

The case-history of Khun Thep Damkham can be used to illustrate the preceding points more clearly. Khun Thep was born forty-six years ago in Bangban, a farming settlement some two hours' boat-ride from Ayutthaya. At the age of twelve he left the village and came to study in town. During term-time he boarded at *Wat* Senasanaram as a part-time monastery boy (*dek wat*) and in his early teens he was ordained at that *wat* as a novice for one Lenten season. Khun Thep was intelligent and had worked very hard to win a scholarship to read law at Thammasat University in Bangkok. When he graduated at the end of a four-year course he returned to Ayutthaya, not to practise law, but to teach at a boys' secondary school in the town. He taught there for fourteen years, his main subject being English which he taught himself from gramophone records whilst living in the capital. He

---

[14] These observances are obviously more optional than life-crisis ceremonies, which must be observed, in however perfunctory a manner.

could moreover read and write with some degree of fluency, although his spoken English had deteriorated from lack of use.

In his mid-thirties Khun Thep became bored with the teaching profession, and was able to obtain a position with the Education Section (*phanek suksa*) as *suksathikanchangwat* or Provincial Education Officer. In this capacity Khun Thep was concerned amongst other things with the management of land belonging to deserted monasteries (*wat rang*) which had become the property of the Church as a whole, and as such was the concern of the Department of Religious Affairs in the Ministry of Education. He was also responsible, at the local level, for helping to implement programmes for restoration and excavation of ancient monuments which were initiated by the central authorities in Bangkok. After four years as *suksathikanchangwat* Khun Thep received a new appointment in the Ministry of Fine Arts as Curator of the two museums in Ayutthaya, with supervisory powers over projects sponsored by the Ministry in the neighbouring Provinces of Ang-thong and Lopburi. He obtained this position not only by virtue of his educational qualifications and his interest in local history, but also because of his command of the English language. It was felt that the latter would be a useful asset in the Curator of the Chao Sam Phraya Museum, which figures on the itinerary of most state visitors to Thailand.

Khun Thep was married but had, much to his disappointment, no children. His wife, who came of a middle-class Ayutthaya family, was part-owner of a private school in town where she also taught. Two nieces, the daughters of Khun Thep's elder sister, shared the house with the Curator and his wife. The older girl, Baew, worked as a guard in the Museum during the day, whilst her sister Lang attended an Ayutthaya secondary school. These two girls occupied a rather anomalous position in the household, being treated neither as daughters nor as servants, but as something in-between. In the evenings and at weekends they performed chores around the house and did the cooking under their aunt's supervision. Only occasionally did they go to Bangban to visit their mother, who lived with her father, her younger children, and a variety of other relatives in the rambling wooden farmhouse, which stood on stilts in a strip of bamboo forest, some two hundred yards away from the river bank. Their father had deserted the family some years before and was believed to be living in Bangkok.

Khun Thep, who felt that he had now very little in common with his relatives, also visited his natal home only infrequently, and much preferred urban life. His own house, which was one of the perquisites of office, had a modern bathroom and lavatory and was furnished in western style with tables, chairs and sofas, and with beds rather than with sleeping-mats. Occasionally the Curator was required to provide accommodation for inspectors and for visiting officials from Bangkok, as well as to entertain important guests who came for the day.

As a civil servant of the second grade Khun Thep earned a monthly salary of 2,600 *baht*, whilst his wife earned 1,500 *baht* over the same period. Evidence of the considerable size of their joint income was not difficult to find, in that their home contained, amongst other luxury items, a television-set, a refrigerator, a radiogramme and numerous electric fans. Khun Thep owned an expensive camera, and his wife was well provided with jewellery and elegant clothes. The Curator also ran a jeep which was in part provided by the Government as being a necessary item of equipment for an official with authority and responsibilities in three Provinces.

Being wealthy, of senior civil service rank, and sufficiently mature in years, Khun Thep appeared to possess the most important attributes of *phu yai* (Elder, eminent person; lit. Big person) and yet he was not regarded as such by the citizens of Ayutthaya. He felt, with some justification, that he was more sophisticated than most of his neighbours and seemed intimate with very few people in the town although he had lived there for the best part of his life.

At the same time, he felt that his peers in the government bureaucracy, most of whom commuted daily from Bangkok, looked down upon him as being a mere 'provincial'. Furthermore, Khun Thep considered that he had been denied the promotion he deserved, because he was frank and outspoken, unwilling to flatter or to modify his opinions for the sake of appearing more agreeable to his superiors in the Department. His dearest wish seemed to be to retire from the service, and to live on the monthly pension of 1,500 *baht* which would be owing to him, supplemented by the interest from land investments in Bangkok. As his wife would continue with her teaching they would still be quite well-off by Ayutthaya standards.

It is clear that the extent to which any householder participates in the religious life of the community depends to some degree upon his tastes and temperament, but as I have remarked clearly, the actor's socio-economic status is also a crucial factor for consideration. It appeared to me that Khan Thep's religious behaviour was fairly typical of individuals in that stratum of Ayutthaya society to which his income and occupation assigned him. Although it may well be that because he has comparatively few friends or clients, the Curator is obliged to make fewer contributions to merit-making ceremonies sponsored by other people than are other individuals of comparable wealth and position.

Between September 1966 and September 1967 Khun Thep spent 450 *baht* in contributing to the religious ceremonies listed below.

Date	Occasion	Amount contributed (in *baht*)
27 November 1966	*The marriage ceremony of an ex-pupil from the Ayutthaya boys' secondary school*	100

Khun Thep had been particularly fond of the boy, to whom he had taught English several years previously, before he had become *suksathikanchangwat*. The groom, now aged 28, was employed in the Department of Accelerated Rural Development in Bangkok, and a senior official from this Department presided over the civil ceremony, which took place in Ayutthaya, as the parents of both bride and groom were residents of the town.

29 November 1966	*The cremation of the wife of the headmaster of Pratuchai School, Ayutthaya*	50

Although they had not been close friends both Khun Thep and Khun Watani had for a long time been acquainted with the headmaster and his deceased wife, who had been a teacher at one of the many schools in Ayutthaya. The Curator felt it would be appropriate to make some contribution to the costs of the cremation as a sign of their respect for the dead woman and for her husband. The ceremony took place at *Wat* Senasanaram where there was a *men* or crematorium. The Governor, who was very westernized, did not follow the traditional Thai practice of holding as lavish a ceremony as one can possibly afford. It is usual for an interval of one year or eighteen months to elapse between the death of an individual and his subsequent cremation. During this time the deceased's family save up money and make the necessary preparations for the *ngan*. The mother of the Governor was however cremated only two months after her death, and very few people outside the immediate circle of family and friends had been invited to the ceremony. The opinion generally held in Ayutthaya was that all schools and civil service departments, hospitals, banks and other institutions in the town should have been represented! Khun Thep had not been invited to the ceremony and only chanced to hear about it on the actual day it was to take place. He thought that it would 'look bad' if he, as a leading citizen, did not make some effort to attend, and consequently he arrived at the *men* just in time to pay his respects to the Governor and to hand over the sealed envelope which contained his contribution, before the other guests began to disperse. The sum of 50 *baht* was nicely calculated to express Khun Thep's respect for the host (*chao phap*) and for the subject of the ceremony, whilst at the same time it was not sufficiently generous as to imply that the donor was equal in status to the recipient, or that the two men were on familiar terms.

27 April 1967	*A* suat chaeng *ceremony held on the occasion of the cremation of Khun Thep's mother's sister at* Wat *Maphrao, Bangkok*	100

When she had become a widow several years earlier, the deceased woman had moved from her home in a village adjacent to Bangkok to live with her youngest daughter, whose husband worked for a firm of hauliers in the capital. She had died during the previous year, leaving a considerable sum of money which she had inherited from her late husband, a farmer of some substance. A proportion of this money was used by her children to finance a *suat chaeng*[15] ceremony during which 500 monks recited in unison certain portions of the *Abhidhamma-pitaka*, prior to the burning of the coffin. The Curator and his wife, and the elder girl, Baew, spent the whole day in Bangkok and stayed with relatives overnight, as the ceremony took place in the evening. It was a good opportunity for them to see kinsmen and friends whom they did not meet in the normal course of events.

29 April	*A ceremony held at* Wat *Suwan to celebrate the promotion of the Abbot to a higher honorific rank*[16]	50

The Abbot of *Wat* Suwan also came from Bangkok and was in fact a distant relation of Khun Thep. As *suksathikanchangwat* the latter had had some professional contact with the Abbot, and had been a frequent visitor at the *wat*. In the afternoon of 29 April he went to the monastery to pay his respects to the Abbot who was receiving guests – including many monks who had been his pupils – in his *kuti* (living quarters).

1 July	*The ordination of Khun Siri Imchai's three sons at* Wat *Nang Plum*	50

Khun Thep and Khun Siri Imchai did not know each other well, although they had 'known of' each other for many years. Khun Siri, who worked as a clerk in the Education Section in the Ayutthaya Town Hall, had encountered Khun Thep when the latter held the position of *suksathikanchangwat*. Khun Thep on the other hand knew that Khun Siri played a prominent part in religious affairs; that he frequently acted as a 'broker' between members of the monastic and the lay communities in town, and as a leader of the congregation (*makhanayok*) at ceremonies held in the *wat*. My staying in Ayutthaya increased their mutual awareness if not their intimacy. Khun Thep contributed 50 *baht* to help Khun Siri shoulder the expenses of ordination, and to avoid 'hurting my feelings'.

[15] See Wells (1960, p. 273).
[16] He became *Phra Racha Khana Chan Rat.* See Appendix 4a.

One of the numerous and underworked guards from the Chao Sam Phraya Museum became ordained for one Lenten season at *Wat* Na Phramen, which was situated very near to his parents' house. The Curator's niece, Baew, helped the boy's female relatives in preparing food for the guests who were to attend the ceremony. Khun Thep was not present throughout the whole proceedings but made a brief visit to the *wat* just prior to the ritual, when he handed his contribution to the host, with a brief expression of his good wishes for the occasion. He then got into his jeep and drove back to the museum. Khun Thep thus contrived both to honour his obligations, and to avoid the probable boredom and embarrassment entailed in attending a gathering of his social inferiors. His behaviour was moreover quite acceptable to the latter, who were not only pleased to receive the money but also grateful to be spared the constraint of his continued presence amongst them.

It can be seen from the foregoing paragraphs that each of Khun Thep's religious expenditures was made in fulfilment of some specific social obligation. He did not spend any money at shrines or at fund-raising monastery fairs, nor did he contribute to collective offerings presented to the *Sangha* as *kathin* or *pha pa*. Although the amount of money spent might vary between individuals – and indeed from year to year for any one individual – the size and nature of Khun Thep's expenditures seemed fairly typical of householders from the wealthier ranks of Ayutthaya society.

Apart from the actual cash he gave as contributions to merit-making ceremonies, the Curator spent an unknown amount of money in providing alms-food for one *bhikkhu* every day. He felt that because he was the head of the household and its chief source of financial support, most of the merit gained by giving rice to the monk must accrue to him, even though the food was prepared and presented by his nieces whilst he was still in bed. The same *bhikkhu* called at the house each morning, as Khun Thep had instructed Baew to invite (*nimon*) a monk – any monk – who passed by on the main road, to accept food from them on a regular basis. The home of the Curator stood back from the road at the end of a long drive and had previously been by-passed by the *bhikkhus* on their begging-rounds.

Khun Thep took no interest in religious affairs other than on the occasions mentioned. He was not on friendly terms with any *bhikkhu*, nor did he serve on any *wat* committee in Ayutthaya. Indeed he recognized no particular affiliation to any monastery although there were a number of *wats* situated less than ten minutes' walk from the house. It seemed probable that had he needed to invite monks to officiate at any merit-making ceremony he would have applied to *Wat* Suwan, whose abbot he knew and whose monks he respected as intellectuals.

Khun Thep however, represents only a very small part of Ayutthaya society, a part which is composed of high-ranking civil servants and professional people, though it is also true that the spending patterns of individuals from old-established Ayutthaya families are, in some cases, not dissimilar from those described for Khun Thep. But some of these people – the remnants of aristocratic families who moved to Bangkok after the fall of the old capital – tend to be more conservative in outlook despite the fact that the size of their income, which is in most cases derived from property-holdings in and around the town, would seem to align them with the more sophisticated professional classes.

It appeared to me that in terms of religious expenditure and participation most householders from these old local families fell somewhere between the two extremes; they tended to sponsor fairly lavish merit-making ceremonies, and it was they who made the really large individual contributions to the *wat*. The fact that these laymen gave generously to the *Sangha* did not however, necessarily prevent them from acquiring highly valued luxury goods – cars, refrigerators, perfume – from the West, nor from investing more rationally in extending their property-holdings. In addition, many of them were well-educated and rather sceptical of the 'magical' elements in Buddhism and of associated Hindu rituals. It was felt that interest in such activities, along with attendance at monastery festivals and fairs, was more appropriate to the 'ordinary people' than to themselves. It is obvious that these householders, like the people from the professional classes, were in no position to act as religious brokers in the town, not only because they were somewhat aloof from the rest of the community but also because very few of them had served in the *wat* on an other than temporary basis.

The larger and more wholly conservative sector of Ayutthaya society comprises individuals from the lower civil service ranks and from the urban service classes. In both their income and their style of life these laymen are sharply differentiated from the more affluent townspeople. It is observable moreover, that religious affairs tend to represent a more important element in their day-to-day social existence, although this naturally varies between individuals. My research showed that those householders who took the most active interest in affairs pertaining to the *Sangha* came from the lower clerical grades of the civil service. Unlike individuals who belonged to the urban service classes these junior officials had an assured income which, though not large, enabled them to make small, but fairly frequent expenditures for merit-making activities of all kinds. On the other hand, they lacked both the considerable cash surplus and the mental habits which made newer economic opportunities so attractive to Khun Thep. Furthermore, many of these laymen occupied an interstitial position in Ayutthaya society which meant that they became involved in religious affairs as liaison officers between the *Sangha* and the lay community, as well as between the *Sangha* and the bureaucracy.

Khun Siri Imchai seems to be fairly representative of the larger and more conservative sector of Ayutthaya society, although he was regarded as being exceptionally active in religious affairs, even by laymen in comparable social circumstances.[17] Nevertheless, the way in which he performed the householder's role is by and large fairly typical of the behaviour of less affluent members of the lay community, and all of the individuals who were prominent in this sphere of activity were of similar socio-economic status to Khun Siri.

He was born in 1901 (B.E. 2444) in Paknampran, a small coastal village in the Southern Province of Prachuap. His family, who were of Chinese descent, made their living by growing fruits and vegetables for sale in the locality, as well as by running the village store which was stocked with patent medicines and cheap manufactured goods, brought from the neighbouring town.

When he was old enough to fend for himself Siri was sent as a *dek wat* to *Wat* Paknampran where he helped the *bhikkhus* with domestic chores around the monastery, and received some rudimentary education in return. Khun Siri told me that it was in fact more congenial to him to live in the monastery, not only because his family home was overcrowded but most of all because he was not on good terms with his stepmother, his father's second wife.

In his early teens Siri went to Bangkok, where he lived in the house of an aristocratic Thai family. He was introduced into the household by two servants already employed there, whose families lived in Pranburi, the market town adjacent to Khun Siri's natal village. During the three years he spent in the capital the boy studied in the school established at neighbouring *Wat* Yanawa, and made good progress, although his duties as a house-boy in the home where he lodged left him little time to do his homework. However, when Siri had just begun his third year of secondary education, at the age of fifteen, his father died, and he was forced to return home to Paknampran where he helped to support his numerous siblings and half-siblings by entering the family business.

[17] I have given the biographies of both Khun Thep and Khun Siri in some detail not only because it is necessary to have an understanding of their respective backgrounds in order to appreciate their religious behaviour, but also because some of this biographic material is illustrative of points made in my concluding chapter concerning the nature of Thai social structure.

Six years later, when he was just 21, Siri decided to become ordained temporarily. After the ceremony of *upasombot*, which was sponsored by his deceased father's younger brother, the new monk took up residence in the local monastery, *Wat* Paknampran, where he had formerly been a *dek wat*. His original intentions were to remain in the Order for only a few months, as he had already reached an understanding with a local girl that he would marry her in the near future. However, Siri quickly adapted himself to the life of the *bhikkhu*, and moreover, found a real vocation as a teacher. He reorganized the education of novices and monastery boys at *Wat* Paknampran by introducing the more modern teaching methods which he had seen applied in Bangkok. After two years in the *wat* the 'temporary' monk had no immediate plans for disrobing although he still intended to marry Mali, the girl to whom he was unofficially betrothed.

But one day a young man came to the *wat* and on meeting Phra Siri declared that he too wished to make Mali his wife, although the girl had rejected his proposal, on the grounds that she was already engaged to Siri. In relating his history the latter remarked that it was very clear to him that Mali did indeed wish to marry her second suitor, otherwise she would have refused his offer outright. By giving him the reason for her reluctance she had also indicated a possible solution to the dilemma. Siri, for his part, had no wish to return to lay life immediately, and consequently he decided to transfer to a monastery in Bangkok, so that his presence should no longer be an embarrassment to the young couple.

Accordingly, Phra Siri went to the capital and to *Wat* Suan Phlu, several of whose residents came from the same coastal area of the Southern Region. He lived there for ten years, during which time he continued both to teach and to pursue his own ecclesiastical studies; he passed the *Nak Tham* examinations quite easily, although he failed repeatedly to acquire the more advanced *Barian* grades. The fact that his academic aspirations had thus been thwarted, allied with a certain amount of discord between himself and the abbot, made Siri dissatisfied with his life in the *wat* and he decided to disrobe.

His personal lay sponsor (*upathak*), who had given him a monthly allowance throughout his stay in *Wat* Suan Phlu, equipped him for lay life by gifts of money and clothes.[18] Instead of returning to Paknampran, Khun Siri began his new life as a layman in Ayutthaya where he worked for some time in a restaurant owned by Chinese relatives on his father's side. He also

[18] He had used this sum of money to buy text-books, writing materials and supplementary food. His *upathak*, an elderly spinster who lived near *Wat* Suan Phlu, had been attracted by the *bhikkhu*'s devotion to scholarship and requested permission to become his sponsor. See above, p. 128.

made himself useful to the wider Chinese community in their dealings with the Thai bureaucracy, by filling in forms and tax returns for the many individuals who were not literate in Thai. After two years as a waiter and general helper, Khun Siri, now 34 years old, felt anxious to better himself, and so volunteered to teach in the school, by that time under state control, which stood in the compound of *Wat* Nang Plum.[19] He was accepted, largely on account of his teaching experience in the Order, and received a salary of 10 *baht* per month. In addition to this Khun Siri made 18 *baht* per month from his part-time job with the Police Department, which involved the weekly collection of the names and numbers of guests who checked into the eleven hotels in Hua Ro market, most of which establishments were owned by Khun Siri's Chinese friends and relatives.

In B.E. 2484 (1941), nine years after he had left the *Sangha*, Khun Siri married an Ayutthaya girl and rented a plot of land, at the rate of 5 *baht* per month, in the compound of *Wat* Nang Plum, where, with financial assistance from relatives on both sides, they were able to build a house. Siri had by this time changed his occupation once again, having obtained a post as a clerk in the Education Section in the Town Hall.[20] As an official in this branch of the civil service he frequently came into contact with members of the monastic community in Ayutthaya, particularly so since at that time the financial affairs of inhabited as well as deserted (*rang*) *wats* were managed by the Education Section, rather than by individual monastery committees as is now the case.[21]

Although he is now, at the age of 67, semi-retired, Khun Siri still goes each day to the Town Hall (*Sala Klang*) to help out with clerical work, and with other odd jobs around the office. His monthly wage of 500 *baht* is supplemented by the 100 *baht* he receives for his part-time work for the Police Department, and by smaller irregular payments, both in cash and in kind, made to him by grateful Chinese shopkeepers and restauranteurs whom he has assisted in some way or other.

Khun Siri still lives in the compound of *Wat* Nang Plum, where he is also a member of the monastery committee (*kammakan wat*). The original

---

[19] At the end of the nineteenth century a national education system was adopted. New schools were built and the monastery schools previously run by the *bhikkhus* have gradually been taken over by the civil authorities.

[20] On entering the civil service he also changed his name from the Chinese name 'Chum' to his present appellation 'Siri' which is recognizably Thai. His Chinese friends and relatives in Hua Ro and outside Ayutthaya continued however, to call him 'Chum'.

[21] As far as I could make out, officials from the Education Section collected rents from monastery lands, and placed the money with the bank on behalf of individual *wats*. In fact this situation still prevails as many junior officials from this branch of the civil service are members of *kammakan wat* (see below).

house, which has been extended several times and in several directions to accommodate the growing family, is now rented at the rate of 50 *baht* per month. At the time of writing the Imchai household consists of Khun Siri, his wife and five children, although the two elder sons both work in the Post Office in Bangkok and spend only weekends and holidays in Ayutthaya. A third son works at the Town Hall, whilst the fourth boy, and the youngest child, Khun Siri's only daughter, still attend secondary school in the town. His wife's widowed mother, now 83 years old, an unmarried sister-in-law, and two nieces on his wife's side, one of whom is married with one child, complete the family. There are no servants as such, although the young female relatives just mentioned to some extent fulfil this function.

The house is, in typical Thai fashion, sparsely furnished. The family usually takes its meals seated around a square of oilcloth which is spread on the polished wooden floor. They use cheap aluminium cutlery and enamel plates. Visitors who call at the house may however be invited to sit in wooden armchairs, which are grouped around a table on the outer verandah.[22] There is no bathroom properly speaking, and members of the Imchai family bathe by ladling over themselves water which is stored in large stone jars inside the house.

When he goes to work Khun Siri wears a khaki tunic and trousers of a civil servant, and always wears western-style shirt and trousers when he leaves the house, though when he is relaxing at home, in common with more sophisticated Thai men, he wears a type of loin-cloth or *phakhoma*, or a pair of baggy Chinese trousers. The women of the household are on the whole much less westernized in their manner of dress; Khun Siri's wife Khun Pa usually wears the sarong-style *phasin* of cotton or silk both at home and when visiting, although she may for very special occasions wear a western-style 'suit' consisting of a blouse and matching skirt. The younger girls however, never appear in western dresses or skirts, although elasticated ski-style trousers are considered an acceptable alternative to the *phasin* for casual wear.

The womenfolk supplement the family income by selling home-made sweetmeats in the market, and by the sale of surplus vegetables grown in the land around the house, although this garden produce is mainly for home consumption. The three elder sons, who are all junior civil servants, also make occasional contributions to the household budget. Aside from the cost of renting the house-plot, clothing, food, and water and electricity charges form the major items of expenditure. The best part of the little money which remains after these bills have been paid is spent on entertainment of various

---

[22] The Thais do not make a habit of entertaining outsiders in their homes, although visitors may call in for brief periods to chat and drink tea.

kinds; this includes the purchase of lottery tickets, of cigarettes, and betel-nut for Khun Siri's wife, occasional visits to the cinema for the younger members of the family, and trips to local beauty spots for everyone. And finally a proportion of this small cash-surplus is spent on merit-making activities, such as those described below.

During the year of my fieldwork in Ayutthaya (1966–7) Khun Siri Imchai made the following religious expenditures.

Date	Occasion	Amount contributed (in *baht*)
29 November 1966	*The cremation of the wife of the Pratuchai school*	10

Although the headmaster was Khun Siri's social superior they had become quite friendly; Khun Siri's position in the Education Section had first brought the two men into contact.

28 December	*The* Nak Tham *examinations at* Wat *Monthop, Ayutthaya*	10

The *Chao Khana Amphoe* (Ecclesiastical District Head) who was in charge of the proceedings had asked all his lay friends and acquaintances in town, as well as members of the *phuak Wat* Monthop to make contributions in cash or in kind towards the provision of refreshments for the examinees throughout the day. The *Nai Amphoe* (District Head) and most of the officials from the Education Section were present for the sermon given on the first day by the *Chao Khana Amphoe*. Khun Siri who was acting as unofficial organizer of the affair spent the whole of the first day and part of the second at *Wat* Monthop, where he helped to serve the drinks, to give out the examination papers and to fix up the microphone through which announcements were made to the assembly at large. His wife and her two nieces helped the other womenfolk to prepare soft drinks and food, some of which they had themselves contributed.

1 January 1967	*New Year's Day celebration at* Wat *Mongkhon Bophit*	16.50

Several hundred people gathered outside the *vihara* at 6 a.m. on New Year's Day to present rice to the 150 *bhikkhus* who had been invited to attend by the officials in the Division of Education. Most of these monks came from nearby monasteries. Khun Siri and his wife brought a tureen of rice (cost unknown) as well as several tins of condensed milk, some salted eggs, and sweetmeats bought in the market beforehand. They stationed themselves at one of the tables which had been set up on either side of the road leading to the *wat* and placed a portion of this food into the bowl of each *bhikkhu* who filed past.

| 2 February | Thet Mahachat *at* Wat *Prasat* | 5 |

The ceremony was organized at the instigation of the abbot, a friend of Khun Siri's, with a view to raising funds to complete the *bot*. Khun Siri went to listen to the Thai version of the recitation which took place in the afternoon.

| 8 February | *A fair held at* Wat *Phanan* *Choeng to mark the Chinese* *New Year* | 2 |

This small sum of money was used to purchase the candles, incense sticks and gold leaf necessary to pay homage to the Buddha image. Khun Siri did not patronize the food-stalls or the side-shows, one of which featured a monk renowned for his powers of conferring good health and longevity.

| 9 February | *A visit to Phraphutthabat (The* *Shrine of the Buddha's Footprint)* | 152 |

Khun Siri hired a taxi (140 *baht*) to take himself, his wife and his two youngest children to visit the shrine, which was situated some thirty miles north of Ayutthaya. They made a short detour to see Phra Non (the Reclining Buddha), another famous place of pilgrimage outside Saraburi. Khun Siri was lucky enough to meet a Chinese relative from Hua Ro market who had set up a noodle-stall at Phraphutthabat for the duration of the pilgrimage season. Consequently the family Imchai and myself were treated to a meal 'on the house'. It was however necessary to spend a small sum of money (6 *baht*) on the ritual items placed before the Buddha image, and a further 6 *baht* for cool drinks during the afternoon.

| 24 February | Makha Bucha *ceremony at the* *Buddhist Association Building,* *Ayutthaya* | 5 |

This ceremony commemorates the four miracles which took place three months before the death of the Buddha.[23] As *Makha Bucha* day is a Thai national holiday the ceremony was organized by the civic authorities and presided over by the Provincial Governor. Khun Siri contributed 5 *baht* to the collection taken earlier in the Town Hall, and on the day of the ceremony acted as lay leader of the congregation (i.e. the *makhanayok*) in requesting the Five Precepts from the *bhikkhus*.

| 15 March | *The wedding of his wife's* *niece which took place at* Amphoe *Uthai, Ayutthaya Province* | 20 |

The wedding was a comparatively quiet affair as the bride was a divorcee.

23 See Wells (1960, pp. 78–80).

However, the female members of Khun Siri's household felt it necessary to spend the two days prior to the ceremony at the bride's house, in order to help with the preparations. They took with them several baskets of fruit and vegetables as a contribution to the 'wedding breakfast'. Khun Siri went by boat to the house on the morning of the ceremony, arriving just before the monks from nearby *Wat* Khok Chang began to recite their chants of blessing over the young couple.

| 19 April | *The planting of the* Sima *(Boundary) Stones at* Wat *Kuti Lai* | 5 |

Eight *Sima* or Boundary Stones were buried at the climax of a ceremony held to consecrate the area within which the *bot* is built. Khun Siri spent this sum of money to purchase gold leaf which was affixed to the *Sima* prior to their burial.

| 29 April | *A ceremony held at* Wat *Suwan to celebrate the promotion of the Abbot to a higher honorific rank* | 12 |

Khun Siri, who knew and respected this *bhikkhu* very much, purchased a tin of his favourite China tea to present to him.

| 7 May | *The ordination of a monk at* Wat *Prasat* | 5 |

The ordinand (*nak*) had been ordained as a novice at *Wat* Prasat but had since moved to *Wat* Arun, Bangkok, to pursue his studies. As he was a local boy whose parents still lived in Ayutthaya, he returned to *Wat* Prasat to be ordained as a monk on reaching the eligible age. As the *nak* came of a poor family, the abbot of *Wat* Prasat was to sponsor the ordination, although the guests were also invited to contribute. The names of donors and the amount each gave was broadcast over a loud-speaker by the *waiyawachakon* after the ritual of *upasombot* was performed in the *bot*.

| 9 May | *A chapter of five monks came to chant at Khun Siri's house on behalf of his mother-in-law who was very ill* | 70 |

Three monks came from *Wat* Nang Plum and two from *Wat* Salapun to recite certain portions of the scriptures to make merit for the ailing woman, who did indeed revive some days later. After taking their first meal at the house the monks were each presented with 10 *baht* and the traditional ritual objects of incense-sticks, candles, and lotus-buds.

| 23 May | *Visakha Bucha ceremony held at the Buddhist Association Building, Ayutthaya* | 5 |

This ceremony takes place during the full moon of the sixth month which is the time when the Buddha was born, later attained Enlightenment, and finally died.[24] The ceremony was arranged by the officials of the Education Section. Khun Siri contributed to the collection taken in his office.

1 July	*The ordination of Khun Siri's three elder sons at* Wat *Nang Plum*	8,000

This occasion is described in detail below and need not be considered here, save to say that the sum of money received as contributions from relatives and friends exceeded 8,000 *baht*.

18 July	*The ordination of the adopted son of the Manageress of the Thai City Bank, Ayutthaya*	10

The ceremony took place in Bangkok at *Wat* Maphrao which was near to Khun Wachana's weekend home. She and Khun Siri were firm friends despite the fact that the Manageress was some twenty years junior to him in age, and considerably senior to him in social status. Their friendship was initially founded on the fact that Khun Siri had introduced Khun Wachana to many of the abbots in town, with the result that most of the *wats* had opened acounts with the Thai City Bank.

22 July–19 October	*The provision of* Kaeng Wian *for the monks of* Wat *Nang Plum*	50

The Imchai household provided food for the community of eight monks on three days during Lent. On two of these days the rice was contributed by another member of the *phuak wat*, whilst Khun Siri's family gave the curries and relishes.

22 October	*The presentation of* kathin *robes to* Wat *Kuti Thong, Chiengmai*	10

Khun Siri led the *kathin* party, which consisted of many members of *phuak wat* Nang Plum as well as other friends and relations of the Imchai family. The abbot of the *wat* in question was also a kinsman of Khun Siri's wife.

Over and above the religious expenditure listed above Khun Siri spent an unknown amount on alms-food for the monks. The women of the household gave morning rice to the monks about ten times each month on average, according to their inclination and the availability of cooked food at the moment when the *bhikkhus* passed the house.

If we compare the merit-making activities of Khun Siri with those of Khun Thep we can see that the former not only spent more time on religious

---

[24] See Wells (1960, pp. 71–2).

affairs, but also a larger amount of money.[25] Leaving aside the exceptional outlay on the *ngan upasombot* (ordination ceremony) for which Khun Siri had been saving money for several years, it can be seen that even so the poorer man spent a larger proportion of his income than his wealthier neighbour. The individual contributions made by Khun Thep, though fewer in number, were somewhat larger in size than the amounts given by Khun Siri. It is interesting to see however that contributions made tend to vary within traditional limits, which is to say that it is unusual for any individual to give less than 10 *baht* or more than 100 *baht* on any one occasion. It follows from this that a layman who is twenty times richer than his neighbour does not necesarily give twenty times more money to merit-making activities.

As the material presented in this chapter shows quite clearly, the amount of money given at any one time also reflects the relative statuses of donor and recipient. An individual tends to make very small contributions, or no contribution at all, to *ngan* sponsored by his superiors, although he may feel obliged to attend the ceremony. Khun Siri for example, attended the cremation of the Governor's mother but gave no monetary contribution, as he was of much lower social status than the Governor and to have given him money would have been both ridiculous and over-familiar. On the other hand a householder of high rank should give generously to his subordinates and dependants although he need not attend the *ngan* in person; appropriately enough, reciprocal exchanges of equivalent amounts of money usually takes place between individuals who are of the same social status.

The two laymen under discussion differ not only in the amount of money they spent but also in the nature of these expenditures. Khun Siri had a wider and more varied circle of acquaintances, as the list of his religious expenses shows quite clearly. Furthermore, unlike Khun Thep, Khun Siri spent several tens of *baht* on religious activities which can be characterized as 'optional' in that they are not associated with the fulfilment of specific social obligations. He did, for example, attend several ceremonies and fairs sponsored by monasteries in town; and he contributed to a *kathin* presentation, and also paid a visit to Phraphutthabat. All of which activities he regarded as great fun, as well as highly meritorious.

It has been argued that the practice of Buddhism inhibits economic growth in that it involves the expenditure of large amounts of money which might otherwise be invested more productively.[26] But as far as the householders of

[25] In the year 1966–7 Khun Siri spent 8,387 *baht* on religious affairs; 8,000 *baht* went towards the cost of ordaining three sons. Over the same period Khun Thep spent 450 *baht* on religious activities.

[26] See Max Weber's *The Sociology of Religion*, trans. Ephraim Fischoff (Beacon Press 1963). Also Pfanner and Ingersoll (1962, pp. 341–61).

Ayutthaya are concerned, my observations suggest that laymen who spend a smaller proportion of their income on religious activities do not necessarily invest their cash surplus in some profit-making business enterprise, nor place it at the bank's disposal. Although Khun Thep had invested some money in land he spent a considerable proportion of his income on consumer goods. This seems to suggest that the practice of Buddhism does not in itself inhibit economic growth, as by and large it is true to say that the Thais have not yet acquired the habit of investment but prefer to spend their money on jewellery or clothes; on supporting relatives and dependents; on merit-making activities, or in the case of the richer and more sophisticated, on acquiring luxury goods from Japan and the West.[27]

THE ORDINATION CEREMONY: ITS ORGANIZATION AND IMPLICATION

I have stated repeatedly in this study that the ordination ceremony is regarded as providing a major opportunity for the accumulation of merit; therefore, in concluding the present chapters, I shall describe the ordination of the three sons of Khun Siri Imchai, Amnuai (25), Chaloem (23), and Kuson (21), which took place at *Wat* Nang Plum on 2 July 1967. I am not in this instance concerned with the actual ritual procedure which has at any rate been described elsewhere.[28] But, I shall attempt to assess some of the social implications of merit-making by analyzing relationships which obtained between the people who attended the *ngan upasombot*, and the material presentations which took place.

It is interesting to see that the monks and laymen who were present at the ceremony, which marked the entry of his sons into the *Sangha*, represented the various chapters in Khun Siri's life-story, which was briefly outlined above. In sociological terms, the *bhikkhus* and householders who were invited can be seen as forming an action-set centred upon Khun Siri as host or *chao phap*, and it seems to me that this kind of sociological grouping is very typical of Thai society where permanent groups are noticeably absent (Wijeyewardene 1967, p. 65) – a point which will be elaborated in the concluding chapter.

The relationships which existed between the people who participated in this ordination ceremony fall into three main types, namely, the relationship between the sponsors and the ordinands, between the host and the

[27] In his book *Economic Change in Thailand since 1850*, Ingram writes: 'No methods have been devised for mobilizing small savings in Thailand. People prefer to keep their savings in the form of gold or cash, and they have not made much use of banks, postal savings or cooperatives for this purpose. Nor are they willing to invest in the stock of a corporation which they do not understand or trust.'

[28] See Wells (1960, pp. 135–50); also Vajirananavarorasa (1963).

bhikkhus, and between the host and his lay guests. Furthermore, each of these relationships can be seen for the purposes of analysis to have three main aspects, the transcendental, the social, and the material, in that an individual makes merit by fulfilling his social obligations which almost inevitably involves the transfer of material goods. The case-material presented in subsequent paragraphs is intended to illustrate these statements more clearly.

It may be recalled that the Thais believe that a youth's ordination makes merit not only for himself but also for his parents who have supported him throughout life. Khun Siri Imchai, who had been planning for several years for one or more of his sons to be ordained, decided that the three eldest boys should enter the *wat* during the Lenten season of 1967. He felt that it was best to hold the *ngan* whilst he and his wife, who were both in their mid-sixties, were still able to finance and organize the affair. He saw the ceremony as having a triple function, in that it would in the first place result in an increment of merit to their spiritual account; secondly it would serve to silence any (imaginary) allegations that he was stingy or negligent in his social duties, and in the third place he said quite frankly that it would help him to recoup some of the money which he had spent over the years in contribution to merit-making ceremonies sponsored by his friends and relatives.

Khun Siri decided that the ceremony should take place at *Wat* Nang Plum, where he was both a tenant and a member of the *kammakan wat*, although he would have preferred his sons to be ordained at *Wat* Salapun whose abbot, besides being a close personal friend was highly respected as a scholar. To ignore the local *wat* however would have been socially maladroit, as it would look like an act of deliberate insult to the *bhikkhus* resident there, and both parties would 'lose face'; the monks, because of the reflection on their competence, and the lay host because of his failure to observe the correct social form. Nevertheless, Khun Siri originally intended that Amnuai should transfer to *Wat* Salapun when the Lenten season began on 22 July, but this scheme was vetoed by his wife who intended to present food to her son throughout *phansa*. She protested that *Wat* Salapun was less conveniently located for her purpose than was *Wat* Nang Plum, a fact which was beyond dispute.

Amnuai, who had spent five years with the civil service, was allowed to spend the whole of the Lenten season in the *Sangha*. His younger brothers on the other hand were only able to stay in the *wat* for the fifteen days' annual holiday to which they were entitled, which meant that they did in fact return to lay life before the Lenten season proper had begun. Sunday 2 July was chosen for the ceremony, not on the advice of an astrologer as is often the case, but because it seemed to be convenient for most of those people directly involved. None of the boys was able, even had he wanted, to spend any time in the monastery prior to the ordination, in order to prepare himself for leaving lay life. Khun Siri was however, determined that they should do him credit and accordingly spent many hours on instructing them as to the phrasing and intonation of the Pali formulae to be used during the ritual.

Amnuai, Chaloem and Kuson were each to be sponsored by a different person, although Khun Siri, who was to sponsor the second boy, was alone regarded as being the *chao phap*, largely because he organized the *ngan*, as well as shouldering any extra expenditures for food and entertainment on the day of the ceremony. The eldest son was to be sponsored by an elderly unmarried female relation on Khun Pa's side of the family. This person was allowed to finance the ordination of the oldest boy in deference to her seniority, not in terms of years (she was three years younger than Khun Siri), but in terms of social placement. Phi Nak had for most of her life held an honourable position as nanny with an aristocratic Bangkok family, and had once spent six years in England when the head of the household was posted to the Thai Embassy in London. Much of her prestige dated back to this sojourn in foreign parts, to which she referred at the slightest opportunity. She felt that it was only right that she should do her humbler relations a favour, by helping to sponsor the ordination of one of their sons, which was also a highly meritorious action in itself.

Twenty-three-year-old Chaloem, who was also employed in the Post Office in Bangkok, was his father's particular responsibility, whilst I volunteered to sponsor Kuson, who was two years younger than myself, with a view to repaying Khun Siri in some measure for the assistance he had given.

The main duty of the sponsor, besides giving his signature to the *nak*'s application form, is to provide the ordinand with the equipment he needs for life in the *wat*. In theory the Buddhist *bhikkhu* requires only a set of robes, an alms-bowl, a razor, one needle and some thread, a filter for straining living organisms from the water he uses, and a girdle to secure his lower robe; these articles are known as the Eight Requisites of a monk. Nevertheless the 28 items listed in Table 5.1 were considered by Khun Siri Imchai to be the minimal requirements, and were provided for each boy by his sponsor.[29] In Hua Ro market place, as in any Thai town, there are shops which specialize in the provision of robes, bowls, fans and other monkish paraphernalia. The crockery, cutlery, and other utensils presented to the candidates for ordination were of ordinary cheap brands which are in common use. Their umbrellas were however, of the old-fashioned Thai type, made from waxed paper and with wooden ribs. Most *bhikkhus* prefer

[29] See Table 5.1.

western-style umbrellas made from nylon and aluminium as they are both lighter and more durable, though somewhat more expensive, being imported from Japan. But Khun Siri prided himself on his strictness in these matters, and considered that an umbrella of the traditional Thai type was not only cheaper, but also more appropriate to a monk. According to the same principles the towels, flannels and quilts presented were of a plain orange or yellow colour, without the garish multi-coloured designs favoured by most laymen.

TABLE 5.1 *Equipment provided for each ordinand by his sponsor*

Article	Price (*in* baht)	Explanation
One set of robes (3 garments)	150	In the early days of Buddhism *bhikkhus* made their own robes from cast-off rags and scraps of cloth. The ready-made robes of today are fashioned from 108 patches as a reminder of this practice (Yalman 1967, p. 157). Robes which are of too brown or too yellow a dye are considered 'impolite'
1 Begging-bowl	30	This is made from iron and fitted with a brass lid
1 Umbrella	13	Made of waxed paper and wood. Used to shelter the *bhikkhu* from both rain and sun
1 Sleeping mat	38	Made from coconut-matting
1 Pillow	25	With a pale yellow cover
Mosquito-net	35	To be suspended from the ceiling above the sleeping-mat
1 *Pinto*	26	An enamel container with several tiers to receive different curries and relishes offered by the householder in the morning
Spittoon	3·25	A round enamel bowl, also used for cigarette-ash, tea-leaves, the stones and peel of fruit eaten, discarded betel-leaves, etc.
Razor	55	Of German make. Used to shave the face each day, and the head and eyebrows once every month
Spoon and fork	7	Made from aluminium
Plate	5	Enamel dinner plate
Khan (ladling bowl)	3	Made of aluminium, with an embossed design. Used in bathing to ladle water over oneself from a large stone storage jar
Sandals	12	Made from rubber, with a thong between the first and second toes. Easily removed when entering a home, or a religious building
Fan	12	Made from hardboard and covered with a cheap silky material. The number of the Buddhist Era (2510) and its Chinese emblem (the Goat) were embroidered upon it. Used when a *bhikkhu* pronounces the Three Refuges formula, and when he gives the Five Precepts (Rajadhon 1961, p. 87)
Monk's bag	15	Made from brightly coloured silk and embroidered as the fan. Used for shopping, and to carry money, books, cigarettes, etc., when the monk leaves the *wat*
Water filter	2	A toy model made from tin, to remind the *bhikkhu* of the prohibition against taking life. I saw a full-scale water filter in regular use at only one monastery, namely *Wat* Senasanaram, the only *Thammayutika* foundation in Ayutthaya

Article	Price (*in* baht)	Explanation
Tin cannister for water	2	A toy model of a utensil used by *bhikkhus* to clean themselves, 'before the invention of lavatory paper'
Towel	10	Of a plain orange colour
Quilt	28	Also as close as possible to saffron in hue, and un-patterned
Flannel face-cloth	28	Orange in colour
Kettle	12	For making tea. Made from aluminium
Cup & saucer	5	Chinese-style, i.e. a small handleless cup with a matching saucer
Bathing robe	10	A plain skirt-like garment. Similar to the lower garment (*sabong*) of the monk's robe
Robes for wear during the ordination ceremony		White in colour. Worn by the ordinand during the ritual before he dons the yellow robe
Upper robe	18	
Lower robe	15	
	Total 420 *baht*	

Several weeks prior to the *ngan upasombot* Khun Siri began to contact *bhikkhus* whom he knew and respected, with a view to inviting them to perform the necessary ritual. However, as the Lenten season was fast approaching many monks whose services he requested were already engaged to perform ordination ceremonies elsewhere on that day. The abbots of both *Wat* Suwandararam and of *Wat* Phanan Choeng were not free to attend for this reason. The names of the *bhikkhus* who eventually came to officiate at the ceremony are set down in Table 5.2, together with some details as to the nature of the relationship with *chao phap*.

It can be seen from a brief examination of this table that several of these *bhikkhus* were invited to attend because they had specific links with Khun Siri. One of them, the abbot of *Wat* Yanasen, is a relative who has become a monk, whilst others are *bhikkhus* with whom Khun Siri became friendly, either during his own period of service in the *Sangha* or since his return to lay life. Some of the monks on this guest-list were invited on the basis of a more generalized sense of obligation the host felt towards them, the *bhikkhus* of *Wat* Nang Plum for instance were included essentially because Khun Siri did not wish to slight them by holding the ceremony elsewhere.

TABLE 5.2 *The cast for the performance of the ordination ceremony which took place at* Wat *Nang Plum, Ayutthaya, on 2 July 1967*

1. The *upacha*
The *bhikkhu* who acted as *upacha* was the abbot of *Wat* Arun, Bangkok, and second in seniority to the Supreme Patriarch in the national ecclesiastical hierarchy. He was a native of Paknampran, Khun Siri's natal village in the south, and had been ordained at *Wat* Paknampran some twenty years earlier than Khun Siri himself. Although the

two men had never met, the fact that they had been born in the same village and had been resident in the same *wat* was felt by Khun Siri to have created some kind of a bond between himself and the *bhikkhu*. Consequently, in the middle of June he travelled to Bangkok to invite (*nimon*) the abbot to act as *upacha* on the appointed day. He had previously put forward an informal request to the *bhikkhu* when the latter attended the ordination of a pupil at *Wat* Prasat on 7 May.

2. The *khu suat* (2 monks)

(*a*) The *Chao Khana Amphoe* (Ecclesiastical District Head) who was the abbot of *Wat* Borommawong, Ayutthaya, acted as *khu suat* (tutor, witness) during the ceremony. He had met Khun Siri, whilst the latter was still a monk, when they had both been invited to take part in a ceremony held in Ayutthaya which had been sponsored by a common friend. The two men had in fact been ordained in the same year, the one in Paknampran and the other in Ayutthaya, and each considered that this might indicate that they had been close friends in some previous existence. The *Chao Khan Amphoe* teased his lay friend by saying that the yellow robe had become too hot for him (*pha ron*) and he had had to return to lay life, at the same time praising Khun Siri's industry and his experience in religious affairs. When this *bhikkhu* had been the abbot of *Wat* Monthop, before receiving promotion to the position of *Chao Khana Amphoe*, Khun Siri had in his spare time collected rent from the tenants of land which belonged to that monastery.

(*b*) The abbot of *Wat* Salapun, who was in addition the Deputy Ecclesiastical Provincial Head (*Rong Chao Khana Changwat*), also performed the role of *khu suat* at the ordination of the Imchai sons. This monk had become very friendly with Khun Siri when he had been the abbot of *Wat* Nang Plum. When he was appointed as *Rong Chao Khana Changwat* he transferred to *Wat* Salapun, to which this office was attached. Khun Siri remarked that the abbot had on several occasions lent him money to help him out of financial difficulties, usually arising from the costs of educating his numerous offspring.

3. The *phra andap*

Khun Siri invited twenty-two monks as *phra andap* who act as a kind of chorus during the ceremony.

Phra andap   1–5 came from *Wat* Nang Plum. Khun Siri invited the abbot, whom he knew personally, and requested that he should bring four other members of the community.

6–7 came from *Wat* Arun, Bangkok. The abbot was asked to bring two *bhikkhus* with him, which is to say that their invitation was of the *kho song* variety.

8–9 came from *Wat* Monthop. One of these monks was the acting abbot of that monastery (i.e. the *phuraksakanthaen chao awat*); both were pupils of the *Chao Khana Amphoe*, and also friends of Khun Siri. Accordingly they received specific invitations (*nimon cho chong*) from the host.

10–12 came from *Wat* Salapun. The abbot who was acting as *khu suat* was invited to delegate two other *bhikkhus* to attend.

13 came from *Wat* Yanasen. This monk was related to Khun Siri's wife, Khun Pa, and was invited on this basis.

14 lived at *Wat* Chonlaprathan, Bangkok, but toured round the provinces teaching morals (*sinlatham*) to pupils in state schools. He had first become acquainted with Khun Siri when the latter began to work in the Division of Education in the Town Hall, Ayutthaya. The monk sometimes stayed with the Imchai family when he was teaching in the area.

15–17 were the abbot of *Wat* Prasat, a friend of Khun Siri's and two junior members of the community invited (*kho song*) by the host.

18–19 came from *Wat* Tuk. Khun Siri asked the abbot, whom he knew slightly, to officiate at the *ngan* and to bring one other monk.

20–21 were the abbot of *Wat* Wongkhong and a more junior member of his community. This abbot was invited largely because he had given me a great deal of help with my research. He was perhaps motivated in part by the fact that I knew the family whose ancestor had restored *Wat* Wongkhong in the 1850s. He stated quite openly that he hoped this charitable gesture would be repeated.

22 was a monk from *Wat* Samwihan whom Khun Siri had invited (*kho song*) to make up the numbers.

NOTE: For detailed explanation of terms *kho song* and *nimon cho chong* see above, chapter 2.

As this material shows, some of the monks, unknown or only slightly known to Khun Siri, were invited to make up the number.[30] In several cases they accompanied a fellow member of the monastic community who had a specific personal tie with the *chao phap*, whilst in other instances monks were invited because they were resident in a *wat* which was situated in the vicinity of the Imchai home.

The *upacha*, the most illustrious member of this chapter of monks, fits into none of these categories as his presence was requested primarily for reasons of prestige, even though Khun Siri might explain the monk's being invited with reference to the bond which he felt to exist between them because of their common birthplace. It is unlikely, however, that the abbot of *Wat* Arun would have even heard of the ordination of Khun Siri's sons had he not been invited, let alone have felt slighted on this score. On the other hand, the monks of Ayutthaya who were close friends of the *chao phap*

---

[30] In fact, as Vajirananavarorasa writes (1963, p. 4): 'five bhikkhus were enough to form the quorum and carry out the processes of ordination. This has been practised up to the present time.' Nevertheless most laymen like to invite as many monks to officiate at this ceremony as they can afford. Wells writes (1960, p. 141): 'For any ceremony involving only the Sangha the favourite number is 25 – allowing for five monks for each one hundred present at the First Council after the Buddha's death.'

would almost certainly have felt offended had they not been invited to officiate at the *ngan*.

At the close of the ceremony, offerings of money and material goods were given to the *bhikkhus* who had taken part, the costs of these presentations being shared equally between the three sponsors. It can be seen that each sponsor spent approximately 720 *baht*, taking into account the money spent on equipping the new *bhikkhus* (see Tables 5.1 and 5.3).

TABLE 5.3   *Offerings presented to the* bhikkhus *at the close of the ordination ceremony*

The Monk	The offering	The cost (*in* baht)
The *upacha* received:	A lotus bud, two candles and three incense-sticks; cigarettes, China tea, and other groceries; a vacuum flask; a chit for 100 *baht* to be presented to the *waiyawachakon*	150
The *khu suat* each received:	Ritual items and groceries identical with the above; a chit for the sum of 50 *baht* to be presented to the *waiyawachakon*	100 (for each offering)
The *phra andap* each received:	Ritual items and groceries identical to those given to the *upacha* and *khu suat*; a chit for 10 *baht* to be presented to the *waiyawachakon*	25 (for each offering)
	Total cost of presentations was 900 *baht*; the expenses were divided equally between the three sponsors	

The material given in Table 5.4 shows that, in all, 266 laymen and women contributed a total of 12,040 *baht* at the time of the ordination ceremony, a sum which more than covered its costs. Several weeks before the ceremony was due to take place Khun Siri had sent out over forty invitation cards to his relatives and friends. Each of the twenty-three people on the list of contributors, to whose *ngan tham bun* Khun Siri had at some time contributed, received an invitation to attend. The remaining 28 cards were sent to other kinsmen and acquaintances with whom he also had close personal ties. Khun Siri felt that they should receive some notification of the ceremony as they would wish to pay their respects to him, a process which in this instance involves contributing an appropriate sum of money. Khun Siri in fact sent invitations to all people from whom he felt a contribution was justified. All except two of these did indeed respond in a positive manner. The majority of these individuals came in person to the *wat* whilst those who were for some reason unable to attend sent their contributions through a third party or by post. The two laymen invited who made no contribution, both relatives of Khun Pa, lived at some distance away, and consequently the links between themselves and the Imchai household had become rather attenuated.[31]

The list of subscribers shows quite clearly that the majority of laymen who made contributions had not in fact been invited. For several of them the ordination ceremony provided an opportunity to repay Khun Siri for the assistance he had given them in their business activities; many of the Chinese shopkeepers in Hua Ro, for example, contributed to the costs of the ordination as a way of showing their gratitude for the help the host had given them in their dealings with the Thai bureaucracy.

Unbidden though not entirely unexpected contributions came from some of Khun Siri's social superiors whom he had not presumed to invite. The Manageress of the Thai City Bank who contributed 500 *baht* was of this number. Khun Siri expressed the view that one could not invite such people as it would look like begging; though one might hope for a contribution, one should not expect it, as the *phu 'yai* were within their rights to withhold.

TABLE 5.4 *Details of the contributions made by lay guests at the ordination of Khun Siri Imchai's three sons at* Wat *Nang Plum, Ayutthaya, on 2 July 1967*

This list is the translation of the one which was made out for me by Khun Siri Imchai himself. I have not however written out the names in full for reasons of space, although I have indicated which of the subscribers were female, and which of them came from the Chinese community of Hua Ro. It will be noted that Khun Siri made two errors in his use of arabic numerals; numbers 39 and 66 are omitted, so that there are in fact only 72 contributors listed here. Khun Siri was accustomed to using Thai numerals, and chose this unfamiliar arabic system in making out the list, largely in deference to me.

I have also emulated Khun Siri Imchai in giving fewer details about the people who gave less money; he said that he would keep a fuller record of these donations for his own use, but when I left the field had not yet done so. He said that most of these individuals were local people, relatives, friends and colleagues with whom he was in regular interaction. He had sent invitations to only eight out of this number, as he felt that it was by and large unnecessary to waste money in this way upon people with whom he was so intimately involved. In addition, some of these smaller contributions came from friends and workmates of the three boys who were being ordained. Furthermore, several friends in the *Sangha* who had been unable to attend the *ngan* owing to prior engagements gave small donations; the Abbot of *Wat* Suwan for example gave 20 *baht*; the Deputy Abbot of *Wat* Phanan Choeng contributed 30 *baht* towards the costs of this ceremony.

---

[31] Distance does not inevitably weaken ties of family and friendship. As the list of contributors shows, several lay guests travelled considerable distances (from Chiengmai and Paknampran) to fulfil their social obligations to Khun Siri.

Details of the contributions made by lay guests at the ordination of Khun Siri Imchai's three sons at Wat Nang Plum, Ayutthaya, *on 2 July 1967*

Contributor (by number)	Size of contribution (in baht)	Place of residence	Occupation	Relationship to Khun Siri	Nature of previous assistance given by Khun Siri to contributor
1 (female)	1,500	England	Research student	Friendship & respect	—
2*	300	Samutprakan (Central Thailand)	Civil servant (ex-Governor of Ayutthaya)	Wife's relative	At merit-making ceremonies
3* (female)	500	Ayutthaya	Bank manager	Mutual respect	In business[a]
4*	200	Chiengmai	Civil servant (Governor of Chiengmai)	Wife's relative	At ordination ceremony
5*	300	Ayutthaya	Accountant at tobacco factory	Nephew	At marriage ceremony
6	680	Bangkok	Friends of two elder sons	—	—
7	300	Ayutthaya	Businessman	*Dek wat* at *Wat* Nang Plum	Helped to rear as a child
8*	200	Paknampran (S. Region)	Businessman	Relative	Taught him as a child
9* (female)	200	Paknampran	Businessman	Sister-in-law	Helped at ordination
10*	200	Bangkok	Author & journalist	Became friends as monks	Canvassed for him during election to House of Representatives (1957)[b]
11* (Chinese woman)	200	Hua Ro, Ayutthaya	Property-owner	Relative	Helped at marriage
12 (Chinese)	100	Hua Ro	Hotel keeper	Mutual respect	Helped in business
13*	100	Ayutthaya	Restauranteur	Mutual respect	Helped in business
14*	100	Ayutthaya	Civil servant (Education Section)	Mutual respect	Helped at work
15* (Chinese)	100	Hua Ro	Bread & cake shop	Mutual respect	Helped in shop
16*	100	Hua Ro	Shopkeeper	Mutual respect	Helped in business
17 (Chinese)	100	Hua Ro	Radio shop	Mutual respect	Helped in business
18 (Chinese)	100	Hua Ro	Businessman	Mutual respect	Helped in business

* Indicates those laymen who received invitations.

[a] Khun Siri contributed 10 *baht* to the ordination of this woman's adopted son which took place at *Wat* Maphrao Bangkok on 18 July.
[b] The last election to this ideally elective body took place in 1957. The House of Representatives is a legislative assembly.

Contributor (by number)	Size of contribution (in baht)	Place of residence	Occupation	Relationship to Khun Siri	Nature of previous assistance given by Khun Siri to contributor
19*	100	Bangkok	Housekeeper	She reared one of ordinands as a child	—
20 (female)	100	Hua Ro	Shopkeeper	Relative	—
21	100	Bangkok	Shopkeeper	Relative	—
22 (female sponsor)	720	Bangkok	Housekeeper	Relation	—
23 (female)	100	Ayutthaya	Shopkeeper	Relative & live in same house	—
24	100	Ayutthaya	Schoolteacher	Taught two of sons	—
25	100	Ayutthaya	Schoolteacher	Taught youngest son	—
26*	100	Ayutthaya	Shopkeeper	Mutual respect	Helped with *ngan tham bun*
27* (female Chinese)	50	Bangkok	Shopkeeper	Relative	Helped at cremation ceremony
28*	150	Ayutthaya	Civil servant (Education Section)		—
29	50	Nonburi (C. Region)	Civil servant (retired)	Wife's relative	—
30	50	Ayutthaya	Secondary school teacher	Taught sons	—
31 (Chinese woman)	50	Hua Ro, Ayutthaya	Shopkeeper	Relative	Helped in business
32	50	Bangkok	Civil servant (G.P.O.)	Friend of son	—
33*	50	Ayutthaya	Civil servant	Respect	Helped in merit-making
34* (Chinese)	50	Hua Ro	Owns shop & hotel	Respect	Helped in business
35* (Chinese)	50	Hua Ro	Printer	Relative	Helped with ceremonies
36* (Chinese)	80	Hua Ro	Dentist	Relative	Helped in business
37 (female)	50	Bangkok	Civil servant	Niece	—
38*	50	Ayutthaya	Civil servant	Workmate	—
40*	50	Ayutthaya	Civil servant	Workmate (Education Section)	Helped in merit-making
41*	50	Banpong (C. Region)	Shopkeeper	Went to school together	—
42	60	Bangkok	Shopkeeper	Mutual respect	—
43	40	Auytthaya	Shopkeeper	Mutual respect	Helped in business
44	40	Ayutthaya	Shopkeeper	Mutual respect	—
45	40	Ayutthaya	Shopkeeper	Mutual respect	—

* Indicates those laymen who received invitations.

Contributor (by number)	Size of contri- bution (in baht)	Place of residence	Occupation	Relationship to Khun Siri	Nature of previous assistance given by Khun Siri contributor
46*	40	Bangkok	Civil servant	Born in Paknampran	Helped with ordination
47*	40	Bangkok	Civil servant	Mutual respect	Helped at *ngan tham bun*
48	40	Bangkok	Civil servant	Helped Khun Siri's sons	—
49	40	Ayutthaya	Shopkeeper	Relative	Helped in business
50*	40	Bangkok	Civil servant	Wife's relative	—
51 (Chinese)	40	Ayutthaya	Shopkeeper	Friend of son	—
52*	40	Ayutthaya	Shopkeeper	Fellow member of *kammakan Wat* Nang Plum	—
53*	40	Hua Ro, Ayutthaya	Photographer's shop	Mutual respect	Helped at marriage
54* (female)	40	Bangkok	Shopkeeper	She was *upathak*c when Khun Siri was a monk	Helped at several *ngan tham bun*
55*	40	Ayutthaya	Shopkeeper	Friend	Helped in business
56	40	Ayutthaya	Civil servant	Mutual respect	—
57	40	Ayutthaya	Hotel-owner	Relative	Helped in business
58*	40	Ayutthaya	Shopkeeper	Mutual respect	Helped with merit-making
59*	60	Ayutthaya	Shopkeeper	Relation	—
60* (Chinese)	40	Ayutthaya	Shopkeeper	Mutual respect	Helped with merit-making
61*	40	Ayutthaya	Shopkeeper	Mutual respect	Helped with merit-making
62*	40	Ayutthaya	Shopkeeper	Relative	Helped with merit-making
63	40	Ayutthaya	Shopkeeper	Relative	Helped with merit-making
64* (Chinese)	40	Ayutthaya	Shopkeeper	Neighbour	Helped in merit-making
65*	40	Ayutthaya	Shopkeeper	Mutual respect	Helped in merit-making
67* (female)	40	Ayutthaya	Shopkeeper	Wife's relation	Helped in merit-making
68	40	Ayutthaya	Cinema manager	Went to school together in Bangkok	—
69	40	Ayutthaya	Shopkeeper	Mutual respect	—
70	40	Ayutthaya	Shopkeeper	Mutual respect	—
71	40	Ayutthaya	Civil servant	Taught in same school	—
72	40	Ayutthaya	Shopkeeper	Friends	Helped in business
73	40	Ayutthaya	Hotel-owner	Friends	Helped in business

* Indicates those laymen who received invitations.

c See above p. 157.

Contributor (by number)	Size of contribution in baht)	Place of residence	Occupation	Relationship to Khun Siri	Nature of previous assistance given by Khun Siri to contributor
74*	40	Ayutthaya	Civil servant	Workmate	Helped with merit-making
75*	40	Ayutthaya	Chemist	Mutual respect	Helped in business and with ceremonies
77	40	Ayutthaya	Shopkeeper	Mutual respect	Helped in business
78	40	Ayutthaya	Shopkeeper	Mutual respect	Helped in business

* Indicates those laymen who received invitations.

In addition, 190 people gave contributions of 30 *baht* or less:
  22 people gave 30 *baht* each; Khun Siri had helped 9 of these people with merit-making
  133 people gave 20 *baht* each; Khun Siri had helped 60 of these people with merit-making
  35 people gave 10 *baht* each; Khun Siri had helped 7 of these people with merit-making
The total amount of money received was 12,040 *baht*.
The total amount of money expended was 11,515 *baht*.

Khun Siri claimed to have spent approximately 8,000 *baht* from his own pocket on the ordination ritual and the associated ceremonies of *tham khwan* (calling the *khwan*) and blessing the ordinands, which were held on the day prior to the *ngan upasombot*. Several days after the ordination ceremony the new monks took part in the ceremony of *Chalong Phra Mai* (Celebrating the new *Bhikkhu*) which was also sponsored by Khun Siri.

The major items of expenditure associated with the ordination (*in* baht)

	baht
Total cost of equipping the ordinands	2,500
Total cost of offerings made to the officiant monks	900
Travelling expenses of *upacha* and two other monks from *Wat* Arun, Bangkok (by taxi)	200
Food costs during this period (i.e. this includes money spent on food for days prior to ceremony and afterwards, as many friends and relatives lodged with Khun Siri, and also covers the costs of entertaining the guests on the day of the ordination)	4,100
Cost of soft and alcoholic drinks	1,250
Cost of live orchestra for *tham khwan* ritual (Khun Siri spent a further 600 *baht* at least on hiring the ritual expert, paying for decorations, film show, etc. He did not account for this sum here)	300
Miscellaneous expenditures (flowers, candles, etc.)	285
Offerings to 9 monks who performed blessing chant on evening prior to ordination	180
Costs of food for 3 monks during their sojourn in *wat* and money spent on *kaeng wian* during Lent 1967	1,800

Finally, groups of the ordinands' friends and workmates, who had similarly received no invitation, clubbed together to make a contribution to the cost of the ceremony marking the boys' entry in the *Sangha*.

It can be seen from this description of the personnel – both monk and lay – who were involved in the ordination ceremony sponsored by Khun Siri Imchai that merit-making ceremonies provide people with an opportunity to reaffirm and strengthen the social ties which exist between them. An individual makes merit by fulfilling his social obligations, which is to say that the actions which an anthropologist sees as tending to maintain social solidarity are regarded as meritorious.

In inviting *bhikkhus* to perform the ritual of *upasombot* Khun Siri made merit by enacting an essential aspect of the householder's role as supporter of the *Sangha*; in inviting some *bhikkhus* who were at the same time relatives or personal friends he fulfilled his two-fold obligation to them. The lay guests, on the other hand, expressed their continuing attachment to Khun Siri by contributing to the merit-making ceremony of which he was the host. The sponsors and their respective *nak* also fulfilled their mutual obligations to one another; the former by financing the ordination, the latter by becoming ordained and thus acquiring merit both for themselves and for the sponsor. Finally, all those who participated in this ceremony in any way were at the same time expressing their commitment to the cardinal values of the Thai social order which are rooted in the practice of Theravada Buddhism.

What in summary can we say about the wider implications of merit-making? We have seen that material aid whether directed towards monk or layman brings merit. Perhaps one of the major differences between these two types of transaction lies in the fact that in giving to a monk merit is the prime motivation, whilst in supporting kin or clients merit is conceived of as a by-product of social obligations fulfilled, rather than the prime *raison d'être* of the transaction.

Only where obligations exist do material transfers bring merit; a layman is obliged to support a monk, a patron to give material assistance to his clients, every man is obliged to help his relatives and friends in time of need. In the first two cases the relationship is asymmetrical and the material transfer is not reciprocal, whilst in the third case, where there is little or no status disparity between the parties concerned, reciprocity is the unwritten – even sometimes as in the case of Khun Siri the written – rule. One thing which all these transactions have in common is that they are the outcome of stable and established relationships; even the relationship between monk and householder may be understood as stable, though it is not specific, in that their relative status is unchanging and permanent, and indeed it is this inherent spiritual disparity which forms the basis for intercouse between them.

The fact that in all these relationships rights and duties are entailed on either side distinguishes these transactions most sharply from purely commercial interaction – as between a shopkeeper and his customer – where economic advantage is at a premium on both sides; where the relationship has no degree of permanency; where neither party experiences any sense of obligation towards the other; and where the question of making merit is irrelevant. Presentations such as solicitary gifts to potential patrons whose interest and support may thus be engaged can be seen as a transitional type of transaction, in terms of the variables of merit, moral obligation, permanency and reciprocity with which we have been concerned.

The Buddhist value of merit can thus be regarded as a conservative and stabilizing force in society rather than the reverse. The quest for merit does not mean that one relinquishes all social ties and consequent volitional actions, but rather that one tries if possible to perform meritorious actions which often merely means fulfilling one's social obligations.

6
The loosely structured social system: red herring or *rara avis*?

A recurrent theme in Thai anthropological literature has been a concern with the alleged 'looseness' of Thai society. Since the publication of John F. Embree's seminal article 'Thailand: A Loosely Structured Social System' (in the *American Anthropologist* 52, 1950), his assertion that Thai society is loosely structured has achieved fairly general recognition and acceptance. Embree maintained that in Thailand, by contrast with Japan where the social system is 'closely structured', 'considerable variation in individual behaviour is sanctioned' and that the Thais act in an individualistic manner within their 'loosely integrated social structure'.

More recently a number of students of Thai society have assumed a somewhat more critical stance (see Evers, 1969), but on the whole they have chosen to refine rather than reject the concept of 'loose-structuring', despite the fact that most of them recognize that Embree's knowledge of the Thai situation and his theoretical tools may have been less than adequate. On the whole their attempts to cope with this crippling conceptual legacy only tend to confirm my own opinion that Embree's formulation has been a barrier rather than a stimulus to productive research into the Thai social situation. Nonetheless, we should try to see why the pursuit of this red herring has exercised the talents of so many for so long; what are the precise referents of the concept 'loosely structured'? Is it intended to be an analytical or descriptive device, applicable to Thai society as a whole or only in part? What is the reason for this posited structural singularity? In examining these questions it may be possible to shed some new light on old material, and at the same time to place the monk–layman relationship, which has been the focus of this study, in a broader social context.

Most of the anthropologists to whose work I shall be referring in subsequent paragraphs are represented in the collection of essays cited above, *Loosely Structured Social System: Thailand in Comparative Perspective* (ed. Hans-Dieter Evers, Cultural Report Series no. 17, Yale University Southeast Asia Studies 1969). On the positive side it must be said for most of these authors that on the descriptive level their work is almost always accurate and perceptive; where they seem to me to err is in seeing these features as comprising 'a loosely structured social system', which is, besides, unique to Thailand, and in laying the burden of responsibility for this structural peculiarity at the door of Theravada Buddhism. These shortcomings are in good measure attributable to the insularity of the anthropologists concerned, as they make very little attempt to place Thai society in comparative perspective, either in terms of relevant ethnographic data or current anthropological developments.

This now controversial term 'loosely structured' is usually employed to describe certain features of Thai social roles and their configuration, or absence of configuration, in permanent groups. With regard to the first point it is generally maintained – and the material I have presented would support this – that social roles are relatively simple and unspecialized in content, relatively undemanding in terms of the qualifications required by individual actors. These are features which we have come to expect in role-systems of relatively 'small scale' societies such as we are faced within Thailand. A characteristic which is perhaps less generally recognized, but which seems on reflection entirely predictable is that this simplicity of roles is associated with remarkable ease of movement between them. This stands in direct contradiction to Nadel's statement that 'It is probably true to say that simpler societies lean towards compulsory, and complex societies towards voluntary, recruitment, which lends to the former their more static nature, and to the latter their greater mobility' (Nadel 1951, p. 152). Associated with a high degree of mobility between roles is a considerable emphasis upon their relative status. I would agree with Mosel when he writes of Thai society that 'statuses associated with roles can almost always be distinguished in terms of higher or lower . . . in a sense we might say that in Thai society there are two highly generalized roles: superior and subordinate. Given any two statuses or clusters of social characteristics the average Thai can easily make paired comparison judgements' (Mosel 1965, pp. 4–5). The relationship between superior and subordinate varies very little in content or in outward forms whatever the sphere of activity may be: 'the superior is benevolent, calmly self-assured, authoritative (rather than authoritarian) whilst the subordinate is respectful, attentive, helpful but not necessarily obedient (although face-to-face disobedience would be unthinkable)' (Mosel 1965, p. 5). A person has in effect very similar kinds of relationship with his patron, his teacher, a senior relative and a Buddhist monk, all of whom occupy a position of superiority with respect to him. These relationships tend moreover to have a material component, which is to say that the inferior party receives not only advice and sponsorship but also more tangible benefits in the form of financial support. The details of the religious expenditures of certain lay informants given in chapter 5 illustrate one aspect of this material assistance in operation. With respect to the relationship between monk and householder it should be remembered that, though the former can be regarded as the patron of the latter, the benefits he confers are of a spiritual kind, whereas support of a more tangible nature – money, food, clothing and so on – passes in an upwards direction from the inferior party.

Another feature of the role-playing in Thai society which has been singled out for special mention is the great emphasis placed upon the 'etiquette of one's station' (Hanks 1962, p. 1256), which is to say upon the formal rather than upon the substantive characteristics of a particular role. Earlier in the present study I mentioned that on his ordination the average Thai boy assumes immediately, the mien and deportment appropriate to a monk. Indeed as subsequent discussion revealed, little else may be demanded of a monk, other than that he is orthodox in these outward forms. The monk who fulfils these minimum requirements for conformity is moreover allowed considerable leeway in the interpretation of his role. This 'ritualization' of roles (Gluckman 1962, p. 26) in Thai society is not as in some other societies an outcome of their 'multiplex' nature, but is an aspect of their relative lack of specificity, which entails in turn their being fairly easily assumed or cast aside. Mosel has suggested that this stylization and the emphasis on etiquette which is apparent in all spheres of activity, is designed to facilitate movement between roles by preventing the actor's becoming committed to any one of them (Mosel 1965, p. 10). This would concur with Hanks' view that because of this ability to remain detached the Thais are able to 'equip themselves for mobility and transient position. To a greater extent than in the West the insignia transform the person' (Hanks 1962, p. 1252).

My own data would support this contention that the Thais do indeed place a very great emphasis on diacritical role attributes. Unlike Hanks, Mosel and others however, I would hesitate to imply that this emphasis is deliberate and purposive, but would suggest merely that the importance attached to etiquette and other distinguishing features is consonant with the ease of role-shift in Thai society. Although it makes no sense to see this feature as instrumental in the process of social mobility, I believe it can be thought of as a necessary concomitant, in that it seems probable that in such a fluid situation it is necessary to define more sharply which role an individual is playing at any one time, particularly when there is so strong an emphasis on disparities in status. In some instances this stylization appears to result from an interest in elaboration for its own sake, as is the case for example when in rural settlements the prefix *thit* is placed before the names of laymen who have seen some service in the *wat*, even though their monkly career may have been of very short duration, and may have no repercussions on their subsequent behaviour and social position. Interestingly enough this practice was not followed in Ayutthaya, where there were many other criteria of differentiation, occupational, ethnic, residential, socio-economic, according to which individuals might be categorized.

These aspects of role-playing in Thai society – aspects which have received ample illustration from the data presented in previous chapters – are the very features which cause it to be characterized as 'loosely structured' by those anthropologists who find this label a useful one. The fact that role-playing individuals rarely form corporate groups of any degree of permanency is interpreted by these scholars as being a further aspect of loose-structuring, which in the opinion of many has 'the Buddhist emphasis on primacy of individual action and responsibility' (Phillips 1967, pp. 363–4) as its source. Again, and at the descriptive level the material used in this study provides evidence in support of the assertion that in Thai society permanent groups appear to be relatively rare, but in the matter of interpretation and analysis I would diverge from my colleagues in not sharing their readiness to invoke the religious ethic to explain this alleged antipathy to co-operative action.

Let us examine the issues involved more closely. The question as to whether Theravada Buddhism actively promotes loose relationships – in any sense of the term – will be discussed below. In the first instance I submit that it might be possible, by the use of comparative ethnographic material, to shed new light on the problem of the rarity of on-going corporate groups in Thailand. Leach's study of the Sinhalese village Pul Eliya immediately comes to mind as providing a useful analysis of the factors which promote or inhibit co-operation in a social situation which is in many respects identical with that of rural Thai settlements, on their experience of which most students of Thai society base their generalizations.[1] Leach has shown for example that in Pul Eliya social groups are formed to protect individual interests in scarce property-holdings, and to ensure the day-to-day co-operation essential for the maintenance of the irrigation system. These factors are not however operative in village Thailand where neither technological specialization nor economic need requires the formation of groups to ensure continuous co-operation, and to protect the interests of coming generations. As made clear in my introductory chapter, Thailand has a tradition of abundant natural resources, an economy in which for centuries labour and not land was the scarce factor. However, with a population in-

[1] The Sinhalese have a bilateral kinship system similar to that of the Thais: all children inherit from both parents. (Leach 1961, p. 67.) Kinship is similarly made the idiom for social co-operation, which is to say that in Sinhalese society kinsmen co-operate and, conversely, that people who are in close contact usually come to regard one another as kin. It should be remembered that most of the generalizations concerning the nature of the Thai social system are based on fieldwork carried out in rural areas.

creasing at the rate of over 3% per annum, this situation clearly cannot be of long duration. Already in many areas considerable pressure upon land is reported and it may well be that as this becomes more critical a situation not unlike that described by Leach for village Ceylon may become operative.

Certain features of monastic organization in Thailand, as we have seen, reflect the country's general material abundance. It may be recalled that, outside Lent, Buddhist *bhikkhus* move very freely between monasteries, and that only the abbot, who as office-holder has a stake in a particular monastery, feels committed to remaining in one place. This general freedom of movement is permissible largely by reason of the fact that wherever the monk resides he receives an adequate amount of food, money, clothing and so on, from laymen living in the vicinity. It is generally true to say that individual *wats* are not differentiated with regard to their access to scarce economic benefits, and hence there has been no need to restrict entry into certain monastic communities.

In certain areas of Bangkok however, there have been some significant changes in this traditional pattern of balanced supply and demand. The decline in general interest in religious affairs in the metropolitan area, combined with a number of other factors which were described above, means that many of the larger monasteries are forced to rationalize their economic behaviour in order to make the monastic estates into a 'going concern'. In these circumstances the community tends to become more 'closed' and cohesive, and there is some evidence to suggest that it is more difficult for a newcomer to gain access because of the pressure on the limited resources available.[2]

Following the principles employed in Leach's analysis we can discern the forces which compel, prevent or render irrelevant social co-operation, in other areas of action. In the political sphere for example, it is notable that until relatively recently the formation of permanent groups with political functions has been restricted to those aristocratic families who traditionally took the initiative in managing Thailand's affairs. Among this privileged minority, as might be expected, there has traditionally been a much greater interest in recording genealogies, with the view to establishing rights to titles and property, and excluding false claimants.

It is generally agreed that most people in Thailand, which is to say, the vast rural majority, are not 'involved in politics' which is regarded as 'properly the affair of politicians, or, more broadly, of the ruling class' (Wilson 1962, pp. 57–8). It should be added that the political elite have traditionally preferred urban to rural society, and have consequently always resided in the capital, near to the seat of power. There is in fact no rural

[2] See above, chapter 4.

landlord class as such, and the majority of cultivators own the land which they farm. Furthermore, the fact that the country has escaped colonization may have inhibited the development of political awareness which might have resulted in the formation of groups with political functions.

Although it seems clear that permanent groups are not an important feature of Thai society it is nevertheless inevitable that short-term co-operative associations should be formed from time to time. In this article 'Some Aspects of Rural Life in Thailand' Wijeyewardene writes that Thai society 'is perhaps more satisfactorily characterized as pragmatic, with organisation directed to specific and limited ends' (Wijeyewardene 1967, p. 65). He concludes on a similar note by saying that 'organisations arise to fulfil specific tasks but there is no tradition of on-going associations which may be called on to fulfil any task which might arise' (Wijeyewardene 1967, p. 83).

Organizations of this nature are of course familiar from many anthropological studies of village Thailand; the mechanism for reciprocal exchange of labour between farming households, known as *ao raeng* (to take strength) is perhaps the one most frequently described (Kaufman 1960, p. 30). Furthermore, as we have seen from the foregoing chapters, religious observances and activities also necessitate the formation of co-operative units wider than the individual family or household. The party of laymen which is formed to take *kathin* robes to the *wat* at the close of the Lenten season for example, is sociologically very similar to the gathering of householders who attended the ordination of Khun Siri Imchai's three sons (an event which was described in detail in chapter 5). Both these groupings which came into being for a specific purpose conform to the concept of an 'action-set' as defined by Mayer (Mayer 1966, p. 108 and passim) in that the component individuals are all related, directly or indirectly, to the central ego, although 'a wide variety of bases for linkage are involved' (Mayer 1966, p. 108), which is to say that the grouping includes ego's kinsmen, colleagues, and neighbours, as well as other individuals related to him only through the latter, with whom he is in more direct contact. It might thus be claimed that Theravada Buddhism, in practice, serves to promote social co-operation between individual actors, and that 'the Buddhist emphasis on primacy of individual action and individual responsibility' does not, as Phillips would claim, constitute 'a major source of loose relationships' (Phillips 1967, pp. 363–4). It is certainly true that the *khammic* actions of each actor are believed to determine his future status, and that no Saviour can intervene on his behalf. But the contention made by Phillips that 'The whole complex cosmology relating to the accumulation of merit and demerit is phrased in terms of the individual's lonely journey through cycles of intermediate existences working out his own moral destiny' (Phillips

185

1967, p. 363), bears no relationship to the situation on the ground. As is, I think, abundantly clear from the data already presented, the emphasis in merit-making is not upon the sacrificial aspect of renouncing ones' ties and material possessions, but rather upon giving for a specific return, whether tangible or intangible; the phrase *tham di: dai di* (Do good: receive good) is given a very literal interpretation on a practical level.[3]

There is one further element of the 'loose-structure' controversy which may be mentioned; several students of Thai society have attributed the absence of permanent groups and the relative ease with which interpersonal links are broken to the particular personality dispositions of the average Thai (Phillips 1965). I have suggested on the other hand that there is little pressure upon individuals in Thai society to form permanent groups because there is no permanent need, arising from economic or political considerations, to do so.

My observations further suggest that the Thais are certainly not more individualistic, and indeed probably rather less so than other people. The deference given to seniority of age, the assumption that if you have lived longer then you automatically know better – an attitude which is closely related to the relatively undifferentiated and, until recently, unchanging economic situation – certainly does not suggest that the Thais are a nation of radicals. There is in fact very little value placed on innovation or originality – even at the university level teaching is largely by rote; discussion is not encouraged nor demanded, and the pupil accepts the word of his teacher. Indeed the Thais recognize and approve of their own ability to *lian baep* (to imitate or copy), a talent which enables them to adapt themselves very easily, at least as far as outward forms are concerned, to alien cultural influences from the West, or increasingly, from Japan.

With more general reference to the fluidity of Thai society, I would suggest that it is important to distinguish between the possibilities for upward mobility, and the desire or ambition to achieve it. Leach's dictum that 'a conscious or unconscious wish to gain power is a very general motive in human affairs' (Leach 1954, p. 10) does not hold good for Thai society. This lack of incentive is largely explicable by reference to the political and economic circumstances already described. Many observers have noted that the Thais exhibit a high degree of 'self-acceptance' or, less flatteringly, that 'their self-approval borders on narcissism' (Mosel 1965, p. 4). Cynical observers have expressed the view that the imminent 'population explosion' might be of some service to the nation, in that by creating a little salutary

---

[3] The fact that *khammic* reaction may be immediate or delayed may make it easier for the Thais as Buddhists to accept, and to explain, the very fluid nature of their society, but I would not posit a causal link between ideology and social behaviour.

deprivation it might shake the society from its present state of complacency and indolence. In such a situation it is not surprising that the rare ambitious individual has little difficulty in improving his position, for he meets with relatively little resistance or competition.

I would suggest in conclusion that in some respects the Thai social system presents us with a situation which is the reverse of that with which we are familiar from most of the classic anthropological sources.[4] It is, for instance, generally emphasized that strong local or kin group ties are an ever-present threat to the coherence of the wider social unit. A number of institutions and practices (exogamy, the incest taboo, age-sets, ritual observances and so on) are believed to counteract these fissive tendencies by promoting the formation of cross-cutting links, and creating a relationship of inter-dependence between the parts which make up the whole (Gluckman 1955, pp. 44–7). In Thailand, by contrast, there are very few corporate groups, or permanent co-operative groupings of any kind, which at the level of individual behaviour means that actors move quite easily from role to role both within and between spheres of activity, and freely relinquish social ties which they no longer consider to be of any importance. This fluid situation is largely an outcome of political and economic features as I have already emphasized, and is found in association, and perhaps permitted by, an exceptionally strong sense of identification, on the part of people at all levels of society, to the wider unit, to the State and its symbols: the Monarchy and the Buddhist *Sangha*.

[4] E.g. *The Nuer*, E. E. Evans-Pritchard (Oxford, Clarendon Press, 1940); *The Dynamics of Clanship among the Tallensi*, M. Fortes (London, O.U.P. for the International African Institute, 1945).

APPENDIX 1

A judge from the Law Courts in Ayutthaya told me of a case which had caused him great embarrassment and distress as it involved a member of the Buddhist *Sangha*.

The action had arisen when a woman living in a rural settlement, had gone to the District (*Amphoe*) Office to register the birth of her baby. She had named, as its father, the abbot of the local *wat*. When he heard of her action, from her own mouth, the *bhikkhu* in question indignantly denied his paternity, and decided to sue her for libel.

The judge, as narrator, repeatedly expressed his grief and discomfort at being required to deal with such a situation. After a private interview with the woman he learnt that she was a regular supporter of that monastery. She always attended services there on Holy Day (*Wan Phra*), and frequently presented food to the community.

Over a year before however, her husband had died and the abbot in his turn had given food and money to help support herself and her family. The woman thus felt herself to be under a great obligation towards him, and consequently when he visited her home after dark one evening, she did not like to refuse to 'become his wife'. The abbot made several such visits and in due course she became pregnant.

The judge interjected at this point, that the child in question did indeed bear a strong resemblance to the monk. This heightened rather than simplified the predicament. Clearly it would be unjust to convict a woman whom he believed to be innocent. He considered that her registering the abbot as the baby's father was a simple-minded rather than a malicious act; had she thought at all it would have been obvious that in doing so she could only harm her position as she could not expect to profit by bringing disgrace on her benefactor, who might otherwise be expected to continue to support herself, and all her children.

On the other hand, the judge shrank from bringing disgrace to any member of the *Sangha*. His natural instinct was to try to reach some kind of compromise, in the quietest manner possible. Accordingly, he asked the woman whether the abbot had any distinguishing marks 'below the waist', to which question she replied that she did not know, as all his visits had

b. The case of the unordained 'bhikkhu'

taken place after dark! Had she answered in the affirmative, the judge had intended to ask the abbot, in private, if he would mind proving his innocence by showing that he had no such marks. His reaction to this suggestion would, according to the judge's reasoning, have been sufficient testimony to his innocence or guilt.

As this stratagem had failed to yield the desired results, the judge approached the abbot and confessed the court's inability to ascertain the truth of the matter. He said that the answer lay with the abbot and no-one else. He further suggested that the case be dropped if the woman could be persuaded to go to the District Office and withdraw the *bhikkhu*'s name from the register. The monk readily agreed to this course of action, which as the judge remarked, was evidence enough. The mother for her part did not demur, as she was already terrified by the judicial processes which her unconscious action had set in motion. The baby was registered as having no known father.

CASE-HISTORY B: THE CASE OF THE UNORDAINED 'BHIKKHU'
It was rumoured that there was one man in Ayutthaya who frequently masqueraded as a Buddhist monk. He had shaved his head, and every morning donned his yellow robe in order to go out collecting alms from the laity. When his bowl was full, he returned home to his wife and children. He was said to live in a part of town which was regarded as being very 'wild'. Few people lived in the area, which had largely been reclaimed by trees and undergrowth.

It appeared from various sources however, that the man's own deeply-ingrained respect for the Buddhist *Sangha* prevented him from deriving full benefit from his falsely assumed position of prestige, and might eventually prove his downfall. When he attended ceremonies and fairs which took place at various monasteries in town he could not, for example, bring himself to eat with the other monks, but rather took his meal later, sitting on one side. This behaviour was considered by everyone present to be extremely odd. When anyone enquired as to his place of residence he replied evasively that he was merely visiting from another town. He did not receive invitations from the laity to perform merit-making ceremonies, as his contact with them was largely limited to the *binthabat* (alms-collecting) transaction.

This case shows clearly that a *bhikkhu* cannot perform his role to the full unless he is living in a *wat* and is thus accessible and accountable to the lay community. As was mentioned in chapter 1, the card of identity received on ordination is a necessary permit for entry into the society of the *Sangha*.

APPENDIX 2

I began my questionnaire survey on 28 December 1966, by which time most of the monks who had been ordained for the duration of one Lenten season had already returned to lay life. The forms were distributed on the occasion of the annual ecclesiastical examinations organized by the *Chao Khana Amphoe* (Ecclesiastical District Head) at *Wat* Monthop. They had been printed for me by my chief informant, Khun Siri Imchai, who had access to the typing and duplicating facilities at the Town Hall. Before distributing these questionnaires at *Wat* Monthop I was able to explain the aim of my study to the assembled monks. It was also stated on the forms themselves that I was conducting research for a doctoral thesis, an explanation which was both understandable and most acceptable to my informants.

Questionnaires were given to 187 monks living in twenty monasteries in the municipal area (i.e. to residents of the fifteen *wats* whose incomes and expenditures are analyzed in chapter 4, and to members of five other communities, viz. *Wats* Choeng Tha, Nang Plum, Tong Pu, Tum and Phrayat).

Approximately 100 of these forms were returned, but only 90 of them were complete enough to make possible the correlation of different items of information. It is therefore probable that the results are biased in favour of younger and more educated monks, who would be more willing and able to complete the survey forms.

The answers received are set out here.

A. ORDINATION
1. (a) Average length of ordination, i.e. the average number of Lenten seasons spent in the *wat*: 14.3 Lenten seasons
(b) Average age of monks: 42.25 years old
(Average age of abbots, and their length of service in the *wat*: Average age: 56.3 years old, Length of service: 26.1 Lenten seasons)

2. *Age at which ordained*
Ordained when 20/21 years old: 42 monks
Ordained in late 20s: 10 monks
Ordained in middle-age (i.e. late 40s and upwards): 25 monks
(18 of these men were ordained for the second time in middle-age, 17 of them were married, and the wives of 10 of them were still living)
Total number of monks ordained twice: 28 monks

The results of the questionnaire survey

Total number of monks ever ordained as a novice: 41 monks
  (28 of whom stayed on after reaching the age of 20 to become permanent monks)

3. *Reason for ordination* (75 monks answered this question)
Answers given in terms of interest in study of the *Dhamma*: 47 monks
Ordained because it is a Thai custom: 4 monks
It is the duty of a Buddhist to become a monk: 5 monks
Because of obligations to parents or senior relatives living or dead: 4 monks
Because wanted to: 2 monks
Lay life too arduous: 3 monks
Desire to teach the *Dhamma* to others: 1 monk

(N.B. These different explanations are not of course mutually exclusive)

4. *Views on disrobing* (30 of the 90 monks answered)
Monks who were either fairly sure or quite certain that they would not leave the
  Order: 18 monks
Monks who were unsure as to their future plans: 12 monks

5. *Concerning the previous ordination of the informant's father*
61 monks stated definitely that their fathers had been ordained.
10 monks stated definitely that their fathers had not been ordained. (The fathers of
  two of the monks who answered had been living in China.)

B. MONASTIC RESIDENCE
1. *Number of monasteries lived in*
All except 19 of the 90 monks who replied had lived in two or more monasteries.
Of the remainder, 4 had become ordained recently, and were unsure as to how long
  they would remain in the *wat*;
5 monks had retired into the nearest urban *wat* in old age;
6 monks had chosen their present *wat* because of its status or that of its residents;
4 monks had been ordained at the nearest *wat*, and had remained there.

2. *Reason for living in present* wat
To study the *Dhamma*: 32 monks
To study (with reference to particular facilities offered): 7 monks
Because of relationship with another monk in the *wat*, e.g. *upacha*, respected abbot:
  7 monks
Came on the advice of a lay relation: 4 monks
Came on the instruction of ecclesiastical officials:
  (i) To be abbot: 6 monks
  (ii) To increase the size of the community: 2 monks
    Because this *wat* is pleasant/quiet/peaceful/comfortable: 5 monks
    To teach: 1 monk
    Because lived here as a novice: 1 monk

(N.B. As is clear from their nature these answers are not necessarily mutually exclusive)

3. The number of monks who had at any stage in their career lived in the same *wat*
  as had their respective fathers at some earlier date (the father of none of the monks
  interviewed was in the Order at the time of my study).

  21 monks answered in the affirmative
  34 monks answered in the negative
   6 monks did not know.

  (It should be noted from B.2 that no monk gave as his reason for living in a *wat* the
  fact that his father had once resided there.)

191

C. RESIDENCE PRIOR TO ORDINATION

(a) Number of monks who had lived in a rural area: 58 monks. Of this number 15 had come from farming settlements within *Amphoe Ayutthaya*; 26 had lived in rural districts in some other parts of Ayutthaya Province, but outside Ayutthaya District (*Amphoe*); the remainder came from other Provinces.

(b) Number of monks who had lived in an urban area: 27 monks. Two of these came from Bangkok, 2 from Saraburi (see Map A), 4 from Ayutthaya, 5 from Angthong. The remaining individuals came from other towns outside the region, notably 3 from Mahasarakham (N.E. Region) and 2 from Songkhla (S. Region).

D. OCCUPATIONS

1. *Occupation prior to ordination*

Farmer: 52 monks (This means in many cases that as a boy the informant helped on his father's farm: this is clear from the age of ordination of the individuals concerned.)

Vendor: 13 monks

Labourer: 5 monks

Civil servant (Gd. 4): 5 monks

Soldier: 2 monks

Carpenter: 1 monk

Watchman: 1 monk

Builder: 1 monk

Train-driver: 1 monk

Samlo-driver: 1 monk (*Samlo*: lit. three-wheels, a rickshaw-like vehicle; a pedicab)

The remaining 8 monks who answered had been ordained from school as novices or monks.

2. *Father's occupation* (where known)

Farmer: 48 men

Vendor: 4 men

Labourer: 1 man

3. *The occupation to be assumed in the event of disrobing*

(Some of the monks who said that they would not disrobe answered this question, hypothetically; 23 monks completed this part of the questionnaire.)

(*a*) 13 monks said that they would resume their previous occupation should they disrobe. Of this number 5 had been farmers; 5 had been labourers; 2 men had been vendors, and 1 had been employed as a watchman.

(*b*) 10 had precise plans for a change of occupation should they disrobe, although a number of these were not certain that they would in fact ever leave the Order.

8 of this number said that they would become civil servants; 5 of them had been farmers; 1 man had driven a *samlo* and 2 of them had been vendors. 1 monk who had been a farmer planned to become a vendor.

1 monk who had been a farmer said that he would go to University in England with my sponsorship!

E. KINSHIP POSITION

(*a*) Average number of siblings in the family (incl. monk): 5.75 children

(According to a survey conducted by the National Statistical Office, Bangkok, in 1963 the average family size in villages of the Central Region was 5.6 and in towns 5.4 (See 'Household Expenditure Survey: Central Region' National Statistical Office, Bangkok, B.E. 2506 (1963).)

(*b*) Sex ratio of children: no discernible regularities.

(*c*) Monk's position in the family: there were similarly no discernible regularities, i.e. there was not a preponderance of individuals born first, second, etc etc. in their respective families.

F. MARITAL STATUS
25 monks had been married at some time.
19 had wives still living.
22 of the married monks had children.

G. EDUCATIONAL ACHIEVEMENTS
1. *Prior to ordination*
   (*a*) 14 monks had some secondary education; only one monk had received as many as three years of secondary education.
   (*b*) 43 had received some formal primary schooling; 37 had completed the primary grades (*Prathom* 1–4).
   (*c*) 11 said they had been taught by monks in monastery schools.
   (31 informants had been ordained as novices on reaching the limits of free education provided by the State in their area.)

APPENDIX 3

Ayutthaya is an important centre for ecclesiastical education with schools at *Wat* Phanan Choeng, *Wat* Suwandararam, and *Wat* Senasanaram (*Thammayutika nikai*). Monks with an interest in pursuing formal courses of study thus tended to live in the municipal area, easily accessible to the monasteries mentioned above.

Of the 90 monks who answered my questionnaire 18 only had *Barian* or Pali Grades. Three of this number (all *Barian* Gd. 5) came from Bangkok to teach at *Wat* Phanan Choeng during term-time. The two most highly qualified monks in Ayutthaya, the Abbot of *Wat* Salapun, and the Deputy Abbot of *Wat* Suwandararam held *Barian* Grade 6. Eight monks, including the three from Bangkok mentioned earlier, had passed *Barian* Grade 5. The remaining eight *bhikkhus* had passed Grade 3 or 4.

With respect to the preliminary or *Nak Tham* course, most of the remaining monks studied fairly regularly, though not necessarily to any great effect. Fifty monks had obtained some *Nak Tham* grades:

27 monks had passed Grade 3
14 monks had passed Grade 2
9 monks had passed Grade 1

The *Nak Tham* examinations were held at *Wat* Monthop, Ayutthaya, on 28 December. The monks and novices examined came from the 72 (*Mahanikai*) monasteries in *Amphoe* Ayutthaya. There were in all approximately 434 permanent monks and 97 novices living in these monasteries at that time. The figures presented thus refer to an area much wider than my chosen unit of study. They are nevertheless instructive in that they give some idea of the standards of achievement reached.

Most novices study the *Nak Tham* Grades, but it was rare in Ayutthaya, though not in Bangkok, to find any novice engaged in Pali study.

---

[1] The figures given above were obtained from the *Chao Khana Amphoe* (Ecclesiastical District Head), Ayutthaya.

b. Results of the ecclesiastical examinations 1966–7

I do not have the comparative statistics for the examinations held at *Wat* Senasanaram at the same time. Monks and novices of the *Thammayutika* Sect from the whole of Ayutthaya Province attended. I suspect that the overall academic standard may have been somewhat higher than that of the *Mahanikai*.

Nak Tham Grade 3
Examined: 286 monks and novices
Passed: 156 monks and novices

Nak Tham Grade 2
Examined: 94 monks and novices
Passed: 57 monks and novices

Nak Tham Grade 1
Examined: 63 monks and novices
Passed: 34 monks and novices

The *Barian* or Pali examinations held at *Wat* Phanan Choeng (*Mahanikai*) in March 1967 were attended by monks from the whole of Ayutthaya Province.

The results were as follows:
Barian Grade 3
Examined: 35 monks
Passed: 3 monks

Barian Grade 4
Examined: 5 monks
Passed: 5 monks

The higher Pali Grades were examined in Bangkok. Only two monks in Ayutthaya were qualified to teach up to *Barian* Grade 5, namely the Abbot of *Wat* Salapun, and the Deputy Abbot of *Wat* Suwandararam, both of whom had passed *Barian* Grade 6. They had themselves long since ceased to study, as their administrative duties left them no time. It would have been necessary for them to transfer to a monastery in Bangkok, had they wished to continue their academic pursuits.

APPENDIX 4

There are over forty ecclesiastical titles of this kind. The ranking system is presented in simplified form below. (See Wells (1960, p. 184) for more detailed information.)

Honorific titles are conferred upon worthy monks as a token of the King's appreciation, and appear to involve no extra duties or responsibilities. They are customarily attached to Royal rather than to Commoner *wats*, and *bhikkhus* may thus have to change their place of residence when a title is conferred. Title-holders are given special fans as insignia of rank. These may be used only at ceremonies attended by the King or his representative (i.e. at *phithi luang*: royal ceremonies).

This hierarchy of honorific ranks merges at the top with the official administrative grades, but is elsewhere only partially congruent. The Ecclesiastical Provincial Head (*Chao Khana Changwat*) must for example be of *Phra Racha Khana* status, although his grade within this category is variable. Similarly all *Chao Khana Tambon* are of *Phra Khru* status, though a monk can be a *Phra Khru* and yet not hold the position of *Chao Khana Tambon*.

There is no direct relationship between educational achievement and honorific rank, which is to say that academic standing is neither necessary nor sufficient to acquire one of the titles which are listed below, in order of importance.

1 *Phra Khru* (four Grades)
2 *Phra Racha Khana Yok*: awarded to monks with no *Barian* Grades
3 *Phra Racha Khana Chan Saman Barian*: the holder must have passed at least *Barian* Grade 3
4 *Phra Racha Khana Chan Rat*
5 *Phra Racha Khana Chan Thep*
6 *Phra Racha Khana Chan Tham*
7 *Phra Racha Khana Rong*
8 *Somdet Phra Racha Khana*
9 *Somdet Phra Sangkharat* (Supreme Patriarch)

b. Monks receiving Nittayaphat

The amount awarded appears to vary according to the position of the *bhikkhu* concerned in the administrative hierarchy, although honorific titles and academic honours may also be taken into account. Nevertheless these criteria do not appear to be applied with any consistency and there are several notable anomalies. The Abbot of *Wat* Tong Pu, for example, seems to be underpaid, whilst his counterpart at *Wat* Na Phramen may be receiving more than he deserves. My investigations suggest that the monks themselves are rarely aware of the amount of *nittayaphat* which is granted to their fellows.

Wat	Monk	Administrative office	Honorific rank	Ecclesiastical educational qualifications	Amount received each month (in baht)
Suwandararam*	(1)	Abbot (Deputy Chao Khana Changwat)	Phra Racha Khana Chan Thep	Nak Tham 1	180
	(2)	Deputy Abbot†	Phra Racha Khana Chan Rat	Barian 6	180
Phanan Choeng*	(3)	Abbot (Chao Khana Changwat)	Phra Racha Khana Chan Thep	Nak Tham 3	260
	(4)	Deputy Abbot†	Phra Khru (Gd. 1)	Barian 5	100
	(5)	—	—	Barian 5	80
Senasanaram* (Thammayutika nikai)	(6)	Abbot (Chao Khana Changwat of the Thammayutika sect)	Phra Racha Khana Chan Rat	Barian 3	240
	(7)	Deputy Abbot†	Phra Khru (Gd. 1)	Barian 5	80
	(8)	—	Phra Khru (Gd. 1)	Barian 5	80
	(9)	—	Phra Khru (Gd. 1)	Barian 5	80
Tum	(10)	Abbot	Phra Khru (Gd. 1)	—	120
Borommawong*	(11)	Abbot (Chao Khana Amphoe)	Phra Racha Khana Chan Rat	Nak Tham 2	240
	(12)	—	—	Nak Tham 1	30
Tong Pu	(13)	Abbot (Deputy Chao Khana Amphoe)	Phra Khru (Gd. 1)	Barian 5	80
Phrayat	(14)	Abbot (Chao Khana Tambon)	Phra Khru (Gd. 2)	Nak Tham 3	60
Thammikarat	(15)	Abbot (Chao Khana Tambon)	Phra Khru (Gd. 3)	Nak Tham 1	30

197

Wat	Monk	Administrative office	Honorific rank	Ecclesiastical educational qualifications	Amount received each month (in baht)
Ket	(16)	Abbot (Chao Khana Tambon)	Phra Khru (Gd. 3)	Nak Tham 3	30
Salapun*	(17)	Abbot (Deputy Chao Khana Changwat)	Phra Racha Khana Chan Barian	Barian 6	180
Ratanachai	(18)	Abbot (Deputy Chao Khana Amphoe)	Phra Khru (Gd. 1)	Barian 5	60
Na Phramen*	(19)	Abbot	Phra Khru (Gd. 1)	Nak Tham 1	80
Chang Thong*	(20)	Abbot (Chao Khana Tambon)	Phra Khru (Gd. 3)	—	30
Phoromniwat*	(21)	Abbot	Phra Khru (Gd. 1)	Nak Tham 1	80
Phutthaisuwan	(22)	Abbot (Chao Khana Tambon)	Phra Khru (Gd. 3)	Nak Tham 3	30
Yai Chai Mongkhon	(23)	Abbot	Phra Khru (Gd. 3)	Nak Tham 3	60
Sawangarom	(24)	Abbot (Chao Khana Tambon)	—	Nak Tham 3	30

NOTES:
  (i) *Indicates royal foundation (wat luang).
  (ii) + Monks (2), (4), (7) are centrally appointed officials, unlike deputy abbots in smaller monasteries who are personally chosen by the abbot and receive no formal appointment from higher ecclesiastical authorities.
  (iii) Chao Khana Changwat: Ecclesiastical Provincial Head
       Chao Khana Amphoe: Ecclesiastical District Head
       Chao Khana Tambon: Ecclesiastical Sub-District Head

ESTIMATED ANNUAL INCOME AND EXPENDITURE
(1966–7) OF TWO MONKS

(*a*) Chao Khun Thep: his estimated annual income and expenditure
The figures given are in most cases only approximate as the monk himself
did not keep a close account of his income nor of his expenditure.

Estimated annual income	*baht*
Food allowance (*nittayaphat*) (260 *baht* per month)	3,120 p.a.
Money received in return for his services as *upacha*	4,500 p.a.
Money received for other pastoral services	1,000 p.a.
Total	8,620

He also received various durable goods e.g. an electric
fan, a sofa, vacuum flasks, etc.

Estimated annual expenditures	
Regular contribution to a Cremation Assurance Fund at *Wat* Ratanachai	3,600 p.a.
Contribution to costs of building school for lay children in the compound of *Wat* Phanan Choeng	3,000
Miscellaneous expenses for support for 6 novices and 5 *dek wat*; purchase of text books for ecclesiastical school	1,200
Personal expenditures: travel, betel-nut, food for visitors, etc.	cost unknown
Estimated annual expenditure	7,800

(*b*) Phra Sombat: his estimated annual income and expenditure

Estimated annual income	
From merit-making ceremonies	800
Occasional gifts from kinsmen and friends	200
Total	1,000

Expenditures
The money received was largely spent on buying books,
cigarettes and supplementary food for his own needs

APPENDIX 6

COMPOSITION OF THE MONASTIC COMMUNITY AND EXTENT OF LAY SUPPORT AT FIFTEEN WATS IN AYUTTHAYA

Name of Wat	Lent (L.) Out of Lent (O.)	Monks	Novices	Monastery boys	Nuns	Monastery committee (no. of lay members)	Lay people who make merit (tham bun) on Holy Day	Lay people who observe the precepts (thu sin) on Holy Day	Number of households which regularly present rice (ban pracham)
1 Suwandararam*	L.	44	22	46	—	4	170	15	10
	O.	28	25	43	—		30	35	
2 Phanan Choeng*	L.	45	60	50	2	8	100	35–40	—
	O.	29	52	30			40–50	15–20	
3 Prasat	L.	21	—	11	12	50	50	40–50	1
	O.	11	15	20	10		10–20	20+	
4 Ratanachai	L.	18	—	15	—	—	100	30–40	15
	O.	15	—	12	—		40+	—	
5 Wongkhong	L.	14	7	10	—	11	50–70	20	50
	O.	8	2	5	—		20–40	—	
6 Kluai	L.	11	1	2	—	20	200–300	50	20
	O.	5	1	2	—		100	—	
7 Yai Chai Mongkhon	L.	37	33	3	35	3	5–10	3	Few
	O.	22	11	3	35		—	—	Few
8 Yanasen	L.	4	7	—	—	4	30	7–8	10–12
	O.	6	—	3	—		—	—	

9 Tuk	L.	12	3	7	—	4	50	25–30	30
	O.	16	3	6	—		—	—	
10 Woraphot	L.	7	1	4	—	—	50	5	10
	O.	7	—	5	—		—	—	
11 Na Phramen*	L.	10	—	18	5	3	100	10	10
	O.	9	—	19	4		5–6	5–7	
12 Salapun*	L.	8	2	12	—	21	30	20+	5–6
	O.	5	2	12	—		—	8–15	
13 Thammikarat	L.	13	—	11	5	—	100	20	30
	O.	5	—	10	5		—	—	
14 Borommawong*	L.	14	3	4	—	4	50	25–30	—
	O.	12	—	5	—		—	—	
15 Monthop	L.	12	5	12	—	—	20–50	6–7	3–4
	O.	13	3	15	—		10–15	6–7	

NOTE: * Indicates royal *wat* (*wat luang*)

APPENDIX 7

The duties of the abbot as stated in the Acts on the Administration of the Buddhist Order of Sangha (1902), Part 4, Art. 14, are as follows;[1] The abbot is required:

(i) to maintain and develop the monastery as well as he can,

(ii) to take care not to let his monastery be a robber's hiding place,

(iii) to govern the *bhikkhus* and laymen in his *wat*,

(iv) to maintain law and order and settle disputes and quarrels occurring amongst the *bhikkhus* and laymen in his *wat*,

(v) to undertake to establish the *bhikkhus* and laymen in his monastery in right conduct in accordance with their character and ability.

(vi) to arrange to educate the children under his care in accordance with their tendency and aptitude,

(vii) to provide lay devotees with proper facilities for their merit-making in his monastery,

(viii) to make a list of the *bhikkhus* and laymen in his monastery together with a report to higher ecclesiastical authority,

(ix) to issue the identification card to a *bhikkhu* or a *samanera* (novice), in his monastery who wishes to go on a journey or to live in another monastery. However when the abbot has reason to believe that such a *bhikkhu* or a *samanera* (novice) will behave unbecomingly outside, he may, upon notification to the suspected *bhikkhu or samanera*, withhold his consent.

In the Act of 1902 (Part 4, Art. 17) The abbot's governing power is defined as follows:

(i) He can govern and admonish monks, novices and laymen in his *wat*,

(ii) he can settle disciplinary disputes in his monastery; in the event however, that it is a civil case, the abbot may also do so with the unanimous agreement of both parties,

(iii) a monk, novice or layman cannot stay in his monastery without obtaining permission from him,

(iv) he is empowered not to allow any disobedient monk, novice or layman to stay in his monastery,

(v) the abbot is empowered to impose a penalty upon a disobedient novice or monk.[2]

NOTES:
[1] More recent Acts on the Administration of the Buddhist Order of Sangha (1941, 1964) list the same provisions in a less specific form.
[2] The miscreant is traditionally made to perform some distasteful menial chore (e.g. cleaning the latrines, sweeping the compound).

APPENDIX 8

1. *Ecclesiastical Provincial Head (Chao Khana Changwat)*
   In order to be appointed *Chao Khana Changwat* a *bhikkhu* must possess the following qualifications

(i) He must have been ordained for at least 10 Lenten seasons, and must have lived in a *wat* in the Province concerned for that length of time.

(ii) He must have been Deputy *Chao Khana Changwat* for two years;

OR

(iii) He must have been *Chao Khana Amphoe* (Ecclesiastical District Head) in one of the *Amphoe* in the *Changwat* concerned for at least four years;

OR

(iv) He must have the rank of *Phra Racha Khana Chan Saman Barian* or be of *Phra Khru* (Grade 2) status;

OR

(v) He must have passed *Barian* Grade 6.
   The *Chao Khana Changwat* is chosen by the Ecclesiastical Regional Head (*Chao Khana Phak*) in consultation with the Council of Elders, and is appointed by the Supreme Patriarch (*Somdet Phrasangkharat*)

2. *Ecclesiastical District Head (Chao Khana Amphoe)*
   In order to be appointed *Chao Khana Amphoe* a *bhikkhu* must possess the following qualifications

(i) He must have spent at least 5 Lenten seasons in the Order;

(ii) He must have been Deputy *Chao Khana Amphoe* of one of the *Tambon* in the *Amphoe* concerned for at least four years;

OR

(iii) He must have been *Chao Khana Tambon* (Ecclesiastical Sub-District Head) of one of the *Tambon* in the *Amphoe* concerned for at least four years;

OR
   (iv) He must be of *Phra Khru* (Grade 2) status or be of *Phra Racha Khana Yok* grade;

OR
   (v) He must have passed *Barian* Grade 4.
   The *Chao Khana Amphoe* is chosen by the *Chao Khana Changwat* in consultation with the *Chao Khana Phak* and is appointed by the Council of Elders (*Mahatherasamakhom*).

3. *The Ecclesiastical Sub-District Head (Chao Khana Tambon)*
   In order to be appointed *Chao Khana Tambon* a *bhikkhu* must have the following qualifications

   (i) He must have been ordained for at least 5 Lenten seasons.
   (ii) He must have been Deputy *Chao Khana Tambon* for two years;

OR
   (iii) He must have been Abbot in that *Tambon* for four years;

OR
   (iv) He must be of *Phra Khru* status;

OR
   (v) He should have passed *Barian* Grade 3 or *Nak Tham* Grade 1.
   The *Chao Khana Tambon* is chosen by the *Chao Khana Amphoe* and appointed by the *Chao Khana Changwat*

(Details from *Kot Mahatherasamakhom* (Laws of the Council of Elders), Vol. 2, Bk. v, Sect. 1.27–1.37.)

APPENDIX 9

(a) Cast contributions received from the laity 1966–7

	Wat	Amount received as Kathin presentation (in baht)	Amount received as Pha Pa presentation (in baht)	Amount received from Thet Mahachat Wat fairs, etc. (in baht)
1	Suwandararam*	11,000 (King's representative)	—	10,000
2	Phanan Choeng*	50,000 (Officials of the Department of Fine Arts)	—	—
3	Prasat	2,000 (Private donor)	—	5,885
4	Ratanachai	40,000 (Bangkok Company)	—	—
5	Wongkhong	3,500 (Private donor)	3,000 (Private donor)	7,000
6	Kluai	2,000 (phuak wat)	—	200
7	Yai Chai Mongkhon	24,000 (Private donor)	—	
8	Yanasen	4,000 (Private donor)	4,000 (Private donor)	—
9	Tuk	40,000 (Municipal Offices, Ayutthaya)	2,000 (Private donor)	—
10	Woraphot	24,173 (Yellow Bus Co., Bangkok)	1,500 (Private donor)	—
11	Na Phramen*	5,500 (Private donor)	—	—
12	Salapun*	5,000 (King's representative)	—	—
13	Thammikarat	2,500 (Private donor)	500 (Private donor)	800
14	Borommawong*	79,582 (King's representative)	—	—
15	Monthop	2,040 (Teachers at an Ayutthaya secondary school)	—	—

NOTES: Details in brackets indicate the host (chao phap) or organizing force behind the presentation.

* Indicates Royal foundation (wat luang)

Income and expenditure of fifteen wats

(b) Statistics relating to land ownership and income from land

	Name of *Wat*	*Thi Wat* (rai)	Income p.a. (baht)	*Thi Thoran-isong* (rai)	Income p.a. (baht)	*Thi Kala-pana* (rai)	Income p.a. (baht)
1	Suwandararam*	12	—	83	24–36,000	75	2,000
2	Phanan Choeng*	82	—	42	96,000	42	2–3,000
3	Prasat	11	31,200	2	—	0	—
4	Ratanachai	11	—	9	12,000	0	—
5	Wongkhong	38	—	0	—	0	—
6	Kluai	9	—	0	—	0	—
7	Yai Chai Mongkhon	20	—	631	20,000	0	—
8	Yanasen	26	1,000	0	—	0	—
9	Tuk	17	—	2	—	0	—
10	Woraphot	61	—	0	—	0	—
11	Na Phramen*	6	—	118	5,000	0	—
12	Salapun*	20	—	0	—	0	—
13	Thammikarat	33	—	42	1–3,000	0	—
14	Borommawong*	20	—	38	36,000	0	—
15	Monthop	30	—	50	—	0	—

Miscellaneous items of income

Wat Suwandararam   received 600 *baht* per annum from the owner of the ferry service, the landing stage for which was built on *wat* land.

Wat Phanan Choeng   received 600 *baht* per annum from the source described above, as its land was on the opposite bank of the river from that owned by *Wat* Suwandararam; and received in addition approximately 20,500 *baht* from the shops erected in front of the *bot* which sold ritual items needed in the worship of the Buddha.

Wat Monthop   received 1,200 *baht* per annum as rent from houseboats belonging to the *wat*.

NOTES:
* Indicates royal *wat* (*wat luang*)
(i) £1 sterling is equivalent to 50 *baht*
(ii) 1 *rai* = 0·4 acre

(c) Estimated annual income and expenditure of three wats 1966–7

I would like to stress that the figures given below are only approximate. The accounting system at the monasteries I studied was at best haphazard, at worst non-existent. Consequently the figures given were obtained at random over time, and often from different members of the monastic community. This being the case, many smaller donations and more routine expenditures may have been overlooked.

In the second place these statistics are misleading in that they deal with financial transactions which took place during a single year, and do not take into account such factors as interest accruing from money deposited in the bank or bills outstanding from the previous year. In some cases the fact that the *wat* was financing a building project which spanned several years made the assessment of financial position even more difficult.

Appendix 9

I would refer the reader to Kaufman (1960, p. 106) for details of the income of a rural monastery, *Wat* Bangkhuad.

1. *Wat* Phanan Choeng

Estimated annual income (in *baht*)
i. *Income from land*
(*a*) *Thi wat:*
Money from shops outside the *bot* (this sum represents a
share of proceeds taken by lay owners of shop) 20,500
Rent from ferry owner 600
(*b*) *Thi Thoranisong:*
Rent received 96,000
(*c*) *Thi Kalapana:* 2,500
ii. *Direct cash contributions*
(*d*) *Kathin* presentation 50,000
Estimated cash income in 1966–7 (*baht*) 169,600

(The *wat* also possessed a *munithi* fund of 120,000 *baht*)

Expenditures (in *baht*)
Building and restoration 90,000
Equipment for ecclesiastical school 3,000
Salary for 3 monks sent from Bangkok to teach in the school
(each received 300 *baht* per month) 10,800
Electricity charges (500 *baht* per month) 6,000
Water charges (500 *baht* per month) 6,000
Cost of food for the community 36,500
Estimated expenditure in 1966–7 (*baht*) 152,300

NOTE: I must stress that these figures are only estimates, as the *bhikkhus* tended to forget about smaller donations and occasional expenditures. The system of accounting, where such existed, was usually makeshift and vague.

2. *Wat* Wongkhong

Estimated annual income (in *baht*)
i. *Income from land*
The *thi wat* (38 *rai*) was not rented out.
The *wat* possessed no other land-holdings.
ii. *Direct cash contribution* (in *baht*)
(*a*) *Kathin* presentation 30,500
(*b*) *Pha pa* 3,000
(*c*) *Thet Mahachat* 7,000

Estimated cash income in 1966–7 (*baht*) 40,500

Expenditure (in *baht*)
Restoration of *bot* 20,000
Electricity charges (100 *baht* per month) 1,200
Water charges (100 *baht* per month) 1,200

Estimated expenditure in 1966–7 (*baht*) 22,400

3. *Wat* Kluai

Estimated annual income (in *baht*)
i. *Income from land*
The *thi wat* which was 9 acres in area was not rented out.
This *wat* possessed no other land.
ii. *Direct cash contributions*

(*a*) *Kathin* presentation	2,000
(*b*) *Thet Mahachat*	200
Estimated income in 1966–7 (*baht*)	2,200

Expenditures (in *baht*)

Repairs to the *bot*	500
Water charges (100 *baht* per month)	1,200
Electricity charges (150 *baht* per month)	1,800
Expenditures in 1966–7 (*baht*)	3,500

NOTE: During the year 1966–7 *Wat* Kluai spent more money than it received from the laity. The abbot stated however that there was a little money in the *wat*'s bank account, although he could not be more specific.

BIBLIOGRAPHY

Ames, Michael M. (1964). 'Magical-Animism and Buddhism: A Structural Analysis of the Sinhalese Religious System', in *Religion in South Asia*, ed. Edward B. Harper. Seattle: University of Washington Press, pp. 21–52.

Banerji, S. C. (1964). *An Introduction to Pali Literature*. Calcutta: Punthi Pustak.

Caldwell, J. C. (1967). 'The Demographic Structure'. In *Thailand: Social and Economic Studies in Development*, ed. T. H. Silcock. Canberra: Australia National University, pp. 27–64.

Coedès, G. (1966). *The Making of South East Asia*. London: Routledge and Kegan Paul.

Conze, Edward (1959). *Buddhist Scriptures*. Harmondsworth: Penguin Books.

De Young, John E. (1955). *Village Life in Modern Thailand*. Berkeley: University of California Press.

Dutt, Sukumar (1957). *The Buddha and Five After-Centuries*. London: Luzac & Co. Ltd.

(1960). *Early Buddhist Monarchism*. Bombay: Asia Publishing House.

Embree, J. F. (1950). 'Thailand: A Loosely Structured Social System'. *American Anthropologist*, vol. 52, pp. 181–93.

Evans-Pritchard, E. E. (1940). *The Nuer*. Oxford: Clarendon Press.

Evers, Hans-Dieter (ed.) (1969). *Loosely Structured Social System: Thailand in Comparative Perspective*. Cultural Report Series no. 17. New Haven: Yale University Southeast Asia Studies.

Fitzsimmons, Thomas (ed.) (1957). *Thailand*. Country Survey Series. New Haven: H.R.A.F. Press.

Fortes, M. (1945). *The Dynamics of Clanship among the Tallensi*. London: O.U.P. for the International African Institute.

Gluckman, Max (1955). *Custom and Conflict in Africa*. Oxford: Blackwell.

(1962) (ed.). *Essays on the Ritual of Social Relations*. Manchester: University Press.

Hanks, Lucien M. (1962). 'Merit and Power in the Thai Social Order'. *American Anthropologist*, vol. 64, pp. 1247–61.

and Hanks, Jane R. (1963). 'Thailand: Equality Between the Sexes'. In *Women in the New Asia*, ed. Barbara E. Ward. Paris: UNESCO, pp. 424–52.

Ingersoll, Jasper (1966). 'The Priest Role in Central Village Thailand'. In *Anthropological Studies in Theravada Buddhism*, ed. Manning Nash. Cultural Report Series no. 13. New Haven: Yale University Southeast Asia Studies, pp. 51–77.

Ingram, J. C. (1955). *Economic Change in Thailand since 1850*. Stanford: University Press.

Ishii, Yoneo (1968). 'Church and State in Thailand'. *Asian Survey*, vol. VIII no. 10, pp. 864–71.

Kaufman, H. K. (1960). *Bangkhuad*. New York: J. J. Augustus Inc.

Khantipalo, Bhikkhu (1965). 'With Robes and Bowl'. Kandy, Ceylon: Buddhist Publication Society.

Kingshill, Konrad (1965). *Ku Daeng* (The Red Tomb). Bangkok: Bangkok Christian College.

Leach, E. R. (1954). *Political Systems of Highland Burma*. London: Bell & Sons Ltd.

(1961). *Pul Eliya*. Cambridge: University Press.

Lingat, Robert (1957). 'Vinaya et Droit Laïque études sur les conflits de la loi religieuse et de la loi laïque dans L'Indochine Hinayaniste'. *Bulletin de L'Ecole Française d'Extrême-Orient*, tome XXXVII, fasc. 2, pp. 415–75.

Mayer, Adrian C. (1966). 'The Significance of Quasi-Groups in the Study of Complex

Bibliography

Societies'. In *The Social Anthropology of Complex Societies*. A.S.A. 4, ed. Michael Banton. London: Tavistock Publications, pp. 97–121.

Mendelson, E. M. (1965). 'Initiation and the Paradox of Power: A Sociological Approach'. In *Initiation*, ed. C. J. Bleeker. Leiden: E. J. Brill, pp. 214–22.

Merton, R. (1957). *Social Theory and Social Structure*. Glencoe, Ill.: Free Press.

Moerman, Michael (1966). 'Ban Ping's Temple: The Center of a "Loosely Structured" Society'. In *Anthropological Studies in Theravada Buddhism*, ed. Manning Nash. Cultural Report Series no. 13. New Haven: Yale University Southeast Asia Studies, pp. 137–75.

Mosel, James (1965). 'Some Notes on Self, Role and Role Behaviour of Thai Administrators'. *Asian Studies* no. 502 (Thailand Seminar). Ithaca, N.Y.: Cornell University.

Mulder, J. A. Niels (1969). *Monks, Merit, and Motivation. An exploratory Study of the Social Functions of Buddhism in Thailand in Processes of Guided Social Change.* Special Report Series no. 1. Center for Southeast Asian Studies, Northern Illinois University.

Müller, Max (ed.) (1885). *Sacred Books of the East*, vol. 13: *Mahavagga*, trans. T. Rhys Davids and L. H. Oldenberg. Oxford: Clarendon Press.

Nadel, S. F. (1951). *The Foundations of Social Anthropology*. London: Cohen & West Ltd.

(1962). *The Theory of Social Structure*. London: Cohen & West Ltd.

Ven. Nanamoli Thera (1966). *The Patimokkha*. Bangkok: Social Science Association Press of Thailand.

Narada Thera (1959). *The Dhammapada*. London: John Murray.

Nash, Manning (1965). *The Golden Road to Modernity*. New York: John Wiley & Sons Inc.

Nikam, N. A. and McKeon, Richard (1966). *The Edicts of Asoka*. Chicago: University Press, Phoenix Books.

Obeyesekere, Gananath (1968). 'Theodicy, Sin and Salvation in a Sociology of Buddhism'. In *Dialectic in Practical Religion* (Cambridge Papers in Social Anthropology 5), ed. E. R. Leach. Cambridge: University Press, pp. 7–41.

Pfanner, D. E. and Ingersoll, J. (1962). 'Theravada Buddhism and Village Economic Behaviour: A Burmese and Thai Comparison'. *Journal of Asian Studies* 21, pp. 341–61.

Phillips, Herbert P. (1965). *Thai Peasant Personality*. Berkeley: University of California Press.

(1967). 'Social Contact vs. Social Promise in a Siamese Village'. In *Peasant Society*, ed. J. M. Potter, *et al*. Boston: Little Brown & Co., pp. 346–67.

Punyanubhab, Sujib (1965) (trans. by Siri Buddhasukh). Mahamakuta Educational Council. Bangkok: The Buddhist University.

Rahula, W. (1959). *What the Buddha Taught*. Bedford: Gordon Frazer Gallery Ltd.

Rajadhon, Phya Anuman (1961). *Life and Ritual in Old Siam* (trans. and ed. William J. Gedney). New Haven: H.R.A.F. Press.

Rhys Davids, T. W. (1963). (trans.) *The Questions of King Milinda*, parts I and II (*The Sacred Books of the East*, vol. xxxv, ed. Max Muller). New York: Dover Publications Inc.

Schecter, Jerrold (1967). *The New Face of Buddha. Buddhism and Political Power in Southeast Asia*. London: Victor Gollancz Ltd.

Siwaraksa [Siwarak], S. (1966). 'Thammayut Mahanikai'. In *Sangkhomsatporithat* (The Social Science Review), Special Edition no. 4, August 1966. Bangkok: Social Sciences Press, pp. 79–95.

(1967). 'Interview with Buddhadasa'. *Visakha Puja*, Annual Publication of the Buddhist Association of Thailand. Bangkok, pp. 24–39.

Sobhana, Phra Sasana (1967). 'The Government of the Thai Sangha'. *Visakha Puja*, Annual Publication of the Buddhist Association of Thailand. Bangkok.

Swearer, Donald K. (1968). 'Some Observations on New Directions in Thai Buddhism'. In *Sangkhomsatporithat* (The Social Science Review), Sept.–Oct. 1968. Bangkok: Social Sciences Press, pp. 52–9.

Bibliography

Tambiah, S. J. (1968). The Ideology of Merit and the Social Correlates of Buddhism in a Thai Village'. In *Dialectic in Practical Religion* (Cambridge Papers in Social Anthropology 5), ed. E. R. Leach. Cambridge: University Press, pp. 41–122.

(1970). *Buddhism and the Spirit Cults in North-East Thailand* (Cambridge Studies in Social Anthropology 2). Cambridge: University Press.

Vajirananavarorasa, Prince (1963). *Ordination Procedure (Upasombot withi)*. Mahamakuta Educational Council. Bangkok: The Buddhist University.

Wells, Kenneth E. (1960). *Thai Buddhism: its Rites and Activities*. Bangkok: The Police Printing Press.

Wijeyewardene, G. (1967). 'Some Aspects of Rural Life in Thailand'. In *Thailand: Social and Economic Studies in Development*, ed. T. H. Silcock. Canberra: Australia National University, pp. 65–83.

Wilson, David A. (1962). *Politics in Thailand*. Ithaca, N.Y.: Cornell University Press.

Yalman, Nur (1967). *Under the Bo Tree: Studies in Caste, Kinship and Marriage in the interior of Ceylon*. Berkeley: University of California Press.

Yano, Toru (1968). 'Land Tenure in Thailand'. *Asian Survey*, vol. VIII, no. 10.

Dictionaries and Works of Reference

Acts on the Administration of the Buddhist Order of Sangha. Mahamakuta Educational Council. Bangkok: The Buddhist University, 1963.

The Civil and Commercial Code of Thailand, Bks I–VI. Compiled by Prasobchai Yamali. Bangkok, 1967.

Concise Pali–English Dictionary. Compiled by A. P. Buddhadatta Mahathera. Colombo: The Colombo Apothecaries' Co. Ltd, 1957.

Kot Mahatherasomakhom (Laws of the Council of Elders), Vols. I–3. Compiled by Nai Chot Thongprayun. Bangkok, 1964.

Phrarachabanyatkhanasong (Royal Edicts pertaining to the Buddhist *Sangha*), 1962. Compiled by Nai Chot Thongprayun. Bangkok, 1965.

Thai–English Student's Dictionary. Compiled by Mary R. Haas. Oxford: University Press, 1964.

INDEX

abacus, 135

Abbots: abdication of, 67n, 93; admission of monks by, 87, 89, 95; and alms-routes, 95, 101, 104, 112; annual reports by, 26–7, 91, 96, 123, 202; appointment of, 59, 68, 92–5; average age of, 92n, 190; duties and rights of, 95–6, 202–3; invited to perform ceremonies, 66, 67n, 68; law case involving, 188–9; and monastery committee, 131, 132, 134; *nittayaphat* allowance to, 197–8; and presentations to monastery, 114, 116, 117; selection of monks by, for ceremonies, 65–6, 66–7, 79; as sponsors at ordination, 39, 162

Abhidhamma-pitaka, Buddhist scripture, 19, 58, 153

Agricultural College, Ayutthaya, requests to be put on alms-route, 101

agriculture, in Thailand, 9; monks not allowed to practise, 32

alcohol, prohibited in Five Precepts, 32, 143, 144

alms, monks' collection of, 60–1, 62n, 64, 68, 100–13, 146; contributors to, 154, 163

alms-routes of monks, 60, 95, 97, 112, 136; map of, 101

animistic practices, 21, 24, 49n

application form, for entry into *Sangha*, 39–40

aristocracy, 13, 18, 115, 184; and *Thammayutika* sect, 28

Arun *wat*, Bangkok, 162; Abbot of, as *upacha*, 169–70, 171

astrology, Hindu, 21, 166

Austere Practices (*Dhutanga*), 32, 54

Ayutthaya, 3–7; monasteries in, 86; traditionalist and progressive laymen in, 148–9

Bangkok: commuters between Ayutthaya and, 4, 148; instruction for *Barian* course in, 58; monks' hospital in, 90

banks, deposit of monastery funds with, 110, 129, 158n, 163, 209

Barian or Pali (advanced) course and

examination for monks, 26, 43, 47, 58–59; failures in, 157; monks successful in, 75, 87, 97, 134, 194; number of candidates passing, 195

Baworniwet *wat*, Bangkok: Abbot of, 57

beds, soft: prohibited for lay devotees, 107, and nuns, 88

begging-bowl of monk (*bat*), 28, 32, 106, 168

bhikkhu, see monks

Borommawong *wat*, Ayutthaya, 201; Abbot of, 132, 170, 197; finances of, 109–10, 197, 206, 207

bot (monastery building in consecrated area), 40, 86, 116, 118; expenditure on repairs to, 208, 209

Boundary Stones (*sima*) of consecrated area in monastery compound, 40n, 86; ceremony of planting of, 162

Brahministic ritual, 22, 149

Buddha, the: and Hindu beliefs, 22; images of, 3, 107, 145, 161; and Lenten season, 36, 90; on *Sangha*, 96n; scripture containing Word of, *see Sutta-pitaka*

Buddhism, Theravada: different levels of awareness of doctrines of, 52; philosophical aspects of, 18–21; Precepts of, *see* Precepts; and Thai social system, 1–2, 142, 178, 181, 183, 185; Three Refuges formula of, 58n, 143, 146, 168; and women, 13, 14

Buddhist Association Building, Bangkok, 161, 162

budget, for support of religious affairs, 26

Burma, 3, 31, 57n

bus company director, organizes *kathin* presentation, 116

candles, in offerings to monastery, 161, and to monks, 33, 63, 162, 172

celibacy of monks, 30–1

ceremonies, Buddhist: at life crises, *see* cremation, house-blessing, illness, marriage, new monk, *and* ordination; merit-making, *see* merit-making ceremonies; Royal, 58n, 196; state-spon-

Index

Index

Suan Phu *wat*, Bangkok, 157
suffering, Buddhist view of, 19, 21n
Sutta-Nipata, quoted, 86
Sutta-pitaka, scripture containing Word of Buddha, 18–19; chants in, 62n, 63; stories about Buddha in (*Jataka*), 117
Sutthi, Chao Khun, example of monk with prestige (active type), 75, 120, 194, 195
Suwandaram *wat*, Ayutthaya, 114–15, 200; Abbot of, 132, 153, 169, 173, 197; Deputy Abbot of, 75, 120, 194, 195; ecclesiastical school at, 43, 87, 99, 111, 155, 194; finances of, 110–11, 125–6, 197, 206, 207; *kathin* presentation to, 116; monks of, 88, 98, 109

television sets, presented to monks, 72, 120
textbooks, for ecclesiastical school, 72
Thammasat University, Bangkok, 149
Thammayutika-Nikai (reform sect of *Sangha*), 27, 32n, 43, 97
Thammikarat *wat*, Ayutthaya, 101, 197, 201; finances of 206, 207
Thep, Chao Khun, example of monk with prestige (passive type), 69–73, 199
Thet Mahachat ceremony (recitations on previous lives of Buddha), 117–18, 129, 161; amount received at, 206, 208, 209
title, honorific, for monks, 196; *see also Phra Khru, Phra Racha Khana, and Somdet Phra* titles
Tong Pu *wat*, Ayutthaya, 190, 197
towns, monasteries in, 43–4, 46, 47, 48
tourists, in Ayutthaya, 3, 6, 7
travel: cost of, for ordination ceremony, 177; by monk formerly an engine-driver, 76; of monks by public transport, 36
travellers, accommodated in monasteries, 127
Tripitaka, scriptures of Theravada Buddhism, 18–19
Tuk *wat*, Ayutthaya: Abbot of, 116, 171; finances of, 122, 206, 207
Tum *wat*, Ayutthaya, 190, 197

umbrellas, of monks, 167–8
Universities, Buddhist, in Bangkok, 43, 47, 63
upacha, authorized to confer ordination, 39, 40, 41, 82; gifts to, 172, 199; monks officiating as, 70, 71, 169–70, 171
Uposatha day (fortnightly recitation of *Patimokkha*), 52, 95, 107n

vegetarianism: enjoined in Five Precepts but not often practised, 69–70, 143–4
Vinaya-pitaka, Buddhist scripture, 18, 20, 25, 27, 57; rules of conduct for monks in, *see Patimokkha*
Visakha Bucha ceremony, 162–3

Wachana Bunsanong, Khun, manageress of Thai City Bank, Ayutthaya, 135, 163, 173
waiyawachakon, *see* lay bursar of monastery
wats, see monasteries
water, monastery expenditure on, 122, 126, 208, 209
water filter, for removing living organisms, 32, 167, 168
wills: leaving property to monasteries, 119, 123; of monks, 120
women, in Thailand, 13–14, 15–16; and merit-making ceremonies, 147–8, 174–7; on monastery committees, 132, 134–5; monks and, 31, 36
Wongkhong *wat*, Ayutthaya, 200; Abbot of, 105, 107, 171; alms-routes from, 104–105; finances of, 206, 207, 208
Woraphot *wat*, Ayutthaya, 201; Abbot of, 116; finances of, 206, 207; school in compound of, 122

Yai Chai Mongkhon *wat*, Ayutthaya, 88, 109, 198, 200; finances of, 206, 207
Yanasen *wat*, Ayutthaya, 75, 171, 200; alms-routes from, 104; finances of, 122, 206, 207
Yanawa *wat*, Bangkok, school at, 156